Su Friedrich: Interviews

Conversations with Filmmakers Series
Gerald Peary, General Editor

SU FRIEDRICH

INTERVIEWS

Edited by Sonia Misra and Rox Samer

University Press of Mississippi / Jackson

The University Press of Mississippi is the scholarly publishing agency of the Mississippi Institutions of Higher Learning: Alcorn State University, Delta State University, Jackson State University, Mississippi State University, Mississippi University for Women, Mississippi Valley State University, University of Mississippi, and University of Southern Mississippi.

www.upress.state.ms.us

The University Press of Mississippi is a member of the Association of University Presses.

First printing 2022
∞

Library of Congress Cataloging-in-Publication Data

Names: Misra, Sonia, editor. | Samer, Rox, 1986– editor.
Title: Su Friedrich: interviews / edited by Sonia Misra and Rox Samer.
Other titles: Conversations with filmmakers series.
Description: Jackson: University Press of Mississippi, 2022. | Series: Conversations with filmmakers series | Includes bibliographical references and index.
Identifiers: LCCN 2021040782 (print) | LCCN 2021040783 (ebook) | ISBN 978-1-4968-3816-2 (hardback) | ISBN 978-1-4968-3817-9 (trade paperback) | ISBN 978-1-4968-3818-6 (epub) | ISBN 978-1-4968-3819-3 (epub) | ISBN 978-1-4968-3820-9 (pdf) | ISBN 978-1-4968-3821-6 (pdf)
Subjects: LCSH: Friedrich, Su—Interviews. | Motion picture producers and directors—United States—Interviews.
Classification: LCC PN1998.3.F784 A5 2022 (print) | LCC PN1998.3.F784 (ebook) | DDC 791.4302/33092—dc23/eng/20211210
LC record available at https://lccn.loc.gov/2021040782
LC ebook record available at https://lccn.loc.gov/2021040783

British Library Cataloging-in-Publication Data available

Contents

Introduction

Over a career that spans four decades and counting, Su Friedrich has made more than twenty films about topics as wide-ranging as heartbreak, aging, illness, sexual desire, lesbian childhood, coffee production, gentrification, parent-child relationships, rituals of gender, and totalitarianism. Her work characteristically foregrounds the personal in service of a far-reaching social, cultural, and political reflection and critique. The poignancy and incisiveness of her films rests not only on their deftness connecting the subjective and the social but also on her unwavering sincerity in both serious and humorous registers. With few exceptions, Friedrich shoots and edits her own films, and her adroit attention to image and sound, in concert and in rhythm, appeals to her viewers' bodies and minds. The sensuality and wit of Friedrich's films construct an intimacy that both comforts and unsettles.

Su Friedrich was born in 1954 in New Haven, Connecticut, to an American anthropology and linguistics professor father and German pianist mother. She first attended the University of Chicago before transferring to Oberlin College where she studied photography and earned a BA in art and art history. After graduating in 1975, she made a six-month solo trip through West Africa, taking photographs. When she returned to the states, she moved to New York City where she would soon become a member of the feminist art collective Heresies. In the late 1970s, during the ascendancy of feminist film theory, Friedrich moved from still photography into filmmaking. Just as Laura Mulvey, Claire Johnston, the Camera Obscura Collective, and others delimited the forms most fitting for feminist filmmaking, Friedrich shattered all sense of what was formally and thematically possible for a feminist filmmaker.[1]

Su Friedrich has been described as an autobiographical filmmaker, an avant-garde or experimental filmmaker, a documentary filmmaker, an independent filmmaker, a feminist filmmaker, and a lesbian filmmaker. According to cinema and media studies scholars, she is also a "domestic ethnographer" and a maker of "dyke docs" and "experimental ethnography."[2] But in interviews, Friedrich sprucely dodges such interpellations, pointing to the strictures of such labels and insisting time and again that she is quite simply a filmmaker. Nevertheless, the influences of the experimental film culture and of the feminist and lesbian political ethos out of which she emerged resonate across her films to the present day, even if at times opaquely.

Friedrich is best known for her films from the 1980s and 1990s namely *The Ties That Bind* (1984), and *Damned If You Don't* (1987), and *Sink or Swim* (1990). Friedrich's more recent films, though lesser known, are far from more minor works. They echo the emotional immediacy of earlier works, and they continue to operate outside of "traditional" documentary form even as they adapt to reflect evolving personal and political concerns. Discussing *I Cannot Tell You How I Feel* (2016) and *The Ties That Bind* in an interview with Adam Schartoff, Friedrich notes, "Thirty years later, I still am really interested in picking up my camera and shooting the world in front of me, but that doesn't mean I'm [yet] going to do a talking heads documentary. I have no objection to that kind of film. I see lots of them. I think they're great, but it's not who I am. . . . I think this shows that, in all these years, I haven't really left some of those early principles or ideas that I had." There are profound connections to be drawn across her body of work, some of which are parsed out in the interviews collected here. Yet, there are also notable differences that must be acknowledged, as a result of her move from film to digital video and growing comfort with humor. Through both the directness of her own words in interviews and the continued dynamism of her recent films, Friedrich makes it clear that her career as a resolute yet adaptable filmmaker has heartily carried on since the '90s.

For Friedrich, each new project is catalyzed by a distinct set of formal and thematic preoccupations, many of which are illuminated in the interviews collected in this volume. She typically works on a single film at a time, completing one before moving onto the next. Friedrich approaches each film as a unique text, selecting the modes and approaches most apt in the moment. Frustrating easy categorization, Friedrich's films employ a wide range of aesthetic strategies, which include words scratched into celluloid, recycled found footage, and appropriated segments from canonical works of cinema, original documentary footage that tends toward realism, and montages of voice, text, and image. She blends documentary, avant-garde, and narrative to explore the likewise permeable boundaries between the private and public, inside and outside, self and Other, reality and imagination.

Friedrich's defiance of aesthetic and genre categories is matched by a defiant affect that colors the emotional content of her work, ranging from vulnerability to rage. What binds her films, perhaps more than any mode, method, format, or genre, is a philosophical commitment to that which is most personal and intimate in service of the political. This is a far cry from Hollywood, which lifts up queer love stories by asserting they are not gay or lesbian but universal. Friedrich's films do not let you forget the particularities for their broader relevancy. Instead, she takes you so close to her experience and the experiences of her family, friends, and lovers that they feel as if they might be your own, while also building in formal signs that guarantee you remain well aware that they are not.

The unfamiliar home footage of *Sink or Swim* tells you that this is not your abusive father; nonetheless, in his words and actions, enhanced by Friedrich's arresting editing, patriarchy's rife paternal violence is unmistakable. It might not be your ex-girlfriend's station wagon, with its cigarette smoke-scented brown fabric seats and cranked-up radio dial, that haunts every step of the unseen protagonist of *Rules of the Road* (1993), but Friedrich's narration and the hard cuts of the film's soundtrack remind you of what it's like to have grief triggered by the sight of a certain object or sound of a particular song. Even if you have not witnessed your own neighborhood destroyed by the fast-encroaching capital of big business, you will feel anger and helplessness as Friedrich's camera refuses to look away from the buildings collapsing around her in *Gut Renovation* (2012).

Friedrich's films address our bodies and minds. *Cool Hands, Warm Heart* (1979), *Scar Tissue* (1979), and *Gently Down the Stream* (1981) utilize handheld black-and-white cinematography to examine and caress both people and objects. *Rules of the Road* and its peers of the mid-'90s feature playful soundtracks of non-diegetic pop tunes, cutting across nostalgia and hope alike. Her films of the 2000s are characterized by sardonic voiceovers and onscreen text commentary, which animate the objects before the camera in a humorous flurry. Friedrich works within strict financial limits, but this has never led to artistic paralysis. Her early black-and-white films, shot on a 16mm silent Bolex, are arguably so beautiful because they cannot include synch sound. *The Ties That Bind*, Friedrich's first longer film, provides an early demonstration of her prowess at coupling image and sound. She edited together interviews with her mother about growing up in 1930s Germany, photography of her mother's present-day life in Chicago, archival footage of postwar Germany, and hand-scratched black leader of her own narration inserted as written text.

NEA and NYSCA grants in the mid-1990s allowed Friedrich to experiment with synch sound in crafting *Hide and Seek* (1996), which ambitiously weaves together fiction, nonfiction, and experimental modes to offer a collective treatise on lesbian childhood. When film became too expensive, she was given a digital camera by painter, Cathy Nan Quinlan, her partner and *Hide and Seek* and *Gut Renovation* collaborator (and *Rules of the Road* heartbreaker). *The Odds of Recovery* (2002), Friedrich's film about her decades-long medical struggles, was her last film to be edited on 16mm and to include 16mm home footage (along with digital footage shot in unknowing doctors' offices). *The Head of a Pin* (2004),

Seeing Red (2004), and the six other films she has made since were all shot and edited digitally.

Friedrich's long reluctance to abandon film stemmed from a belief that analog and digital video are simply ugly in comparison. She expresses such anti-video sentiments in the first interview collected here: "I hate the light, I hate the way it looks." However, as the more recent interviews chronicle, her turn to digital video also opened up avenues of expression. Much of *Gut Renovation*—including the long takes of an impenetrable boulder occupying the lot across the street—would have been impossible on film, as the time need to shoot without cutting exceeds the windup Bolex's capabilities. In *The Odds of Recovery*, digital video enabled her to sneak cameras into doctors' offices, recording the neglectfulness of the medical profession. In *Gut Renovation*, Friedrich continues this highly personal, anti-capitalist guerrilla filmmaking, recording open houses in the neighborhood's new luxury condos at hip-level under the auspices of prospective condo ownership. For *I Cannot Tell You How I Feel*, Friedrich was able to capture digitally her mother's move from her home of fifty years in Chicago to an independent living facility in New York, complete with her mother's real-time objections, Friedrich's thoughts and feelings on these matters conjoined through digital intertitles added in postproduction.

This is the first book dedicated exclusively to Su Friedrich and her work. The interviews collected here highlight the historical, theoretical, political, and economic dimensions through which her films gain their unique and defiantly ambiguous identity. In selecting these interviews, we sought a comprehensive perspective on Friedrich's diverse body of work and the conditions in which they were made. We wished to show how they have circulated and become understood within different contexts. Together these interviews underscore central preoccupations of Friedrich and the evolution of her career and life. The repetitions seen at times in her answers reflect the centrality of these sentiments and points of analysis.

This collection contains fifteen interviews with Friedrich and three autobiographical writings. While the majority of scholarly and critical attention to Friedrich's oeuvre focuses on the first third of her career, more than half of the interviews included here discuss those films made in the twenty-first century. This choice does not undercut the immense significance of her earlier work or the value of interviews from the '80s and '90s, but it allows us to focus attention on films that have been much understudied. Su Friedrich is a major filmmaker, early and late.

Interviews such as the nuanced discussion between Friedrich and avant-garde film scholar Scott MacDonald have been foundational in framing her works in terms of both their aesthetic strategies and political resonances. MacDonald's talks with Friedrich detail her early films up to *Sink or Swim*. More recent interviews, such as that with Caroline Berler, reflect on Friedrich's historical positioning, with Berler's particular interest being Friedrich's 1990s work as it aligns with and challenges the decade's lesbian historical imaginary. The volume closes with our "Editors' Interview," which seeks to illuminate areas that remain latent or under-discussed in other interviews. One such area is Friedrich's position as a film professor at Princeton University, in particular how her pedagogy and choice of employment have influenced her career as a filmmaker, and vice versa. This interview also draws attention to Friedrich's projects that supplement her own filmmaking, such as creating a website for the late African American filmmaker William Greaves, and *Edited By*, an online historical resource dedicated to collecting information about and honoring the contributions of women film editors.

Echoing across these various interviews is Friedrich's charmingly sardonic and defiant personality, familiar from her films. Her occasional resistance to an interviewer's line of questioning opens up other, unexpected lines of inquiry as it also provides insight into her distinct philosophy. We must thank Su, who graciously made herself available for any questions we had as we pieced together this project. She also assisted us in tracking down potential interviews and other writings to include in this collection, as well as providing contact information for authors as we worked to secure copyright permissions. It has been a pleasure to collaborate with her on this project. It is our hope that, by perusing this collection, readers may get to know her a little bit better, gaining a sense of her deeply personal filmmaking and the ways in which Friedrich's life becomes intimately entangled with her art.

Notes

1. Laura Mulvey, "Visual Pleasure and Narrative Cinema," *Screen* 16, no. 3 (Autumn 1975), 6–18; Claire Johnston, "Women's Cinema as Counter Cinema," in *Notes on Women's Cinema* (London: Society for Education in Film and Television, 1973); Camera Obscura Collective, "Feminism and Film: Critical Approaches," *Camera Obscura: A Journal of Feminism and Film Theory* 1 (Fall 1976), 3–10; Camera Obscura Collective, "Chronology: The Camera Obscura Collective," *Camera Obscura: A Journal of Feminism and Film Theory* 3–4 (Summer 1979), 5–13; Mary Ann Doane, "Woman's Stake: Filming the Female Body," *October* 17 (Summer 1981), 22–36; Annette Kuhn, *Women's Pictures: Feminism and Cinema* (London and Boston: Routledge and Kegan Paul, 1982); and E. Ann Kaplan, *Women and Film: Both Sides of the Camera* (New York and London: Routledge, 1983).
2. Michael Renov, "Domestic Ethnography and the Construction of the 'Other' Self," in *Collecting Visible Evidence*, ed. Michael Renov and Jane Gaines, 140–55 (Minneapolis and London: University of Minnesota Press, 1999); Chris Holmlund, "When Autobiography Meets Ethnography and Girl Meets Girl: The 'Dyke

Docs' of Su Friedrich and Sadie Benning," in *Between the Sheets, In the Streets: Queer, Lesbian, and Gay Documentary*, ed. Chris Holmlund and Cynthia Fuchs, 127–43 (Minneapolis and London: University of Minnesota Press, 1997); and Catherine Russell, "Hide and Seek: Looking for Lesbians," in *Experimental Ethnography: The Work of Film in the Age of Video*, 148–56 (Durham and London: Duke University Press, 1999).

Chronology

1954	Su Friedrich is born in 1954 in New Haven, Connecticut.
1971–72	Friedrich attends the University of Chicago.
1972–75	Friedrich attends Oberlin College where she studies photography and earns a BA in art and art history.
1976	Friedrich makes a six-month solo trip through West Africa, taking photographs. Friedrich moves to New York City. She soon becomes a member of the Heresies Collective, a feminist art collective, and contributes to their journal *Heresies: A Feminist Publication on Art and Politics*.
1978	Friedrich attends Super 8mm workshops at the Millennium Film Workshop and starts making films.
1981	Friedrich curates the program "Women's Film Feast" at the Millennium Film Workshop.
1982	Friedrich receives a grant from the New York State Council on the Arts, which supports the production of *The Ties That Bind*.
1983	*Cool Hands, Warm Heart* wins the Special Merit Award at the Athens Film Festival.
1984	Friedrich releases her first long film, *The Ties That Bind*, touring Europe with the film and receiving a DAAD (German Academic Exchange Service) grant. She spends six months as artist-in-residence in Berlin.
1987	Friedrich releases her first explicitly lesbian film, *Damned If You Don't*. The film screens at dozens of film festivals, including gay and lesbian festivals in New York, Los Angeles, San Francisco, and Vancouver.
1989	Friedrich receives a Guggenheim Fellowship, as well as grants from the New York State Council on the Arts, the Jerome Foundation, and the New York Foundation for the Arts, which help support the production of *Sink or Swim*. Friedrich is featured in the Whitney Biennial.
1990	Friedrich releases *Sink or Swim*, which wins the Grand Prix at the Melbourne Film Festival and the Special Jury Award at the Atlanta Film Festival. Friedrich is awarded a Rockefeller Foundation Fellowship, which helps support the production of *First Comes Love*.

1992 Friedrich is named by B. Ruby Rich as part of the group filmmakers changing the international film festival circuit with irreverent "homo pomo" films in the critic's field-forming *Sight and Sound* essay "New Queer Cinema."

1994 Friedrich receives a National Endowment for the Arts Fellowship, which supports the production of *Hide and Seek*.

1996 Friedrich releases her biggest budget and most collaborative film to date, *Hide and Seek*, about lesbian childhood. The film was photographed by Jim Denault, and Friedrich wrote the script with her partner Cathy Nan Quinlan. The film wins the Special Jury Prize at the New York Gay and Lesbian Film Festival and the Outstanding Documentary Feature Award at Outfest in Los Angeles.

1998 Friedrich begins teaching video production at Princeton University.

2000 Friedrich receives the Peter S. Reed Lifetime Achievement Award.

2001 Anthology Film Archives hosts a retrospective of Friedrich's films. Friedrich receives a New York State Council on the Arts grant, which supports the production of *The Odds of Recovery*.

2002 Friedrich releases her first film that includes footage she shot on digital video, *The Odds of Recovery*.

2003 *The Odds of Recovery* wins the Femmedia Award–Best Documentary at Identities, Vienna's International Queer Film Festival.

2004 Friedrich releases her first film entirely shot and edited on digital video, *The Head of a Pin*.

2005 *The Head of a Pin* receives a Director's Citation/Honorable Mention at the Black Maria Film Festival. Friedrich receives a New York State Council on the Arts grant, which supports the production of *From the Ground Up*.

2006 The Museum of Modern Art hosts a retrospective of Friedrich's films called "The Personal Films of Su Friedrich." Outcast Films releases a DVD boxset of Friedrich's films.

2008 Friedrich curates the film program "Genre Trouble" at Light Industry in Brooklyn.

2009 Friedrich curates a program for the "Then and Now" series at Anthology Film Archives. Friedrich receives the Continuing Excellence in Documentary Filmmaking Award at Wellesley College's New Directions in Documentary Film Festival and Symposium.

2012 Friedrich is a featured artist at the Flaherty Film Seminar. *Gut Renovation* receives the Audience Award at the Brooklyn Film Festival. Friedrich is commissioned by the Brooklyn Academy of Music to make the short film *Practice Makes Perfect*.

2015 The United States Library of Congress selects *Sink or Swim* for preservation in the National Film Registry.

2019 Friedrich launches the website *Edited By* (https://womenfilmeditors.princeton.edu/).

2020 Friedrich is commissioned to make a short film, *5/10/20*, as part of the Wexner Center for the Arts' *Cinetracts '20* project. Friedrich creates and launches a website for the late filmmaker William Greaves (http://www.williamgreaves.com/).

Filmography

HOT WATER (1978)
Director: **Su Friedrich**
Cinematographer: **Su Friedrich**
Editor: **Su Friedrich**
Production Company: Su Friedrich Films
Distribution: Vimeo
Super 8mm, black & white, 12 minutes

COOL HANDS, WARM HEART (1979)
Director: **Su Friedrich**
Screenwriter: **Su Friedrich**
Cinematographer: **Su Friedrich**
Editor: **Su Friedrich**
Cast/Interview Subjects/Voiceover Performers: Donna Allegra Simms, Sally Eckhoff, Jennifer MacDonald, Rose Maurer, Marty Pottenger
Production Company: Su Friedrich Films
Distribution: Outcast Films; Canyon Cinema
Super 8mm and 16mm, black & white, 16 minutes

SCAR TISSUE (1979)
Director: **Su Friedrich**
Screenwriter: **Su Friedrich**
Cinematographer: **Su Friedrich**
Editor: **Su Friedrich**
Production Company: Su Friedrich Films
Distribution: Outcast Films; Canyon Cinema
Super 8mm and 16mm, black & white, 6 minutes

I SUGGEST MINE (1980)
Director: **Su Friedrich**
Screenwriter: **Su Friedrich**
Cinematographer: **Su Friedrich**

Editor: **Su Friedrich**
Production Company: Su Friedrich Films
Distribution: Private Collection
16mm, color and black & white, 6 minutes

GENTLY DOWN THE STREAM (1981)
Director: **Su Friedrich**
Screenwriter: **Su Friedrich**
Cinematographer: **Su Friedrich**
Editor: **Su Friedrich**
Cast/Interview Subjects/Voiceover Performers: Jennifer MacDonald, Marty Pottenger
Production Company: Su Friedrich Films
Distribution: Outcast Films; Canyon Cinema; Film-Makers' Cooperative; Canadian Filmmakers Distribution Centre; Freunde der Deutschen Kinemathek; Light Cone
Super 8mm and 16mm, black & white, 14 minutes

BUT NO ONE (1982)
Director: **Su Friedrich**
Screenwriter: **Su Friedrich**
Cinematographer: **Su Friedrich**
Editor: **Su Friedrich**
Production Company: Su Friedrich Films
Funding: New York State Council on the Arts
Distribution: Outcast Films; Canyon Cinema
16mm, black & white, 9 minutes

THE TIES THAT BIND (1984)
Director: **Su Friedrich**
Screenwriter: **Su Friedrich**
Cinematographer: **Su Friedrich**
Editor: **Su Friedrich**
Sound Editor: **Su Friedrich**
Cast/Interview Subjects/Voiceover Performers: Lore Friedrich
Production Company: Su Friedrich Films
Funding: New York State Council on the Arts
Distribution: Outcast Films; Canyon Cinema; Canadian Filmmakers Distribution Centre; Freunde der Deutschen Kinemathek; Light Cone
16mm, black & white, 55 minutes

DAMNED IF YOU DON'T (1987)
Director: **Su Friedrich**
Screenwriter: **Su Friedrich**
Script Consultant: Cathy Nan Quinlan
Cinematographer: **Su Friedrich**
Editor: **Su Friedrich**
Sound Editor: **Su Friedrich**
Cast/Interview Subjects/Voiceover Performers: Peggy Healey (The Nun), Makea McDonald, Cathay Nan Quinlan, Martina Siebert, Ela Troyano (The Other Woman)
Production Company: Su Friedrich Films
Funding: New York State Council on the Arts, Jerome Foundation, and German Academic Exchange Service
Distribution: Outcast Films; Canyon Cinema; Film-Makers' Cooperative; Canadian Filmmakers Distribution Centre; Freunde der Deutschen Kinemathek; Light Cone
16mm, black & white, 42 minutes

SINK OR SWIM (1990)
Director: **Su Friedrich**
Screenwriter: **Su Friedrich**
Cinematographer: **Su Friedrich**, Peggy Ahwesh, Carl J. Friedrich
Editor: **Su Friedrich**
Sound Editor: **Su Friedrich**
Cast/Interview Subjects/Voiceover Performers: **Su Friedrich**, Jessica Lynn, Martina Meijer, Peggy Ahwesh
Production Company: Su Friedrich Films
Funding: Guggenheim Foundation, New York State Council on the Arts, Jerome Foundation, New York Foundation on the Arts, and Art Matters, Inc.
Distribution: Outcast Films; Canyon Cinema; Canadian Filmmakers Distribution Centre; Freunde der Deutschen Kinemathek; Light Cone
16mm, black & white, 48 minutes

FIRST COMES LOVE (1991)
Director: **Su Friedrich**
Screenwriter: **Su Friedrich**
Cinematographer: **Su Friedrich**
Editor: **Su Friedrich**
Sound Editor: **Su Friedrich**
Production Company: Jezebel Productions, Inc.

Funding: Rockefeller Foundation
Distribution: Outcast Films; Canyon Cinema; Film-Makers' Cooperative; Canadian Filmmakers Distribution Centre; Freunde der Deutschen Kinemathek
16mm, black & white, 22 minutes

LESBIAN AVENGERS EAT FIRE, TOO (1993)
Director: **Su Friedrich** and Janet Baus
Screenwriter: **Su Friedrich** and Janet Baus
Cinematographer: **Su Friedrich**, Janet Baus, Jean Carlomusto, Julie Clark, and Harriet Hirschorn
Editor: **Su Friedrich** and Janet Baus
Sound Editor: **Su Friedrich** and Janet Baus
Production Company: Lesbian Avengers
Distribution: Outcast Films; Lesbian Avengers
Video, color, 60 minutes

RULES OF THE ROAD (1993)
Director: **Su Friedrich**
Screenwriter: **Su Friedrich**
Cinematographer: **Su Friedrich**
Editor: **Su Friedrich**
Sound Editor: **Su Friedrich**
Cast/Interview Subjects/Voiceover Performers: **Su Friedrich**
Production Company: Jezebel Productions, Inc.
Funding: Rockefeller Foundation
Distribution: Outcast Films; Canyon Cinema; Canadian Filmmakers Distribution Centre; Freunde der Deutschen Kinemathek; Light Cone
16mm, color, 31 minutes

HIDE AND SEEK (1996)
Director: **Su Friedrich**
Screenwriter: **Su Friedrich** and Cathy Nan Quinlan
Producer: Eva Kolodner and Katie Roumel
Executive Producer: **Su Friedrich**
Cinematographer: **Su Friedrich** and Jim Denault
Editor: **Su Friedrich**
Editing Consultant: Cathy Nan Quinlan
Sound Editor: Juan Carlos Martinez
Cast/Interview Subjects/Voiceover Performers: Chelsea Holland (Lou), Ariel Mara (Betsy), Linzy Taylor (Lizzie), Sarah Jane Smith (Miss Callahan), Alicia

Manta (Maureen), Mindy Baransky, Cindy Bink, Ashley Carlisle, Gina Caulfield, Kelly Cogswell, Marlene Colburn, Dorothy Donaher, Ashley Ferrante, Tracey Frederick, Su Friedrich, Virginia Gravli, Marie Honan, Delritta Hornbuckle, Hunter Johnson, Alisa Lebow, Nikki Michaels, Kirsten Oriol, Lydia Pacifico, Matthew Pavlov, Jane Perkins, Cheryl Perry, Ann Podolske, Pat Powell, Frank Rosner, Linda Small, Claudia Steinberg, Brandon Winston, Maleena Waddy, Jean Edna White, Noah Wilson, Penny Wright, Apryl Wynter
Production Company: Downstream Productions, Inc.
Funding: Independent Television Service, National Endowment for the Arts, New York State Council on the Arts
Distribution: Outcast Films; Canyon Cinema; Freunde der Deutschen Kinemathek
16mm, black & white, 65 minutes

THE ODDS OF RECOVERY (2002)
Director: **Su Friedrich**
Screenwriter: **Su Friedrich**
Cinematographer: **Su Friedrich** and Joel Schlemowitz
Editor: **Su Friedrich**
Sound Editor: **Su Friedrich**
Cast/Interview Subjects/Voiceover Performers: **Su Friedrich**
Production Company: Downstream Productions, Inc.
Funding: New York State Council on the Arts, New York Foundation of the Arts, Charette Communications
Distribution: Outcast Films; Canyon Cinema
16mm and video, color, 65 minutes

THE HEAD OF A PIN (2004)
Director: **Su Friedrich**
Cinematographer: **Su Friedrich**
Editor: **Su Friedrich**
Sound Editor: **Su Friedrich**
Cast/Interview Subjects/Voiceover Performers: **Su Friedrich**, Barbara Epler, Cathy Nan Quinlan, Claudia Steinberg
Production Company: Downstream Productions, Inc.
Distribution: Outcast Films
Video, color, 21 minutes

SEEING RED (2005)
Director: **Su Friedrich**
Cinematographer: **Su Friedrich**

Editor: **Su Friedrich**
Sound Editor: **Su Friedrich**
Cast/Interview Subjects/Voiceover Performers: **Su Friedrich**
Production Company: Downstream Productions, Inc.
Distribution: Outcast Films
Video, color, 27 minutes

FROM THE GROUND UP (2008)
Director: **Su Friedrich**
Screenwriter: **Su Friedrich**
Cinematographer: **Su Friedrich** and Pedro Díaz Valdés
Editor: **Su Friedrich**
Sound Editor: **Su Friedrich**
Music: Kurt Hoffman and Meg Richardt
Production Company: Su Friedrich Films
Funding: New York State Council on the Arts
Distribution: Su Friedrich Films
Video, color, 54 minutes

PRACTICE MAKES PERFECT (2012)
Director: **Su Friedrich**
Cinematographer: **Su Friedrich**
Editor: **Su Friedrich**
Sound Editor: **Su Friedrich**
Cast/Interview Subjects/Voiceover Performers: Kam Kelly
Production Company: Su Friedrich Films
Commission: BAM (Brooklyn Academy of Music)
Distribution: Vimeo
Video, color, 11 minutes

GUT RENOVATION (2012)
Director: **Su Friedrich**
Screenwriter: **Su Friedrich** and Cathy Nan Quinlan
Cinematographer: **Su Friedrich**
Editor: **Su Friedrich**
Editing Consultant: Cathy Nan Quinlan
Sound Editor: **Su Friedrich**
Cast/Interview Subjects/Voiceover Performers: **Su Friedrich**
Production Company: Su Friedrich Films

Distribution: Outcast Films
Video, color, 81 minutes

QUEEN TAKES PAWN (2013)
Director: **Su Friedrich**
Cinematographer: **Su Friedrich** and Carl J. Friedrich
Editor: **Su Friedrich**
Sound Editor: **Su Friedrich**
Cast/Interview Subjects/Voiceover Performers: **Su Friedrich**
Production Company: Su Friedrich Films
Distribution: Vimeo
Video, color and black & white, 6.5 minutes

I CANNOT TELL YOU HOW I FEEL (2016)
Director: **Su Friedrich**
Screenwriter: **Su Friedrich** and Cathy Nan Quinlan
Cinematographer: **Su Friedrich**
Editor: **Su Friedrich**
Sound Editor: **Su Friedrich**
Cast/Interview Subjects/Voiceover Performers: **Su Friedrich**, Lore Friedrich, Maria Friedrich, Pete Friedrich
Production Company: Su Friedrich Films
Distribution: Icarus Films
Video, color and black & white, 42 minutes

5/10/20 (2020)
Director: **Su Friedrich**
Cinematographer: **Su Friedrich**
Editor: **Su Friedrich**
Sound Editor: **Su Friedrich**
Production Company: Su Friedrich Films
Commission: Wexner Center for the Arts Artist Residency Award, Ohio State University (as part of the *Cinetracts '20* project)
Distribution: Vimeo (as a single film); part of the *Cinetracts '20* project at www.wexarts.org
Video, color, 2 minutes

Su Friedrich: Interviews

Su Friedrich to Leslie Thornton, Leslie Thornton to Su Friedrich

From *Idiolects* 13 (1983). Reprinted by permission of Mary Filippo, coeditor of *Idiolects*.

March 4, 1983

Dear Leslie,

I thought I would write in my journal but then I decided to write this to you. Tonight, *Gently Down the Stream* was shown at the Lucky Strike, a club on Stuyvesant Street (across the street from where A. lived after we broke up, down the street from where A. and I lived when we first moved to NY and were happy together, and where we lived also when we split up). It was a group show—I think I earned 75 cents for it. Manuel DeLanda, Benning/Gordon, Kobland, von Zeigesar, et al. Two women from the Heresies Film issue whom I really like were there—and the monitor (E.) from the Millennium which, in some way, rounded out the picture. I was extremely nervous before the film, and got stoned, and hence got more nervous. I was worried about what C. and G. would think. But secretly I felt as if <u>I</u> was about to surprise <u>them</u> with the film—as if the film's strength wouldn't be determined by their response to me (That then i.e. I'd think it was goof because of their response) but that they would be determined by their ability to fall prey to the film. As if I'd laid a trap for them and was waiting to see if they'd fall into it, rather than that the film (and I) was waiting to become "real" as a result of their response. It's one of those reverse cases of confusing hindsight with the original feelings I had when making the film—so I guess it's hindblindness? Does that seem weird? It does to me. And then I watched the film clutching my sides, with a secret smile on my face (embarrassed to show my cowboyish Yippee! Attago! Waowiee! Looker that frame looker that cut! Feelings) because for once <u>I</u> was enjoying the film. I felt as if I'd made it for <u>myself</u>. That it was a gift to myself. That every choice was made completely for my pleasure. And yes. But I also started feeling strange, as if it had its own determined, predetermined trajectory. One that I couldn't see before, because I was making it. And so it took me, forced me, dragged me headlong through the paces until the moment that I knew it was complete (when the words MY TONGUE first appear in the last dream), and whatever that means, I was forced to stare it straight in the face, though I felt like a kid pulling HARD in the other direction from where "grown up" is trying to drag me. So then of course I got the shakes with a vengeance, and when the film ended I was so embarrassed. G. was the first to give me a good word. C. eventually admitted that she thought it was good. And yes, I was pleased and flattered to hear that; I started stuttering and reached for my beer, and we spoke a bit more. But I suddenly felt very apart from them, settling away and down into some private, noisy little corner of myself. Because I knew beforehand that they'd probably like it (though of course I leave the possibility wide open that they wouldn't like it or would have strong objections to something in it—and I could even relish that event, as you'll see—), and I felt discouraged. I knew that I was beyond the experience of that film: not in quality, but in some more horizontal manner. It had done its work on me, I had given it all I had, and so necessarily it would speak some truth to those who would want to hear or would enjoy hearing what I needed to hear and enjoyed hearing when I made it. But somehow, tonight, seeing through the film to the essence of what it afforded me in certain pleasures, I felt as if I'd suddenly turned my hunchback away and started plodding on to the next thing, which at first will/would (must?) seem like a torment until I can find what specific pleasure it will afford me. Because I can't go back to that old film for any (unfamiliar, surprising, unnerving) pleasures anymore—I know them, and I'm still afraid and ignorant of the next ones. A no-man's-land I'm in right now.

When I know what delight or spark of thought I can give or share with someone, I get bored. When I know pretty much how much a film can or can't affect someone (what its strengths and weaknesses, limitations, failings are), I get bored. There always must be something that's unfamiliar, if only so that one can overcome fear enough in order to make it familiar. Yes?

much love,
susi

P.S. [. . .] Has anyone ever talked literally about what happens when they "break up" with a film they've made?! And what we stand to learn and suffer from that?

Dear Su—from a list of things to tell you—

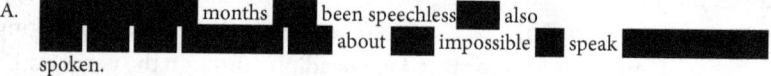

A. [redacted] months [redacted] been speechless [redacted] also
[redacted] about [redacted] impossible [redacted] speak [redacted]
spoken.

B. [redacted] I [redacted] people [redacted]
spark [redacted]
talk around [redacted] cannot say
circumscribe [redacted] incompletability [redacted]
no "idea" [redacted] wound [redacted] healed?
[redacted] covered [redacted]
figures [redacted] excess [redacted] shrill [redacted] awful.

C. [redacted] turns [redacted] erases. [redacted] Maurice Blanchot's writing,
sentences, passages [redacted] moving [redacted]
jack-knife [redacted] drop off or [redacted] turn around. [redacted]
the fiction [redacted] the writing [redacted]
tension [redacted] foregrounded [redacted]
. [redacted] thrill [redacted]
dread? [redacted] seeing [redacted] working [redacted] writing [redacted] seduced [redacted]

D. [redacted] shyness [redacted] wish [redacted]
involvement [redacted] viewer [redacted]
circuit [redacted]
don't instigate [redacted]
We get nowhere [redacted]
stop thinking [redacted]

E. [redacted] dynamic [redacted] communication [redacted]
work [redacted] lover, tric[redacted]kster,
seductress, student victim [redacted]
never reducible to one (or the other) [redacted]
strong [redacted] life [redacted] never contained [redacted] hermetically sealed [redacted]
pleasure, labor and trail, yours and others.
work [redacted]
"first person" [redacted] confidence [redacted] self [redacted] questioned,
questioning. [redacted]

F. [redacted] Last night [redacted] elderly woman [redacted]
tape-recording [redacted] silent film [redacted]
laughter and silence [redacted]
reconstituting [redacted]
film [redacted] aural braille [redacted] same
woman [redacted] screening of Adynata [redacted] —"You know, I loved your film,
but I was just wondering if you could maybe be a little more clear." [redacted]
wonderful [redacted] again [redacted]

G. [redacted] writing [redacted] real [redacted] overheard
[redacted] re-invented [redacted]
framing [redacted] (a verbal snapshot) [redacted]

"That's the way she is. That's the way she is. She's like that. That's all she is. That's what she is. I know what she is. I know. I know. I don't think she trusts herself. Unh unh. Uh huh. It ain't like that. She is evil"

"That's family. That's as low as you can get. Anything she does that's OK. That's A-OK. Yeah, that's her. Hey, I'm not surprised. Hey, that's the way she is. You see what I'm saying?" (Hands up in the air.)

"Something went on in her mind she thought she was married. She sent out the invitations. She's not married. She thinks she's married. But when the story really came down she's not married. So she's got alot of problems thinking she was married. It's psychological."

"She got her hair waved on our like this. Makes your head look big. She was in a real deep slum and depression. What I'm tell you she did it for the wrong reasons. It's an investment but she did not do that for any right reasons."

"She did not need none of that stuff. Nothing. She did not need that car. She did not need that foster child. She doesn't know what she needs. She just wants men and then runs them away. And that's the kind of person she is."

H. [redacted] share with you [redacted] letter [redacted] grim [redacted]

[redacted] strange [redacted] letter [redacted] jokes? [redacted] wastebasket [redacted]

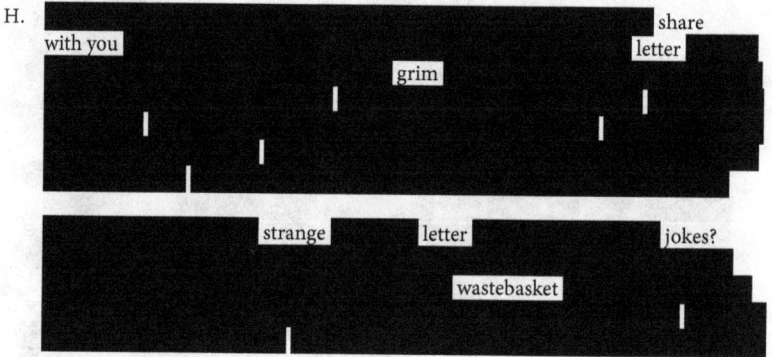

Much love,
Leslie

Interviews with New York Filmmakers: Su Friedrich

Stephanie Beroes / 1986

From *Cinematograph* 2 (1986). Reprinted by permission of Stephanie Beroes.

Stephanie Beroes: How did you get started making films?

Su Friedrich: I don't think I would be a filmmaker if it wasn't for Millennium Film Workshop, because when I began making films in 1978, I was doing paste-up work to earn a living, but not earning very much. Since the Millennium fees were so low, I managed it so that I didn't have to work at a job that much, but still get a lot done on my films. I was making short films, between six and fifteen minutes long. I was working in black and white, and doing all the technical work myself. I would shoot and edit in Super 8mm and blow-up to 16mm the sections I wanted. That made it affordable. I was spending only a couple hundred dollars on each film. I spent over one thousand making *Gently Down the Stream.*

SB: What about grants? You recently received a DAAD to live in Germany.

SF: I think psychologically, it's not good to depend on grants. Because it's important for me that if a grant does not come through then I can still work, otherwise it makes me feel desperate and helpless. Also, writing grant applications can be frustrating. I've written six this year, which is the most I've ever done. It just makes me feel really angry that I'm writing out these descriptions and trying to second guess what they might want to hear. And I can assume that one place is fairly open to experimental film or feminist film but another place is really conservative and so I have to tailor my description for them. And it gets me so confused because I end up not knowing what my film is about. But I can earn the money doing graphic arts work and put it into filmmaking. My standard of living hasn't changed in the last couple of years. I would like to receive grants to make films, however. I work hard enough, and most artists I know work hard enough that we deserve to get grants. Filmmaking is a tremendous amount of labor. I don't know what it is about experimental filmmakers, that we are all willing to work so hard and assume that we shouldn't get paid for the work—our work! And that was something I had encountered a lot in the feminist community. That we did an enormous amount of work for free, just for the cause. And I feel like I worked for free for years in feminist organizations. And I finally said I'm not doing this anymore. I have to have time to earn money to spend the remainder of my time being a filmmaker.

SB: How about exhibitions and tours? Do you depend on that for money?

SF: I have been able to do so only this year. Before 1981, I had done a lot of work putting on group shows, because I wanted to show my films, but I also wanted to show other people's films and to feel that I was working with other filmmakers in some way. And so I did a lot of shows around the city in churches, galleries, at the Women's Center. I think that made me appreciate programmers and the trouble they go through. But it was a good experience because it gave me a feeling of independence from the Millennium and the Collective for Living Cinema. I felt that there were other places I could show and didn't have to think of those as the only showcases for experimental film. But now today, if somebody asks me if I want to work with them organizing an event in a gallery, I get cold feet, because it's too much work. I have too much work to do just to get my films distributed; you know how much work it can be. Anyway, *Gently Down the Stream* rented a lot, and then when I finished *The Ties that Bind* in 1984, I had a show at Millennium and then at the San Francisco Cinematheque. Then I went to Germany for six months, and I felt like I dropped off the face of the earth. The film was with the New York Filmmakers Cooperative by then, and Women Make Movies had decided to take it, but I wasn't around to do any promotion for it, but I did have a lot of shows in Germany. I did nine shows in Germany and five in London. While in Europe, it seemed like suddenly it was possible to get more one-person shows, and also when I got back to the States, because I had this longer film. So I did a huge mailing when I got back, probably wrote to one hundred places, sending out reviews and personal letters, and I did arrange a few shows for the spring at a couple of universities. It seems like it's taken people about six months for them to register that the film is available and that they can rent it. From March of 1985 until March of 1986 I probably earned about three thousand dollars with shows where I might get paid between $200 to $500, less travel, and also from rentals. And this is more than I would have expected.

SB: Travel expenses can take up a lot of the fees earned.

SF: I really covered a lot of my travel. Some places paid that in addition to the rental. But I know what you mean because Leslie Thornton and I *did* a joint tour in California in 1982, we showed at five places, and we each lost $700 in travel and expenses. Some places paid us $125, which we split between us. But it was a learning experience for both of us. It was fun, because each time we presented the films, we would order them differently. We saw our films in every possible context. But that particular tour was a financial disaster. After that I thought, well, that's what touring is all about. But now I know it can actually be worthwhile, but it is really exhausting work.

SB: You were in Germany in 1985?

SF: Yes, 1984 to March 1985. And then I spent the fall of 1985 doing five shows outside of New York City. And the only other good money was getting *The Ties that Bind* shown on WNYC, for which I got $1,100. Then I was asked to be on Channel 13 (PBS) and found out that I couldn't because the broadcast premiere had already been on WNYC so it couldn't be on Channel 13, and I would have made three times as much money.

SB: How do you feel about the avant-garde film in general? Some people think not many good films are being made today and this means that "the avant-garde is dead."

SF: I think it's really funny for anyone to say that. I think a filmmaker who says that presumes that they've made a good film. I don't think it's ever been any different. I think that if it was 1973 or 1963, some filmmakers would feel that no good films are being made. My introduction to experimental filmmaking was reading Mekas's articles in the *Village Voice*, and feeling like there was no end to the excitement that had been generated during the 1960s.

SB: Right, but let's talk about the last five years. What is the state of things today in 1986?

SF: Yeah, but I think that's partly just the way things seem when you read about it in a book. Reading about a movement in a book makes it seem more cohesive and I think that if somebody in 1990 were to write a book about independent filmmaking in the 1980s it would be an exhilarating thing to read, because it would seem like there was so much going on. So sometimes, when I get the feeling "there's nothing going on," I think, well, it must be because I'm not editing right now, and so it seems like life isn't very interesting when I'm not editing. But I don't know, I think that video did make a difference. I just suspect that but it seems like it started happening in the early '80s when people were switching over to video. I'm still too new as a filmmaker to really know what effect that would have on the larger world of filmmaking. All I knew was that I just wasn't going to start making video.

SB: And today, how do you feel about working in video?

SF: I still don't want to work in video. I hate the light. I hate the way it looks. So, video has affected the avant-garde, and also the "New Narrative." I think there are a number of experimental filmmakers who decided to do something more narrative . . . I have no problems with somebody wanting to do a crossover film or to mix film styles . . . I mean I think that is what it's all about . . . But I think if you are going to be directing actors, you should know how to direct. I think most people who are experimental filmmakers who decided to do narrative can't direct worth shit and also don't find people who can act and that's really a problem because it just makes the film boring . . . and those films don't have to be boring . . . But I do think it's giving "avant-garde" a bad name . . . Like there are a lot of people in the larger world who kept away from experimental film and have now become more interested in it because there is something more narrative about the films with actors or whatever. But I don't think that brought the audience any closer to *real* experimental film.

Su Friedrich

Scott MacDonald / 1986–1990

The critique of conventional cinema that is articulated in Su Friedrich's early films—*Cool Hands, Warm Heart* (1979), *Scar Tissue* (1980), *Gently Down the Stream* (1981), *But No One* (1982), *The Ties That Bind* (1984), *Damned If You Don't* (1987), and *Sink or Swim* (1990)—has roots in two different cultural projects: the development of North American avant-garde cinema and the 1970s–1980s feminist reassessment of modern society (including both popular and independent cinema). During the 1980s, she demonstrated her loyalty to these projects through her extra-film activities: Friedrich was instrumental in getting the 1990 *Film-makers' Cooperative Catalogue* finished and published, and for years she was an active member of the Heresies collective. As filmmaker, her particular gift has been to find ways of combining cinematically experimental means and a powerful feminist commitment in films that are accessible to a broad range of viewers, even to viewers unaccustomed to enjoying either experimental or feminist filmmaking. This accessibility is, to a large degree, a function of Friedrich's willingness to use her filmmaking to explore the particulars of her personal experience. And her success in reaching audiences represents a powerful attack on the assumption that viewers will only respond to conventional film rhetoric.

At the very beginning of her filmmaking career, Friedrich's films were fueled by a relatively grim feminism, personal only in the most general sense. *Cool Hands, Warm Heart* documents several women performing conventional, but normally private, women's rituals—one woman shaves her legs; another, her armpits; and a third braids her hair—on a crowded street on New York's Lower East Side, as a way of rebelling against canons of "feminine modesty" in commercial media and against those independent filmmakers who were arguing that films shouldn't polemicize an identifiable politic. *Scar Tissue* presents physical gestures recorded on New York City streets, revealing the subtle workings of patriarchy in a mood of numbed horror.

Gently Down the Stream is more specific to Friedrich's personal experience. Friedrich spent months paying attention to her dreams, writing them down, and etching the most powerful and suggestive into the emulsion of black-and-white film, word by word. At times there is no imagery except for the hand-scratched words; in other instances, the words, which are always the foreground of the film, are combined with photographed imagery, much of which provides metaphors for our voyage along Friedrich's stream of consciousness (a woman exercises on a rowing machine, another swims). In general, the dreams recorded in *Gently Down the Stream* reveal a conflict between Friedrich's Roman Catholic upbringing and her lesbian desires. Indeed, the words that tell these dreams often seem to quiver with the intensity of this conflict. *But No One*, made soon after *Gently Down the Stream*, has much in common with the earlier film.

The Ties That Bind, Friedrich's first long film and her first 16mm film with sound (an early Super 8 film, *Hot Water* [1978], no longer in distribution, had sound), combines elements of documentary (on the soundtrack she interviews her German-born mother about her experiences growing up in Germany during the thirties as an anti-Nazi German) with elements familiar from avant-garde forms of cinema: the visuals are a mix of Friedrich's hand-scratched questions of her mother (we hear only Lore Friedrich's responses on the soundtrack, not the questions that provoke them); photographic footage recorded with a handheld Super 8 camera during Friedrich's visit to Germany to investigate her roots; 16mm footage of her mother in her Chicago environment, and of her own trip to a demonstration at the Seneca Army Depot in upstate New York (the arms race and thermonuclear were much on artists' minds in the early 1980s); archival footage recorded during the Second World War in Germany; and home movies made soon after Friedrich's mother arrived in the United States with her GI husband at the end of the war. Diverse as the film's sources of information are, they are bound tightly by Friedrich's intricate editing, which develops a range of thematic and formal "ties" between image and sound. *The Ties That Bind* is a consistently engaging record of a filmmaker's coming to terms with her mother's troubled past and her own cold-war threatened present.

Friedrich's decision to explore her German background confronted what was at the time an implicit cultural taboo. Like many of us who have German roots, Friedrich was haunted by the specter of the Holocaust. Even if we grew up after the Holocaust ended, our genetic inheritance seemed to condemn us. At the time when she talked with her mother, Friedrich could not be sure what her mother might reveal about herself. And even once she had learned of her mother's fervent disapproval of the Nazis and what this stance may have cost her, Friedrich was well aware that whatever suffering her mother and the rest of her family endured could not compare to what went on in the camps. *The Ties That Bind* is useful and revealing in many ways, not least of which is that it allows people of German heritage to admire the courageous example of those Germans who resisted the Nazi horror and to feel their own progressive urges reconfirmed. Of course, Friedrich's decision to use the production of a film as a space within which to try and resolve her personal conflicts with regard to her mother and their shared heritage was a departure from the detachment of conventional cinema and of much independent cinema, as well.

In *Damned If You Don't*, Friedrich returned to the issue of Catholicism and lesbian sexuality. But where *Gently Down the Stream* grimly dramatizes the psychic trauma this conflict seems to have created in Friedrich early on, *Damned If You Don't* is as good-humored as it is daring. Friedrich imbeds a narrative about a nun (played by Peggy Healey) pursued by another woman (played by Ela Troyano) within an informal investigation of some of the ways in which the issue of nuns and sexuality has played itself out in Western culture.

Like *The Ties That Bind*, *Damned If You Don't* is an amalgam of elements from disparate cinema traditions—still, in 1987, a breakthrough formal choice. The film begins with an amusing voiceover précis/critique of the Michael Powell–Emeric Pressburger melodrama *Black Narcissus* (1947), which the woman protagonist is watching on television. The woman's subsequent pursuit of the nun is interwoven with documentary imagery of nuns and convents; with formally lovely and metaphorically suggestive passages focusing on swans, swimming snakes, and white whales at the New York City Aquarium; and with a variety of information on the soundtrack, including an interview with a high school friend (Makea McDonald); her partner Cathy Quinlan reading passages from Judith C. Brown's *Immodest Acts: The Life of a Lesbian Nun in Renaissance Italy* (New York: Oxford University Press, 1986), and moments of self-reflexive conversation. The beautifully choreographed final scene of the nun and the Troyano character making love is the culmination of the narrative.

Damned If You Don't was a courageous film on two different levels. Obviously, even to expose sexual desire in nuns was highly unusual, and to do so with humor and in the name of an open expression of lesbian desire had to be shocking for some viewers; the lovemaking scene where the Troyano character undresses the nun is as outrageous as it is sensual. The second level of Friedrich's courage was her rejection of what, during the 1980s, was understood as a central tenet of feminist filmmaking. Once the filmic gaze was recognized as essentially (or at least traditionally) male, some filmmakers and critics came to see traditional film pleasure as an implicit acceptance of the workings of patriarchy and felt the need to expunge female nudity and sexuality from serious cinema. Other forms of film pleasure also seemed questionable: the sensuous rhythms, textures, and structures of personal and structural forms of avant-garde film were seen as self-indulgent.

Friedrich may have originally been in sympathy with a somewhat puritan feminist position (*Cool Hands, Warm Heart* and *Scar Tissue* suggest she was), but by *Damned If You Don't*, she had come to see it as a dead end, an attitude that implicitly reconfirms patriarchy. If male films are sensual and pleasurable, while female (or at least feminist) films are rigorously unsensual and pleasureless, males are defined, once again, as having something females lack. Traditionally, women have been damned to function as cogs in an exploitative male cinema that thrives on female sensuality. In some feminist films, women are damned a second time, to wander through ideologically pure but pleasureless (or, at least, sexless) narratives. *Damned If You Don't* was Friedrich's declaration of independence from this pattern. It energizes the feminist response to patriarchal cinema by locating it within a context of two forms of reappropriated film pleasure: the excitement of melodramatic narrative and the sensuous enjoyment of cinematic texture, rhythm, and structure.

Friedrich's decision not only to include a representation of female sexuality but to use it as the triumphant conclusion of the film was crucial. In *Damned If You Don't* Friedrich cinematically reappropriated the pleasure of women's sensuality for women, though her use of imagery of a male and female tightrope walker to announce the lovemaking of the two women suggests that the sexual pleasure of women need not be confined to women. In fact, at one point during the film, Friedrich quotes Mr. Dean in *Black Narcissus*, when she laughingly sings "No I won't be a nun; no I shall not be a nun. For I am so fond of pleasure, I cannot be a nun."

In *Sink or Swim*, which can easily be seen as a companion piece to *The Ties That Bind*, Friedrich returns to her family history to explore her relationship with her father, anthropologist/linguist Paul Friedrich, who left the family when Friedrich was a child. In *Sink or Swim*, Friedrich confronts the brutality built into the conventional nuclear family by virtue of societal gender assumptions, directly and personally, though with subtlety and thoughtfulness. Her goal is not simply to respond to the long-term effects of painful childhood experiences but to aid viewers—men and women—in thinking about their own experiences as children and their own approaches to parenting.

As is true in *The Ties that Bind* and *Damned If You Don't*, Friedrich's desire to enhance viewers' willingness to interact in humane ways within and across gender lines is reflected by her cinematic approach, which is, on one hand, to bring together filmmaking traditions that are usually considered distinct and, on the other, to edit her visuals and her soundtrack so that these separate sources of information intersect in a wide range of obvious and subtle ways. *Sink or Swim* is a personal narrative recorded in an often gestural style, but its organization evokes "structural film," particularly Hollis Frampton's alphabetically organized *Zorns Lemma* (1970). The individual stories that make up *Sink or Swim* are presented in reverse alphabetical order, according to the first letters of their one-word titles: "Zygote," "Y Chromosome," "X Chromosome" . . . Whereas Frampton's film uses the alphabet to trace a classic sense of the stages in the development of the intellect, *Sink or Swim* implicitly argues that the evolution of intelligence is also deeply affected by family structure and family trauma, in her case, the trauma of divorce. While *Sink or Swim*, like her other early films, is deeply resonant with the history of American avant-garde film—particularly Maya Deren, Stan Brakhage, and Frampton—Friedrich tells her story clearly and powerfully enough to be accessible to both cinephiles and general audiences.

Friedrich and I discussed her films up through *Damned If You Don't* in March 1986 and again in September 1987. We discussed *Sink or Swim* in June 1990.

■ ■ ■

Scott MacDonald: I find *Scar Tissue* and *Cool Hands, Warm Heart* hard to look at. They seem to have been made within a small circle of friends as feminist exercises. The change from those two films to *Gently Down the Stream* seems considerable, even though the style of all three films is related. I feel somewhat the same way about the jump from *Gently Down the Stream* and *But No One* to *The Ties That Bind*. Do you see big leaps in power from the earlier films to the later ones?

Su Friedrich: I think of those early films as being too obvious, or too much about a single issue or image. *Cool Hands* is about these acted-out women's rituals; *Scar Tissue* is about certain midtown men and women. *Scar Tissue* was made with a small audience in mind. I think it was made in part as a response to Dave Lee and his film *Remembering Clearing Space* [1976, 1979], which was made with black and clear leader and footage from the Margaret Mead film *Trance and Dance in Bali* [1952]. We'd had this ongoing debate about what happens when you use clear and black leader. When I made *Scar Tissue*, I was doing the opposite of what he did. We were very close then, and we talked a lot about film. I do tend to think of just one or two people when I'm working on a film. Actually, after I made *Scar Tissue*, I made a film that you haven't seen. It had two titles: first it was called *Someone Was Holding My Breath*; I changed it to *I Suggest Mine*. I didn't like that film; it was so personal, about such neurotic aspects of my self-image, that I re-edited it, but I still didn't like it. Then I started working on a film about excision in Africa.

SM: That's the removal of the clitoris?

SF: Yes. And sewing up the vagina and the labia. I was really freaked out about the subject. I'd seen Ann Poirier's film *Primal Fear* [1978]. In it there was this brief bit of footage of an excision being done on a little girl in Africa. When I saw that footage at the New York Film Festival, I screamed out, "No!" But then I got interested in doing a film about excision. I read lots of material, and I started doing scratched-word tests because I wanted to make the film a conversation. One voice would be the "experts," like Western doctors or African men and women who would talk about why it's done, and the other voice would be the women describing what it felt like and their memories of it. I did a lot of tests with scratched words, but then I realized that that was a completely inappropriate form for such a film, which would have to be a much more accessible sort of documentary. Since I didn't want to work in a documentary style, I gave it up.

I started working on *Gently Down the Stream* because I was having a lot of trouble, and I wanted to reread my journals and then burn them all. Instead I got interested in many of the dreams I'd recorded. I developed *Gently Down the Stream* from those dreams.

When I made *I Suggest Mine*, I thought I should try to do something very personal, entirely about me. I failed miserably. I was much too self-conscious about exposing myself. By the time I got around to *Gently Down the Stream*, I had accepted the idea of using personal material, but I had also found a way to work with it with some sort of distance. At first, when I was reading the dreams and thinking about them, I felt really embarrassed about revealing them. But by the time I began to see how they looked when they were scratched out and saw what images went with them, I had lost some of that personal investment.

When I was doing *Cool Hands* and *Scar Tissue*, I was much more rigid in my thinking, both about film and about myself as a woman. With *Scar Tissue*, especially, I wanted to be very extreme, to just use a few elements and be very aggressive with them. In both films I wanted to convince people of something; I wanted to show them some little corner of the world and say, "You see, this is the way it is, and it's not good that it's this way." When I made *Gently Down the Stream*, I felt differently. I had certain assumptions about what my dreams meant, and I certainly had ideas about what it meant to be involved with a woman and then involved with a man. I had ideas about how to work with dreams and how I felt they were useful. But I also liked the idea that, being less doctrinaire, I was leaving things more to chance. I wasn't saying that all women are good or that it's only good to be with women. I was saying, well, you know, things are kind of messy in our private lives and in our dream worlds and that's just the way it is. At first it seemed that if I was going to be a "good" feminist I should show the relationship with the woman to be a good one as compared to the relationship with a man. But I couldn't because the dreams that I had about the relationship with the woman revealed a lot of problems. The dreams revealed that both relationships were pretty much failures, and that seemed more realistic than trying to sell some theory about how relationships *should* be.

SM: Are there a couple of shots from *Scar Tissue* in *The Ties That Bind*?

SF: Yes. There's also a lot of footage from *Hot Water* [1978], my very first film, in *Gently Down the Stream*: the stuff of the woman swimming in the pool and the woman rowing on the rowing machine.

SM: That material looks like found footage from another era.

SF: Yes, it does. I really liked shooting that first film. It wasn't a very good film, but it was fun to do. I liked the footage in it, but I wasn't crazy about the way it was put together. I was low on footage when I was making *Gently Down the Stream*, and I figured I might as well use this stuff. Actually, I was thinking of using some outtakes from *But No One* in *Damned If You Don't*. I like the idea of recycling things and of finding new meanings, in a new context, for images that have appeared in earlier films.

SM: There are some very weird dreams in *Gently Down the Stream*. The dream about making the second vagina and the image of the baby that crumbles are pretty powerful. I used the film in several classes this year, and the students found the film outrageous. They were riled up about it.

SF: If people see the film without knowing it's made from dreams, they do tend to get very anxious. But if they recognize that the texts are dreams, they tend to accept the film. We all have weird dreams.

SM: Well, there's also the question of admitting what you dream or feel. We may know we have embarrassing dreams, but publicly admitting what they are is something different. I'll bet most people repress confusing dreams very quickly.

SF: I've been surprised when I've traveled with *Gently Down the Stream* how many people tell me that they never remember their dreams or if they do, they never bother to write them down. They don't take them seriously. I find that I go through periods when I don't remember any of my dreams, and I feel terrible after a while because I feel like I really need to remember them and look at them. When I went through my journal to find dreams for *Gently Down the Stream*, I found great dreams I hadn't remembered—the one about making the second vagina was one of them. I thought, "What a great image. It's so loaded and says so much"—and I'd forgotten about it! I would never have come up with that image during a conscious moment; I feel grateful for the images we create while dreaming.

The dreams that ended up in the film are suggestive in different ways. Remember the dream where I say that the woman sitting on the stage asks a friend from the audience to come and make love to her? Every time I show the film and I'm in the audience, I think about how somebody in the audience feels. As a filmmaker, I'm doing just what the woman in the dream is doing. I think there's something about making work that has to do with your wanting to please people, to make love with the audience. This dream is a bald statement of a desire that I think is part of a lot of films.

SM: How many dreams did you start with?

SF: Ninety-four. I asked my current lover, who was a man, and a former lover, who was a woman, and one male friend and one female friend (both of whom are gay) to read all the dreams and tell me which ones they liked.

After I got all their responses, I studied them to see which ones the men liked and which ones the women liked. I didn't really use that as the basis for making a final decision about which to use but it did help me to think about the dreams. Finally, I chose to do the dreams about women with moving scratched words and the dreams about men with optically printed freeze-framed scratched words. I did about forty dreams, some with images, many without. I put it all together and showed it to a few people. They said, "It's just horrible; it's way too long! Nobody could ever make any sense of it." So I went through a painstaking process of cutting dreams out: each one I eliminated felt like such a great loss. But that experience was a crucial lesson for me because I learned that no matter how painful it is to let go of material, a film usually benefits from a very severe editing process. As I whittled the film down, I also started developing more ways to use images; I started combining images with dreams that hadn't had any before.

SM: Your use of text reveals a strong sense of poetic timing. Do you read much poetry?

SF: No. I read Walt Whitman one summer—almost nothing but him. The only other poets I've read closely are Sappho and Anna Ahkmatova. But I have trouble reading poetry. I get impatient with it.

SM: There's something about the timing and the spacing in your films that reminds me of William Carlos Williams.

SF: Well, the timing is important. I started out with each dream on an index card, and kept whittling down the phrasing until it was really succinct. Then I started breaking it up into lines to see how it should be phrased in the film. I heard the rhythm of each dream very clearly in my mind before I started scratching. I would scratch them onto the film and project the results. If something wasn't right, I'd cut out a few frames or add a few frames.

SM: I remember Hollis Frampton saying that once you *can* read, you can't *not* read. When the words appear, the viewer has no choice about reading them. You participate in this film on a different level from the way you participate in a conventional film.

SF: I have a fantasy that one day I'll show *Gently Down the Stream* and the audience will say the whole thing out loud.

I'm at a strange point now, as far as using text goes. I had so much fun making *Gently Down the Stream* that I ended up making a second, similar film, *But No One*. I liked what I did in *But No One*, but I wasn't crazy about it. *But No One* is made out of a certain amount of repression and depression, and it shows.

SM: Even the device of scratched texts doesn't work as well.

SF: I feel very intimate with that device, but I also feel that I might not be able to use it much longer. Actually, I pushed it further in *Gently Down the Stream* than I did in *But No One* or *The Ties That Bind*.

SM: You may articulate it more in *Gently Down the Stream* than in *The Ties That Bind*, but in the longer film you found a way of using it without its dominating the entire experience.

SF: One large area that I haven't really worked with is scratching words over images. I mean I did that a little in *The Ties That Bind* (when I go to my mother's house, for example) and at the end of *Gently Down the Stream*, where "blindness" is spelled out over the water with that incredible movement. That's one area I'd like to explore more. I'm interested in what would happen if I started using scratched text to comment on the images that you're seeing or to completely confuse the image, to have them be so contradictory that you couldn't, or wouldn't, want to be looking and reading at the same time.

SM: What got you started on *The Ties That Bind*?

SF: Well, I remember that I was in California on tour with Leslie Thornton, showing films. I wanted to make a movie, and I kept thinking of the phrase, "She built a house"—just the phrase. I was doing a lot of drawings and making little notes to myself about having a sense of home, and one day I suddenly thought of my mother. She was someone I thought of as without her own home—although she's lived in the United States since 1950 and is settled here, she'd always seemed a little bit uprooted to me, partly because I'd never met any of her relatives.

Suddenly, I thought that her life was something I absolutely had to find out about, something I had to work with. I went to Chicago to see her. I had to lie a little bit, to make it seem like this wasn't such a serious project. I was very diffident about it when I talked to her, and then I showed up with lots of equipment. I think she was suspicious. But she was great about the filming. She was so unselfconscious, and *I'm* the sort of person who *hates* to be in front of the camera, still or movie. I thought she would be very uptight; I thought she would worry about the way she looked, but she was completely indifferent. She just went about her business, paid no attention to me. One or two times, she said, "Oh, stop that filming for a minute." She'd be having a conversation with me, and I'd be behind this big camera grunting and saying, "Oh yeah? Oh yeah?" and I think after a while she felt uncomfortable with it. But she never refused to let me film anything.

SM: You recorded the tapes later?

SF: No. I did all the interviewing and some shooting on my first visit there, but the film was ruined because my filter holder wasn't completely in and the light was coming through. I went back about a month later and shot all the material of my mother that you see in the film.

I felt really distressed about the project. I had started on it so quickly because I had such a passion about it, but I hadn't really thought it through. I was still insecure. When I saw the ruined footage, I felt *really* discouraged and almost didn't continue.

SM: How much taping did you do?

SF: I taped for five evenings. I was embarrassed about it. I had originally said to her that we were doing it so that the tapes could be transcribed, so that she could pass on her stories to her children. I was misleading her, and I was afraid that if I pushed certain issues too far, she might wonder what was going on. When I realized how upset she was becoming as a result of the discussions, I was worried. I thought she might just fall to pieces. Maybe suddenly I would say the wrong thing, and it would be the last straw for her, but she came out with a lot more than I expected.

SM: She seems very at ease. She's a good storyteller.

SF: Well, that might be my editing too. I did a lot of editing. There's always a certain artifice in even the most "natural" footage or sound of someone. For example, my mother became very upset when thinking and talking about certain experiences, and she tended to slow down and have long pauses between passages of a story. At first I thought those pauses should remain so that the viewer would feel her searching through her memories, but I realized that the effect would be boring, rather than moving. So I spent a lot of time cutting out silent passages.

SM: The story itself is interesting—the idea of knowing what it felt like to be anti-Nazi in Germany in the thirties. Even if she wasn't a member of The White Rose [an anti-Nazi underground organization discussed in *The Ties That Bind*], it took nerve to be who she was. The audience can empathize with her and admire her. Is she pleased with the film?

SF: If I ever hear myself on tape, I always think, "Oh my god, I sound like such a fool!" She had the same reaction at first, and she also felt that a lot of other people had suffered much more than her, or had been a lot more courageous, and that therefore she wasn't appropriate material for such a film. But the last time she saw the film, she seemed pretty comfortable with it.

Before I made *The Ties That Bind* I had such bad feelings about being German, being the daughter of a German; and my father is half German too. I don't think I really trusted the material I had. When I was working on the film, I told myself to stop worrying, to stop thinking I shouldn't be doing it, to stop disbelieving her, to trust her. I figured if the film was a failure in the long run I wouldn't show it.

At some point I just stopped carrying on about it. It was strange to suddenly be thinking of my mother in this respectful way, to really be admiring her for what she did, for surviving. I had never thought of *her*.

SM: She's a remarkable person.

SF: Well, it took me a lot of time to figure that out. I think part of being a teenager is that you're so interested in forming your own identity and not being identified with your parents that you only see their bad side. One night when I was making this film, I was talking to Leslie [Thornton] about it, and said, "It just occurred to me that I learned some really good things from my parents." I was developing a better sense of myself; I was respecting myself more as a worker. I was proud that I could support myself, and I thought, "You know, this came from something; somebody taught me how to do this for myself, and it must have been them."

SM: You said at the screening tonight that you edited *The Ties That Bind* section by section, for seven hundred hours. The subtle interconnections between the imagery, the text, and the sound make it an easy film to see again and again.

SF: I was really scared about editing sound and picture. It was completely unknown territory for me. The temptation was to have this strong sound carry the image, but I was afraid of the image getting lost. I started with a forty-five-second bit (when she says she feels so horrible that she's a German) and inched my way along from there, going to a two-minute section, then to a five-minute section, and finally I could work on a ten-minute section comfortably.

I think part of my process as a filmmaker has been to start at a point where I think nothing is allowed, where you have to work with the barest minimum. I've needed to see what I can make from that minimum and then move in the other direction. I find I'm letting more and more things into my films now, and sometimes it worries me. I'm afraid I'm going to get to be too indulgent, too entertaining and engaging.

But I always want my films to be very sensuous. I want the rhythm and the images to be gratifying. I think it would be foolish, and false, for me to make a film simply in order to be "difficult," to respond to a certain part of the film world that expects that of a film. I enjoy going to films that are both sensual and entertaining, that engage me emotionally as well as intellectually. I'm so bored by most of the films that are made in response to current film theory, and I've never felt obliged to use that sort of language in my own work. I'm perfectly aware of all the pitfalls of the identification that happens when we watch narrative films, and I think that's an issue worthy of serious discussion. But I'd never deny the necessity and pleasure of storytelling, because I've learned so much from being engaged by other people's stories of their lives. I've always wanted to make films that are as emotionally honest as they can be, and then I hope that other people will learn something from seeing them or feel that a part of their own life is being honored in the films.

SM: While I understand the resistance of some filmmakers to the idea that watching films should be a pleasure, I sometimes have a suspicion about the "moral purity" of this stance. I mean, if you're against sensuality in film, you don't have to go through the painstaking process of learning how to create a sensual experience.

SF: Right, right. It's the same thing with humor. I really envy people who can make funny films. That's a great talent. I would love my next film to be funny to a certain degree, but that's very difficult to do. I think there's a difference between humor that you laugh at, and wit, where something is clever and surprising and pleasing in a more subtle way. I think there are witty moments in *Gently Down the Stream* and in *The Ties That Bind.*

SM: One of the things I found really interesting about *The Ties That Bind* is your mother's perspective on the arrival of the liberating allies. She goes into some detail about how they destroyed her house; you can feel how violated she felt by that.

SF: When I talked to my father about it, he said that as far as he was able to observe (and he was never in combat; he came in at the end of the war to work in the denazification program), the first soldiers to come in were the combat troops who had seen a lot of action and were just sick and tired of everything. They came through and went home. It was the service and supply guys who hadn't been in combat, who were looking for some kind of action, that caused trouble. The combat troops had probably gotten rid of a lot of the aggression they felt toward the Germans, but the supply guys were doing it this other way. My mother told me a story about two friends of hers, neighbors, who were raped and killed by American soldiers. I was going to use that story in the film, but I decided that what I had was strong enough. She had many stories about being harassed by American soldiers. She was almost raped one time but got away.

SM: You mentioned earlier that you feel your parents gave you the skills you needed to be able to support yourself. How do you earn money?

SF: I do pasteup. I haven't worked lately but when I do, I get eighteen dollars an hour. I hate it passionately, but I learned how to do it by pasting up the first couple of issues of *Heresies* (with some other women). You just take the text and the picture and set it all up for the printer. It's very exacting, mechanical manual labor. Actually, I think it's affected my filmmaking. My ability to be precise with the scratched texts is partly a result of my experience as a pasteup person. At this point I don't want it anymore as an influence, but I don't know what else I would do to earn a living. During the past two years, I've also been able to earn about twenty percent of my income by doing one-person shows at schools and museums. It gets pretty difficult at times to answer the same questions over and over, but it's important to make contact with the audience, to know the people "out there" who still support these sorts of films. I've also gotten a few grants, which were a real blessing; it would have taken me twice as long to make *Damned If You Don't* without them.

SM: When you took on *The Ties That Bind*, did you assume its length would generate more shows?

SF: I had no idea that *The Ties That Bind* was going to be as long as it was, and I also didn't think that people were going to be that interested in it. It just got longer and longer and more expensive, and then I found that because I had an hour-long film it was easier to get shows. Before that, I had always been in group shows. (Actually, I started out doing some programming myself, setting up shows in galleries in the East Village, in churches.) I had never really worried much about getting one-person shows because I kept making these short films and it didn't seem possible. But once I did *The Ties That Bind*, I got lots of invitations. It's always hard to be businesslike about your own art products, but I decided I had to force myself to accept that part of the filmmaking process, to deal with the hard work that comes *after* the hard work of getting the film made.

SM: I would think *The Ties That Bind* could have a pretty good-sized audience, certainly more than just the avant-garde film audience.

SF: I've shown it in a number of places where it seemed like a lot of people in the audience don't see experimental film. Afterward people would come up to me and say, "I've never seen a film like this. I was confused at first, but by the end I really understood and enjoyed it." When I was making the film, I was hard on myself about the relationship of sound and image. I wanted to be very precise, to push the two elements in a way that doesn't happen in a standard documentary, but I also wanted the film to be accessible to people. I respect people's intelligence enough to think that if they were shown this sort of film more often, they would be able to understand it. I don't think people will necessarily run screaming from experimental films, and I wish some programmers had more respect for their audience's intelligence.

And I think people might enjoy playing the games the film sets up. I certainly feel the difference between a film in which the person is trying to be communicative and one where a person is just trying to be obscure and go over everyone's head. I don't think *The Ties That Bind* feels deliberately obscure.

SM: Avant-garde film is always going to have technical "weaknesses," compared to commercial cinema. The secret is to use them to your benefit. When the viewer of *The Ties That Bind* hears the mic bang on the couch, the home-movie feeling of the film is enhanced; it's as if we're sitting in somebody's den looking at the slides of their trip. Your film is technically screwed up just enough to make the viewer feel at ease; it's the polar opposite of Leni Riefenstahl's *Triumph of the Will* [1936], which I've juxtaposed it with in courses a number of times.

SF: I have a very uneasy relationship with the technology of filmmaking. I think I'm careful only up to a point, and it's usually the point where redoing something would mean spending more money than I have. Past that point I think, "Fuck it."

SM: Has *The Ties That Bind* been shown on TV? Has it earned income as a semi-commercial theatrical film?

SF: It was shown at a number of festivals, and it was shown on WNYC in New York.

SM: Do you think your work suffers when it's transferred to video?

SF: Scratched words don't look good on video. They lose the crisp articulation and rhythm that's there on film. And the material in *The Ties That Bind* that's blown up from Super 8 to 16mm looks terrible on video. It just falls to pieces. I have a horrible feeling about that because in the past—let's say five or ten years ago—when I would go to a screening of films by women, many of them would be technically poor. There would be this urgency about getting the film made and saying this important thing, and if you didn't expose the image right or if the sound was bad, well those were the breaks. When I've seen my film on video, I've thought, "My god, if somebody just turns this on and doesn't know me and hasn't seen the film projected, they'll think, 'Oh god, another film by a woman that looks like shit.'" Of course, these days many women are making technically competent films. And I think that that earlier period in our history—of making films out of a breathless sense of urgency despite technical limitations—was absolutely crucial. The same process happened in third-world countries when they were first developing their own film industries, and some incredibly powerful films were made despite the lack of technology.

SM: One feminist reaction to conventional cinema has been to confront patriarchal exploitation by eliminating the kinds of pleasure that conventional films thrive on. I'm assuming that in *Damned If You Don't* you're taking the position that there's no reason why feminist films shouldn't be as sensuously pleasurable as conventional cinema.

SF: I think I did have that plan when I started. I wanted to make something that I (and viewers) would enjoy. But I don't think I set out to contradict any other person's film or any other kind of filmmaking. It's true that when I go to films that are determined *not* to provide traditional pleasure, I end up being really frustrated or bored or angry. My reaction to such films has been building for a long time. Even when I was making *Gently Down the Stream*, I had a combative stance toward antipleasure films, but at that time I wasn't able to do as much as I wanted to do in terms of providing pleasure myself. And certainly there wasn't much place for pleasure in *The Ties That Bind*. It wasn't until I was actually into making *Damned If You Don't* that I realized I could create some of the visual (and aural) pleasures I had wanted to experience in other people's films. Maybe it took me this long to be able to begin to work with pleasurable material because I had my own reservations about it. As much as I was angry about what other people were doing, I knew that I wasn't prepared politically or emotionally to do something different. I had to overcome my own backlog of things I *shouldn't* do.

SM: The subject of *Damned If You Don't* doesn't seem a very likely place for humor, and I'm sure to some people it isn't at all funny.

SF: I have a tendency to look at things too seriously. When I made *Damned If You Don't*, I was particularly close to someone who has a really good sense of humor and who definitely pushed me into putting more humor into the film. Also, when I told my brother I was working on the film, he said, "Oh god, why don't you just once make a film about a light subject!" He imagined, rightly, that I was planning another anguished exposition. His saying that really stuck in my mind.

SM: The woman who delivers the critique of *Black Narcissus*, Martina Siebert, does a terrific job.

SF: I chose her partly because she's German and has a German accent. Initially I thought of it as a joke on the expert German scientist in fifties documentaries. But her delivery didn't come through that way. Her English is good, but she didn't always understand the cadence I intended, so a lot of times she said things in an odd way I couldn't have anticipated—which ended up working out for the best.

SM: Another section of the film that's pretty funny, and I assume consciously so, is when the text from *Immodest Acts* is juxtaposed with the shots of the nuns walking around. When the reader says, "I saw Christ coming," one nun looks up as though she sees something coming. It's as if the nuns are unwittingly acting out the story. At the end of the film you apologize to those nuns. Was that because you felt you had made jokes at their expense?

SF: Well, I started the film feeling very angry toward nuns and toward the Catholic church, and I wanted the film to be a condemnation of everything about the church.

SM: Why were you angry at nuns in, particular?

SF: Priests had some influence too, but the nuns were more immediate for me because they were my teachers for eight years. And, of course, they're women and they set what I thought was a bad example for me as a woman. But as I worked on the film and remembered more about the nuns, I realized that there was also a very good side to them, and I found myself feeling a lot of affection for some of them. Later, when I had the footage, I just wanted to look at them and remember them somewhat affectionately through this footage.

In the passage you asked about, the nuns are just walking around on the street looking very ordinary. I would look at that material and think about the nun in *Immodest Acts* who's in a delirious state because Christ is supposedly removing her heart while another nun watches from behind a curtain. By combining that text with the footage of nuns looking like they lead a fairly normal life, I wanted to create an uneasy feeling. When you see the nuns, it's hard to imagine that they would go so far as to believe that their hearts could actually be taken out of their bodies. Yet there's an ambiguity: maybe they've all had that kind of experience.

But to answer your earlier question: I apologized at the end because I'd had to lie to the nuns at the convent so that they would let me shoot, and I felt guilty about it.

SM: What did you tell them you were doing?

SF: I said I was making a narrative film about a woman lawyer who's working on a case and struggling with some ethical problem that causes her to have a flashback about a nun she'd had in grade school who taught her an important moral lesson. They were very flattered and liked the idea of my filming. When we were there, they kept coming in and out of the convent and saying hello. If any of them had spent time watching what we were doing, they would have sensed that something else was going on. I mean, here was this nun looking out from behind a tree while another woman was walking by. I don't know if they figured anything out.

SM: At the Flaherty seminar [Friedrich was a guest at the thirty-third Robert Flaherty Seminar in August 1987], after the screening of Johan van der Keuken's *The Way South* [1981], you were very angry at his manipulation of the people he filmed. I thought then and still think someone could ask a very similar question of you.

SF: Of course, it's convenient for me to be able to see a distinction between the two.

SM: I'm interested in hearing the distinction.

SF: Well, I would never have interviewed any nuns on film or on tape and then have used the material without their knowing the complete context of the film. All the nuns I shot were in the public domain; they were out in the world. And I wasn't making a direct connection between any of those particular nuns and specific material in the film. I think it would be very different and completely unacceptable for me to interview nuns and then reveal their private lives, the way van der Keuken revealed the people in his film, without their permission. I gave my mother final approval of *The Ties That Bind*. I certainly could have thought, "Fuck her, she's my mother; I can do whatever I want with the material." But if she had said that any part of that film was not permissible to use, I would have removed it. When I filmed at the convent, I very deliberately didn't show the name. I tried not to create a context by which people could identify the convent. I wanted the material to be anonymous.

SM: I would argue that were van der Keuken to explain his politics to the people he films, they would be comfortable about appearing in his film. On the other hand, if the nuns whose images you use understood the politics of your film, I'd guess they would be horrified.

SF: Again, this may be splitting hairs, and the nuns definitely wouldn't be interested in my hair splitting, but I made a conscious choice not to use any images of them over any explicit sexual material. I thought that would be going too far. I'm sure you're right that they would all be incensed to find themselves in the film, but what can I do? There *are* nuns who have either come out or have gotten involved with men and left the convent, so the issue in the film is legitimate. I don't think it's sacrilegious or vulgar to suggest that some nuns might be sexually frustrated by their vows and might go to certain extremes to break away from their past beliefs and practices.

SM: *Damned If You Don't* seems related to the tradition of psychodrama and trance film—what P. Adams Sitney has called "visionary film"—where an entranced character (a dreamer, a "seer"—in any case, a representative of the film artist) is pursuing Beauty, Vision, whatever. The Troyano character's pursuit of the nun strikes me as an emblem of your pursuing the subject of nuns as a filmmaker.

SF: I haven't really thought about it that way. I had already shot a fair amount of footage about nuns during the spring and summer of 1986, but it wasn't narrative material. And then in the fall I went to London and was staying with someone who had a tape of *Black Narcissus*. That film pushed me into thinking about my film more in terms of a sexual confrontation between this nun and another woman, rather than as a personal documentary about my experiences growing up Catholic.

So in a way it is true that *Black Narcissus* functioned for me the way I had it function for Ela in the film.

I guess I thought when I was doing *Damned If You Don't* that it was really about my finally coming to terms with my own fear of sex and of dealing with people about sex. The film was going to be a celebration of sex. I guess I did identify with Ela as the aggressor, the one who represented sexual freedom. And I was a little bit scornful of the nun because she embodied my fear. I think that as I went along I felt more and more for the nun, and when I was finished with the film and some time had passed, I realized the film was very much about that fear. My fear must have been pretty great for me to make a film about it.

SM: You know, both characters look a bit like you, but like different parts of you. It's almost like one part of you is being pursued by another part, and the goal of the film is to help you bring the two parts back together, to put them in balance.

At first it looks like the sensual person is following the spiritual person, although as the film develops, you realize that if the nun weren't sensual, she wouldn't be having a conflict about sex, and if the Troyano character weren't spiritual, she wouldn't be putting dozens of candles around her bed before they have sex.

SF: I think this kind of psychoanalyzing is a problem in public discourse. Audiences don't know that much about my character and shouldn't need to. The way I would talk about these issues is to focus on one abiding problem within Catholicism, the split between the spiritual and the sexual. One of the really profound lessons I learned as a Catholic—and I don't mean "lesson" in a good sense—was that on the one hand there's a general love for the world, a love that leads one to serve the world, to serve people and God. And then there's another kind of love, a sexual love for someone. The church always splits those two things. Within the context of loving an individual in a marriage with children you are expected to serve your community, but still there is married love and, distinct from it, the love that a person within the church—a nun or a priest—has with God and toward the world. I find that terribly schizophrenic. I think it really fucks people up. I chose Peggy Healey to play the nun character because she has a very sensual face, and I wanted someone who would embody a certain sensuality within a supposedly unsensual context.

SM: It's interesting that you introduce the Other Woman alone, not as part of a community, whereas the nun implicitly does have a community.

SF: That's true. Toward the end of the film, when Ela gets dressed up to go out to the party, I'd planned to show her within a community, and at one point, I thought of her having a friend or a lover. But that sort of fell by the wayside. It is funny to have her be such a lone wolf. A very powerful thing about being a nun is that you're part of a community of like-minded souls.

To come back to the issue of sex for a moment, in a lot of public discourse sex is defined as something anarchistic and divisive. The sex drive is what ideally unites two people in a very intense way, but it creates a great discord in the world at large, in the form of jealousy, hysteria, whatever. Sex is allowed to function in people's lives when they're young, when they don't have responsibilities; but once responsibilities set in, somehow it gets put on the back burner. Once people are married or coupled, sex with a person outside the marriage creates a terrible problem. I think the church is very aware of that and controls it. It knows that if it were to say that God loves sex as much as he loves anything else—go right ahead and enjoy yourself—it wouldn't be as successful in convincing people to live in strictly monogamous marriages. This idea is implicit in the film. You have this one woman who is part of a coherent community where becoming sexual puts her at great risk. You don't see a context for the other woman so you can never be sure whether she's just picking this nun up or whether she's looking for love and romance and a life happily ever after. That they come together at the end and that sex is what unites them doesn't mean the problem is solved. Although the end is very celebratory within the context of the film, there's still the possibility that in the long run sex will create the same problems for these women that it's created for other people.

SM: There's something almost sad about the fact that it takes so much conflict and self-questioning for this moment to happen. The bells going off at the end not only celebrate their union, but seem a campy way of laughing at our difficulties with sex: why is it so *difficult* all the time?

SF: Right! [laughter] Actually, some people have said, "Well, that nun sure looked like she knew what she was doing." I guess they feel she should have looked more awkward or innocent. Obviously, it would have made the scene much less erotic if I'd shown her fumbling around and complaining and saying, "Oh, don't!" I wanted that final scene to be beautifully choreographed. But I think there's some truth to their lack of awkwardness. All of the stuff that leads up to the moment when you're finally in bed with somebody is where most of the awkwardness and hysteria happens. A lot of times, once you're there, you only think, "God, what a relief! Let's go!"

SM: It's interesting that we see *Black Narcissus* within your black-and-white film. You may know that *Black Narcissus* won an Academy Award for best color.

SF: Oh really? I didn't know that, but the color is beautiful.

SM: Your critique of the film in *Damned If You Don't* doesn't allow the viewer to experience that film's sensuous levels.

SF: Well, that's not completely true. Or I hope it isn't. The way I frame the imagery, very close, is to me a way of appreciating the really high drama of *Black Narcissus*. A lot of narrative films seem to have some very exciting moments connected by a lot of filler, and it was fun to pare *Black Narcissus* down to the bone, to string the exciting moments together and really focus on the sexual hysteria at the core of the film. Powell and Pressburger used lighting to such great effect and created a lot of expression in the faces, which is all you have to work with when you're dealing with characters who are completely covered. I tried to bring some of that out.

Some people have reacted negatively to the roll bars that happen when you film from a TV screen. They think the roll bars are there because I had no control over the technology. When I saw *Black Narcissus* in London, I thought, "This is a fantastic film; I'm going to use it," and the next day I set up my camera and shot it. I came home, developed the film, and there were the roll bars. I thought, "Okay, I can either go back and work it so that there aren't roll bars or I can keep going the way I've begun." Once I had decided that the roll bars were part of the image, it became really interesting to edit for the rhythm of gestures within the shot, combined with the rhythm of the roll bars, combined with the cadence of the speech at the moment. It became an elaborate game to play, though my eyes were on the floor when I was done.

SM: One of the things that draws me to your films is their precise rhythmic control, which I connect with a certain tradition of sixties film—Brakhage, for example.

SF: Actually, a long time ago when Marjorie Keller first showed *Daughters of Chaos* [1980; at the Collective for Living Cinema in New York City], I saw it and liked it. I talked to somebody afterward who said, "It's one of those films that was made on a Steenbeck." At that point I had never worked on a Steenbeck, so I didn't even know what he meant. He said, "Well you know, it all gets done in the editing." Part of me thought, "Well, that's an interesting criticism; maybe it is a problem," but on the other hand, I found myself thinking that I liked the film and wondered how the method could be so bad if it resulted in something so intricately woven together? I guess I do admire Brakhage's editing, though I don't always admire what he's making the film about. To me the most fantastic part of constructing a film is taking many disparate elements and making some sense out of them, making them work together and inform each other. That process was really hard in *Damned If You Don't* because I had shot so much for a more documentary film, and the more the narrative took shape, the less that other stuff worked with it.

Also, at times I felt really angry at myself for getting caught in this bind between narrative and experimental. That was something I had always warned myself about and critiqued other people for. I had felt that once you start dealing with narrative, there really isn't the room for serious experimentation that there is when you don't use narrative at all. I don't know what will happen the next time I make a film, but in *Damned If You Don't* I do manage to create certain moments I really enjoy, which are a result of the film's mixture of very different approaches.

SM: You could say that the film reclaims certain kinds of pleasure that are the stuff of commercial cinema without accepting the commercial cinema's ideology and that the film reclaims certain kinds of pleasure that are particular to avant-garde film without necessarily accepting the ideology of the films in which these avant-garde pleasures are usually experienced.

SF: It seems that the issue is always giving yourself the maximum amount of freedom. If you make narrative film, then—some people would argue—you have more freedom because you're making something that will be accessible to people and will get to more audiences. Other people would say that only if you're doing something extremely experimental do you have absolute freedom, because you never have to worry if anyone understands anything you're saying.

There are drawbacks to both positions, and advantages to both. Actually, I think when they're good, experimental films are as accessible as good narrative films.

SM: Name some experimental films that you think compete on an enjoyment level with commercial films.

SF: I'd say a number of films by Brakhage or Frampton or Maya Deren. Margie Keller's films. Leslie Thornton's. God, there are so many.

I think that in the past my animosity toward narrative film had to do with not having the usual experience of identification. This was partly because I'm a woman (I saw a lot of films about interesting male characters and stupid female characters) and at times because I couldn't identify with the romantic line of the films. One of the things that changed me was finally seeing Fassbinder's films. I certainly have my differences with his style and with what some of his films are about, but I have a strong identification with many of his films. When I first saw them, I had the feeling that here finally was a narrative filmmaker who was talking about stuff that I wanted talked about in films. Experimental films were mind-expanding for me in other ways that related to my studying art history, especially painting and sculpture.

It's tempting to want to work on every possible level in a film. Narrative is tempting in its way, but I can't imagine eliminating the footage that deals with elements of the materiality of film. There is a danger. You can make something that's terribly compromised, that doesn't do either thing well. To me *Damned If You Don't* was risky because I didn't know what I was going to end up with. One of my oldest friends, who had once been an experimental filmmaker, was very critical of *Damned If You Don't*. He saw it as a weak compromise.

SM: I'd say that since conventional narrative cinema and experimental cinema have been ghettoized away from each other, the radical thing to do is to bring them together.

The critique of *Black Narcissus*, which is funny and precise and which, I'm sure, nearly everyone enjoys, builds patience that allows the more materially experimental elements to be accepted by the audience. Because you begin by giving them elements of conventional pleasure, you enable them to go with less conventional experiences.

SF: What I felt I was doing by beginning with the *Black Narcissus* material was saying, "OK, you want a narrative; here, take it: you can have it. And you can have it just for its high points; you don't have to slog through all the bullshit, all the transitions." In a way it was a joke on the conventional narrative "hook." I do think there's a real awkwardness for about five minutes after the *Black Narcissus* critique is over, when the audience has to shift out of this really safe, funny world into something that's less clear. And I did want the *Black Narcissus* critique to be interesting and amusing on its own terms.

SM: Are Makea McDonald's reminiscences her own or did you write them?

SF: I interviewed seven women who had gone to Catholic schools. One was my sister; four were women I've known from living in New York; and two were women I went to high school with. I had gone to school with Makea and met her again in New York after many years. Some of the other women were gay, but they didn't really talk about their relationship to nuns in terms of being gay. For a while I tried to collage their voices, but it got too confusing and so I settled on Makea. She was the only one who talked about having crushes on nuns, and I really identified with some of what she said, not just about nuns, but about other things too. I particularly love what she says during the Coney Island section, when she talks about her spirit splitting from her body when she had sex with a man. That was really beautiful. It was nice to discover her again and have her be such a crucial element in the film.

SM: She enacts one of the conflicts that the film's about. She talks about being gay and yet she also sings the Lord's Prayer.

SF: Yes. That ambivalence was very appropriate for the film. And since she's a trained soprano she has a powerful voice.

SM: We see two motifs during *Damned If You Don't*: the black-and-white snake that curls through the water and the swan through the fence. On one level both are reminiscent of the nuns because of their formal coloring, but both are also traditional phallic images. I assume that you're reappropriating the imagery so that it represents female sexuality.

SF: The first time the snake and the swan appear is when Ela has fallen asleep after seeing *Black Narcissus*. My alternating between them was meant to be a dream sequence of hers. I was thinking of the snake being the Ela character (its movements are very sensual but sort of dangerous) and the swan being the nun. But actually, I think it was just that I loved the footage and wanted to use it, and worked it in that way!

SM: At the end you announce the women's sexual union by showing a routine between male and female tightrope walkers. It's a convenient metaphor for the nun's doing this chancy thing of coming to the other woman's room. But why did you use a heterosexual tightrope couple?

SF: I liked the dance between them. I thought it was a wonderful ballet of a seduction. I certainly considered that it was a heterosexual moment right before a homosexual moment, but I don't see sex as exclusively heterosexual or homosexual. At a discussion of *Damned If You Don't*, somebody asked whether I was trying to imply that all nuns are lesbians. I really hope that people don't think that that's what I'm saying in the film; it's very important to me that people *don't* think that. To be provocative, I said, "Well, I think it would have happened exactly the same way if it had been a man and the nun." At the time I thought to myself,

"That isn't entirely true!" But I wanted to make people think about it. I think the whole ritual of seduction works out to be pretty much the same thing between a man and a woman or between a woman and a woman—at least that's been my experience. There are differences, but there's also something universal about being attracted to somebody and trying to make something happen about it.

SM: *Sink or Swim* is about your relationship with your father, but the way in which you present your struggle to come to grips with that relationship is unusual. Probably of all your films, *Sink or Swim* has the most rigorously formal organization. The only other film I know that uses the alphabet as a central structural device is Frampton's *Zorns Lemma*. Obviously, your film deals more directly and openly with personal material than Frampton's did, but I wonder, is there any conscious reference to cinematic fathers, as well as to your biological father?

SF: That's a hard question to answer. Offhand, I'd say I wasn't making a conscious reference to any other filmmakers, but that the structure was determined more by the fact of my father's being a linguist. I thought that using the alphabet was an obvious choice for the overall structure. I've certainly been influenced by many filmmakers, including some of the so-called structural filmmakers, like Frampton or Ernie Gehr, but my films are never meant to be a direct comment on or a reworking of ideas from other people's films.

I tend to think of the structural film school as avoiding the use of personal, revealing subject matter; I think they're more concerned with how film affects one's perception of time and space than with how it can present a narrative. Whenever I set out to make a film, my primary motive is to create an emotionally charged, or resonant, experience—to work with stories from my own life that I feel the need to examine closely, and that I think are shared by many people. With that as the initial motive, I then try to find a form that will not only make the material accessible but will also give the viewer a certain amount of cinematic pleasure. In that I feel somewhat akin to the structural filmmakers, since I do like to play with the frame, the surface, the rhythm, with layering and repetition and text, and all the other filmic elements that are precluded when one is trying to do something more purely narrative or documentary.

In the text of *Sink or Swim*, I had to make a decision about form. I was using stories from my own life and began by writing them in the first person, but I got tired of that very quickly. I sounded too self-indulgent. Writing them over in the third person was quite liberating. The distance I got from speaking of "a girl" and "her father" gave me more courage, allowed me to say things I wouldn't dare say in the first person, and I think it also lets viewers identify more with the material, because they don't have to be constantly thinking of me while listening to the stories. Some people have told me afterward that they weren't even aware it was autobiographical, which I like. The point of the film is not to have people know about *me;* it's to have them think about what we all experience during childhood, in differing degrees.

On the other hand, it can sometimes be a problem to impose a structure on a story. I was happy to have thought about using the alphabet, but then that forced me to produce exactly twenty-six stories, no more, no less. I went into a panic at first, thinking that I had either seventy-five stories or only ten, and wasn't sure that I would be able to say all I wanted to say within the limits of the twenty-six. But that became a good disciplinary device; it forced me to edit, to select carefully for maximum effect.

SM: I think the irony is that Hollis, for example, really thought his formal tactics were keeping his films from being personal (his use of Michael Snow to narrate *nostalgia* is similar to your use of the young girl to narrate the stories in *Sink or Swim*). When I talked with him about his films, he rarely mentioned any connection between what he made and his personal life—a conventionally "masculine" way of dealing with the personal in art. But from my point of view, his best films—*Zorns Lemma, nostalgia, Poetic Justice* [1972], *Critical Mass* [1971]—are always those in which the personal makes itself felt, despite his attempts to formally distance and control it.

SF: The issue for me is to be more direct, or honest, about my experiences but also to be analytical. I think there's always a problem in people seeing my films and immediately applying the word "personal." *Sink or Swim* is personal, but it's also very analytical, or rigorously formal.

I don't like to generalize about anything, but I do think it's often the case that the more a person pretends or insists they're not dealing with their own feelings, the more those feelings come out in peculiar ways in their work. Historically, it's been the position of a lot of male artists to insist that they are speaking universally, that they're describing experiences outside of their own and thereby being transcendent. I think conversely that you get to something that's universal by being very specific. Of course, I think you can extend beyond your own experience; you can speak about your own experience while also describing the experience of other people you're close to or decide to know. But I think you have to start at home.

SM: Maybe these things are cyclical. I'm sure those late sixties, early seventies filmmakers who avoided the personal—Frampton and Snow, Yvonne Rainer—were reacting against the sixties demand that art, including film art, had to be personal. You bring two things together—the sixties' emphasis on the personal and the reaction against it—and make the intersection into something that exploits the useful parts of both approaches.

SF: I am a child of both worlds. When I was studying art history, I really responded to conceptual art, minimal art—those approaches which were very much about form and not about personal drama. But then, of course, I grew up through the women's movement and from the start really responded to the personal drama involved there. Not just that: I love fiction, I love to read about other people's lives, to learn about the choices people make and the ways in which they survive, or overcome, their personal histories. So I feel very much caught between the two approaches and I learn from both.

As an artist, it's important to me to keep both issues alive: to remember that my responsibility is to speak honestly about how it feels to be alive, and that my pleasure is to use my medium to its greatest advantage. I wouldn't be happy if I only let film tell a story in a conventional form, but I would feel that the heart of the work was missing if I only worked with the film as a material, if I only investigated its formal properties. The film scene is in a constant state of flux, and I think this effort to convey meaningful subject matter through unconventional form occupies a lot of filmmakers today. Hopefully, the lines between narrative, experimental, and documentary will continue to be broken down.

SM: Now that you've made a film about your father, as well as the film about your mother, it's probably inevitable that the two films will be paired a lot. When you made *The Ties That Bind*, did you already assume that, sooner or later, you'd come back to your history with your father?

SF: I know some people always have three or four projects in mind, but I never know what I'm going to do next until I'm completely finished with my current project. Certainly when I was interviewing my mother for *The Ties That Bind* and she got onto the subject of them getting divorced, it really struck a nerve and I thought it might be something to explore later.

One time a friend said it seemed like all of my films have been about my father—not really about him, exactly, but about reacting to his influence, or trying to get away from his influence, which is, in a larger sense, reacting to patriarchy. That was a pretty good observation, and I suspected there was going to come a time when I would have to deal with the question of patriarchy more directly, to look at how it happened closest to home, not out there somewhere.

SM: This film is clearly going to have a larger audience than some of the other films, just because it's in synch with the pervasive, contemporary issue of child abuse. What's interesting about *Sink or Swim* is its focus not on the most extreme types of child abuse, but on the situations men create because they feel that in order to be men, they have to act in a certain way. On one hand, you uncover the brutality that's gendered into the family situation. On the other hand, as much as there are things your father did that you really dislike, even hate, the film suggests an ambivalence about him and about his influence on you.

SF: Yes. I agree with what you said about gender, that abuse is more likely because of the inhuman situations that are intrinsic to a society that divides roles along gender lines. But *Sink or Swim* is also like *Mommie Dearest*: it's about the damage either parent can do when they're trying to shape their child in their own image. Most parents, either instinctively or consciously, try to instill their values in their child. They have a lot of ambitions themselves and, consequently, a lot of ambitions for their children. They force their children into activities or try to instill certain ideas in them that are not good, not natural for the child. I can see from watching the children of friends and relatives that part of who we are is formed by our parents and part of us is there from Day One. If you have a kid who's not naturally ambitious or aggressive and you try to make him that, you're just going to bend him out of shape. On the other hand, if you have ambitious children and don't encourage them, you can be very destructive.

To answer the second half of your question—about my ambivalence about my father: people have said to me, "It can't be all that bad, because look where you are," or "You're not a destroyed person; you're capable, you've made films, you've lived a relatively good life." I recognize that, and that's the source of my ambivalence. Certainly, I've learned to do things from him that have stood me in good stead over the years, just as I have from my mother.

Moreover, since the film is about how I've been affected by my childhood, it would have been grossly unfair not to acknowledge how my father was affected by his. I tried to speak to that by including the story about his younger sister drowning and showing how he spent many years afterward trying to overcome his guilt and loss. I put that story right before the one about him punishing my sister and me by holding our heads under water for too long, because I wanted to give a context to that punishment, to show that although we were devastated by his punishment, we were being punished by someone who had suffered his own childhood traumas.

One of the most painful things to realize in making the film was that we all inherit so much sorrow and hurt from our parents. We aren't the product of perfectly balanced adults; we are created by people who have a legacy of their own, which goes back through each family line. On my good days, I try to believe that each generation rids itself of a bit of the violence of the prior generations, that with education and greater material well-being we wouldn't have such widespread abuse. But unfortunately I think the solutions are extremely complex, and I can see that simple notions like education are hardly an answer.

SM: The most obvious example of your ambivalence is the source of the title, which refers to the incident of his throwing you into the pool for you to "sink or swim," since you wanted to learn to swim. At the end of that story, you admit you've remained an avid swimmer.

SF: But the swimming was fraught with all kinds of anxiety, which is why at the end of the film I tell the story about wanting to swim all the way across the lake and realizing that maybe I'm not physically capable of it, and am certainly very frightened at the thought of doing it, but feel compelled to do it anyway, because of him. It's at that moment that I finally say, "No, I don't have to do that. I can enjoy swimming, but on my terms, and I won't take on his standards for what makes a good swimmer or a brave swimmer," and then I swim back to shore.

SM: Although there's an irony there, too, because you swim halfway across the lake and then back, which means you actually swam as far as all the way across.

SF: I think the ambivalence reveals a great deal about the stubbornness of human nature. Many children who are born into situations that undermine them in certain ways still manage to survive beyond the situations. The question is why parents build that degree of uncertainty and anxiety and fear into the family setup. If you want your children to learn something, why not teach them in a way that is constructive and supportive, rather than by terrorizing them? It's been standard practice for parents to get children to learn to do something by scaring them in one way or another about what will happen if they don't learn to do it. I don't think that's the way people learn. It's certainly not the way you learn to do something you later enjoy.

SM: I think in his generation there was this feeling that unless you were capable of terrorizing your kids a little, you weren't a serious parent. Scaring them was almost a way of demonstrating how much you cared. As a young parent, I remember debating in many situations whether I was wimping out and doing my child damage by not being tough enough to do something that in the long run would be good, even if in the short run it was bad. And I think your father's generation felt this even more strongly. Did you talk with your siblings when you were making this film?

SF: Yes. My sister is a year older than I, and my brother six years younger, so I was interested in their different memories of childhood. My sister and I shared a lot of the experiences I mention in this film, and we lived longer with my father, so she was able to confirm many of my stories. She had other stories she wanted me to include in the film, but I stayed with those which had the most resonance for me. Since my brother was much younger, and was only five years old when my parents got divorced, he didn't know about, or hadn't shared, some of the events in the film, but I valued his perspective a great deal. He has slightly more distance from my father and was concerned that the material be presented fairly, that it not function simply as vendetta, which was also a concern of mine. In fact, he had a funny reaction to *The Ties That Bind*. He said, "Jesus, I hope you never make a film about me!" I certainly can't blame him for that sentiment; it's a weird and suspect process to make films based so openly on one's own family.

SM: It seems inevitable that at some time or another your father will see the film. What do you think about that?

SF: I dread it. When I first started working on the stories, I had a lot of anger, obviously—I even thought about sending a script to him. I had vengeful feelings. But the longer I worked on it, the less I wanted to punish him, and the more I felt I was not doing it so that he would finally acknowledge my experience, but so that I could acknowledge my experience.

The nuclear family is based on a relationship in which one person (the parent) has a lot more power and control than another (the child). Because of this, I think children are constantly having their feelings denied by their parents. If the child is unhappy and the parents can afford to acknowledge the unhappiness, they do it; but if the parents can't acknowledge the unhappiness because it reflects badly on them, they won't. For me, it was a matter of writing these stories so that I could finally say to myself, "This *did* happen to me, and this is the effect it had on me," regardless of his experience. I'm sure he has a very different interpretation of a lot of the stories, which is understandable—everyone sees things from their own perspective, their own history.

By the time I finished the film, I really felt that I was making it so I could understand what had happened *and* so other people who had the same experience could have that experience acknowledged. I don't think the sole purpose of art is to provide acknowledgment for people, but I think that's one of the things art can do. You can see a film or read a book that in some way corresponds to your experiences, good or bad, and you might feel stronger because you see yourself reflected in it. That's what being in the world is all about—having common experiences with other people. I hope that's the effect the film will have.

SM: During the film's coda, we see a home movie image, of you and hear you sing the ABC song. The last words of that song, and of the film, are, "Tell me what you think of me." Obviously, the song relates to the film in several ways, but is your use of it, on one level, a comment on the whole enterprise of making film? Do you mean that films are attempts to please whatever is left of the father in us and that the audience, which is now going to make a judgment of the film they've just seen, is an extension of patriarchy?

SF: Well, in a way, but that was the joke end of it. When you make a film, you do it to get a response, and presumably most people want a good response. I surely can't imagine making a film and hoping everyone will *hate* it. The conclusion of *Sink or Swim* was more a way for me to acknowledge my absurd ambivalence. A lot of the stories in the film are about doing things to get my father's approval, and then at the end in the last story I decide I'm not going to swim across the lake to please him. I've made a sort of grand gesture of turning back to shore, swimming back to my friends who will hopefully treat me differently than my father has treated me. But then in the epilogue I turn right around and sing the ABC song, which asks him what he thinks of me! I believe that, to a certain extent, we can transcend our childhood, but in some way we always remain the child looking for love and approval.

SM: I would guess that whether or not men like this film is going to have a lot to do with their ideologies about family. I'm sure it will make some men uncomfortable; it will expose them.

SF: A surprising number of men have come up to me afterward and talked about the film from the vantage point of being fathers. That wasn't foremost in my mind when I was making it, but their responses have been interesting: the film brings up a lot of fear in them, a lot of concern about how they're treating their own children. Many of them express a profound hope that they won't do major damage to their kids.

SM: At one point your father takes you to a movie theater and you see this film about people who didn't care about Western culture.

SF: *The Time Machine* [1960]. I used that film because it was one I remember seeing, but also because I could address the issue of people who have abandoned civilization. In the story, the time machine transports the main character into the year 20,000 (or whatever). He goes into the library, which no one uses, and sees that the books are just rotting away. The people, oblivious to history, are living a life of pleasure and yet are slaves to green monsters who control them and finally eat them. In some ways, I feel critical of the idea of people living a hedonistic life, divorced from serious thought and ignorant of the consequences of history. On the other hand, my experience with my father was that he was absolutely indebted to Western civilization and to the world of books and theory. I wouldn't say that he would defend Western culture against other cultures—he's an anthropologist who's spent a lot of time studying other cultures—but in some more profound way his life is organized around the principles and institutions of Western civilization. If you've lived your life in an ivory tower at a university, if you've lived your life in books, that can exclude you from a lot of experiences.

In some ways I was trying indirectly to critique a certain kind of film practice that's been in vogue for the last ten or fifteen years, and a certain kind of film theory that is often quite divorced from normal experience (although I wonder about the word "normal"). The story later on in the film about the kind of articles my father was writing while my parents were getting divorced was meant to be a dig at a lot of the writing that's done about films that I think strips the life out of them. I'm interested in more direct speech, something more visceral, more emotionally honest. I wanted to touch on that, but not directly.

SM: I assume this project was similar to *The Ties That Bind* in that you worked at great length on the editing.

SF: I started editing in November 1989 and worked pretty steadily until April. I had some breaks of a week or two here and there, but I pretty much kept to it that whole time. It took a tremendous amount of juggling decide what the order of the stories would be and what the overall visual theme of each section would be, and how to make the images move. As I've said before to you, when you're working with voiceover, you have to be extraordinarily careful about how your images work so you don't lose your audience. I think we tend to see more than we hear; I think we favor the sensual experience of images. I realized I had written a dense narration, and felt it would be drowned out by the barrage of images if I didn't work really carefully to keep the two elements informing each other.

Some people who have seen *Sink or Swim* have said that sometimes they spaced out, that they couldn't follow every word of every story. I understand that because I don't think I'd be able to either: the film presumes a second or third viewing, but that was something I really struggled with. I also didn't want the film to work just on a symbolic level or to be completely literal, so I go back and forth between the two. For example, there's a story about going over to the neighbors' and making ice cream sundaes and then watching a circus on TV, which is synched with circus imagery; and the story of the chess game, which is illustrated by a chess game. But other stories are accompanied by more symbolic imagery, like the story about the poem my father wrote about going to Mexico, which you hear as you see a glass vase being filled with water and three roses. And there are stories that are somewhere between the two poles, which I like. I most prefer when something is both symbolic and literal, though it's hard to do.

SM: I think probably the dimension that gets lost most easily in your films is the intricate network of connections between sound and image. In both *The Ties That Bind* and *Sink or Swim* the subject is so compelling that the subtleties of your presentation can easily be overlooked.

SF: I think people might not be so articulate about that level of the films because, not being familiar with the field of avant-garde film, they might not have the language with which to describe those effects. But I do think there's an unconscious recognition of that level; that's why the film is working. If I weren't editing well, if I was putting stupid images up against those stories, the stories might have a certain impact, but the images I use produce so many more meanings, and *that's* what people are really responding to, even if they think it's primarily the stories that are affecting them. If they come up afterward and say, "That was really powerful," I think, "Well, it's powerful because it's the right shape, the right texture, and the right rhythm—all those things."

There was a period when I thought it was important to deny myself everything, including all kinds of film pleasure, in order to be politically correct and save the world, but I think if you do that, you deplete yourself and then have nothing to offer the rest of the world. If you want to engage people, if you want them to care about what you're doing, you have to give them something. Of course, that doesn't mean making a Hollywood musical. The discussion tends to be so polarized: some people think that if you introduce the slightest bit of pleasure, whether it's visual or aural or whatever, you're in the other camp.

SM: There's always an implicit debate between the people who seem to want to get rid of cinema altogether, because of what it has meant in terms of gender politics, and the people who want to change the direction of cinema, to make it progressively vital, rather than invisible.

SF: Sometimes it's a case of "the harder they come, the harder they fall." When people hold out against a position—against cinematic pleasure for example— the urge is still there in them. If they hold out too long, they end up doing something that is so much about cinematic pleasure that in effect they've gone over to the other side without really acknowledging how or why. I think that happens a lot and it disturbs me. I really believe in film. I believe in its power. I think it's going to be around for a long time, and if people can't accept their responsibility for producing cinematic pleasure in an alternative form, well, that's their problem, and everyone's loss.

SM: Do you plan to tour with this film? I know you've been having some reservations about the usual way independent filmmakers present their work.

SF: In the case of the last two films, I did go around the country (and a little bit in Europe), showing the films and talking about them. With *The Ties That Bind*, I was eager to do it. For the most part, touring with that film was interesting for me. With *Damned If You Don't*, touring was a way to earn part of my living, and I was curious about the audience's response: since it was about a lesbian nun, I was curious to see whether people would be scandalized or amused, if a lot of lesbians would come to it, whatever.

But I got really worn out from the experience of having to speak after *Damned If You Don't*, and I approach the prospect of doing it with this film with a lot of dread, for two reasons. Making a film that evokes such painful memories is risky; people sometimes look at me afterward as if I have a solution to all the problems, as if I know some way to cope with the pain one feels. I'm afraid I don't really have any answers to give. All I know right now is the importance of acknowledging those childhood expectations.

The other reason is more general: I think the whole setup of having a personal appearance by the filmmaker after the screening is obsolete. I think this structure grew in part out of a feeling in the sixties and seventies that, while there was an audience out there for avant-garde film, it wasn't big enough, and one way to make the film more accessible was to have the filmmaker there. If people were frustrated or confused during the viewing of the film, they would be relieved of their frustrations afterward by having the whole thing explained to them.

Avant-garde film is in a period of crisis. Many independent filmmakers are moving into feature narratives, and there's a feeling that the process of making "smaller" films is dying out. That might make some people think it's still important to go out and proselytize and educate, but I think that's a misguided response to the situation. The idea that I would go to a performance by John Zorn or whomever—some composer or musician—and he would have to get up afterward and explain how to hear his music, as opposed to how to hear Schönberg or Beethoven, is absurd. I think the film community is much too paranoid about the audience's alleged inability to understand avant-garde films.

My experience with *The Ties That Bind* proved this to me. Since it was about an older woman, I often had older people in the audience, people in their fifties and sixties who had never seen an experimental film. Sometimes they told me afterward that they were intimidated at the outset, but by the end of the film they were fine, they understood and enjoyed it. They're adults; they've got minds. There has to be more respect for the audience, and more trust.

Does Radical Content Deserve Radical Form?

Su Friedrich / 1988

From *Millennium Film Journal*, no. 22 (Winter/Spring 1989–90). Reprinted by permission from Grahame Weinbren, Senior Editor of *Millennium Film Journal*, and Su Friedrich.

The theme for this panel was originally "Radical Content Requires Radical Form," although recently Barbara [Hammer] seems to have broadened the parameters of the discussion. But since I've been worrying over the original thesis for the last month or so, I'd rather try to address it . . . which I find to be almost impossible for several reasons, the first of which is the use of the term "radical." It tempts me to start using phrases like, "When I was younger . . ." However, if I were to proceed along those lines, I'd soon be admitting that even back then I wouldn't have used the term to define myself. It always conjured up actions which were far more extreme than my own (such as making posters, publishing magazines, going to demonstrations, and taking photographs). And although I was much more willing then than I am now to take absolute positions about issues concerning, for example, sex or sex-role stereotyping, I was still more interested in finding the nuances, the subtle points which would undermine or recast those absolute feelings. I was always somewhat afraid of, and intimidated by, those who were willing to assert the most radical positions: that lesbian relationships are inherently better than heterosexual ones, that women are better (morally or otherwise) than men, that collectives are preferable to hierarchies, that experimental film is superior to narrative, that monogamy is oppressive, etc.

I agree that it can be bracing or clarifying to have certain patterns described in their most extreme manifestations (e.g., that marriage is legalized prostitution, that narrative is inherently reactionary) and that this has allowed us to see the skeletal structure of certain social institutions or cultural practices; but I think we have to be careful and allow for the countless shades of gray that exist between the black and white of those radical formulations. Saying this makes me very anxious because I don't want to appear as an apologist either for the oppressive characteristics of the nuclear family or of narrative filmmaking, but

I must admit that I'm still invested in certain aspects of both those traditions, and I find it more fruitful to analyze and work—albeit cautiously—with those traditions and save the good of them, than to throw them out entirely in the interests of being a "pure" radical. And then again there's the dreadfully predictable scenario of people who were once considered radical but are no longer able to live with the extremity of their position and flee back to the opposite extreme. Like Catholics who become rabidly antispiritual (and I come very close to that myself), or junkies who clean up and move to the suburbs, or leftists who join the political machine, or experimental filmmakers who end up making Pepsodent commercials (although those are the rarest converts, it appears).

This brings me (somehow) to the question of content, radical or otherwise. If I try to apply the requisite formula to the broad range of experimental films that have been made in the past thirty years, I would be hard pressed to find many that live up to that standard. I don't think the content of even half the films could qualify as radical, if one defines that as something which argues for the drastic overhaul of some aspect of society. Certainly a lot of experimental films have portrayed alternative ways of living and have asserted that there's more to perception or experience than can be conveyed through a linear narrative—and indeed there's a great freedom to be had in seeing those films. But equally often they portray, if through a radical use of the medium, things which are fairly mundane or familiar.

Stan Brakhage is a good case in point. His use of the medium has been truly radical; he has forced us to see through a lens as few others have, to move with his camera and in his editing in a way that few others did before him. But I couldn't say the same for his content. He's made a few too many films about his family, his wife as Muse, and himself as the artist-as-genius. I've felt as aggravated and oppressed watching some of his films as I feel watching a sitcom, even though that feeling was often mitigated by my interest in his formal devices. Therefore, if I were to apply the aforementioned formula to his work, he would have to be relegated to the trash heap—and I have done that with a few of his films. But in the long run, I appreciate the risks he's taken with form enough to allow, somewhat grudgingly, for his conservative sexual politics and his self-mythologizing. He's one example among many in the field, and I've gone to countless screenings hoping to find that synthesis of radical form and content only to be disappointed. After many experiences of the kind, I've come to feel that it's necessary to wrest at least some good from the work, to appreciate it if the person has managed to take some risks, whether in form or content, even if they haven't formed a perfect synthesis. It isn't easy for me to do that, and now I must confess that I constantly hope to see realized in the world of film the marriage of those two radical acts.

But having admitted that, I want to proceed with my defense of those films which fail to meet the standards of this formula.

Stan Brakhage and many others stand as good examples of the split between radical form and content, defending—by the very nature of their genre—the superiority of a radical approach to form. On the other half of that divide exist many fine documentary and narrative filmmakers. It's hard for me to choose an example, but suffice it to say that I've seen innumerable films during the past fifteen years which have exposed me to the lives of people with whom I might never be in direct contact. I've been taught about how others live, think, and feel, and that experience has made me re-evaluate my own prejudices, taught me the narrowness of my own thinking and my own experiences, and compelled me to put my life in the context of all those other lives out there. I'm grateful to those films for giving me so much.

Yet, just as I feel after many experimental film shows, I've come away from these other films distressed by the inconsistency in them; distressed by the fact that they would push me so hard, work such a transformation in my thinking without even beginning to address, let alone challenge, my sense of narrative structure or the alleged veracity of film as a "realistic" medium. It's such a weird feeling to sit at one of those films and watch myself be worked on, watch as the film gradually feeds me all the familiar narrative hooks, pulls me in and keeps me going until we arrive together, breathlessly, at the long-awaited conclusion. If that sounds a bit like having sex, it's no coincidence . . . but enough on that subject for the moment.

I go away from the films again with a sense of loss, a sense of potential only half realized, and I continue to imagine that the combination of a transformative experience through the content and a radical approach to form would take me halfway to heaven. But unfortunately we live on earth, and I still believe in the separation of church and state. Hence I've come to accept, albeit reluctantly, that there are, and will be, many good films made that do provide a fairly radical content without giving the least hint of a radical form. And so it goes.

Being a natural pessimist, I have to force myself at this point to acknowledge that there are a number of film and video makers who come pretty close to synthesizing the two elements, who are willing and able to go beyond the limits set by an earlier generation of experimental filmmakers, who don't insist that a film must only be silent or elliptical or structural or geometric or nonnarrative or apolitical or diaristic or whatever else to be considered "really" experimental. In fact, most people I know can barely define the term "experimental" anymore, which I think is a healthy sign. And now I feel completely confused: because I was trying to say that there is some work which manages to be fairly radical both in its form and content, but on the other hand I celebrate the fact that we can't really define the terms that we're using. I guess the problem for me is that making art is a matter of being in a constant state of evolution—which means that I feel on pretty shaky ground most of the time. I'm always stunned by people who talk about their work with utter confidence and clarity, who seem to have a single, purposeful theory underlying their work. I can't imagine thinking that way; and whatever yardstick I use to measure my work or someone else's on one day may be entirely different from what I use on the next. Hence my reservation about claiming that anyone is actually achieving that synthesis of form and content, and my misgivings about the formula altogether.

If I'm torturing you with my indecisiveness, let me spend a few minutes saying something about my own work; that might clarify why I refuse these days to plant a flag.

I started out making films when I was quite estranged from narrative films, although Fassbinder was one of the few exceptions that proved the rule of my contempt. I was bound and determined to use the medium for all its most extreme potential: to speak about states of mind and being that I didn't see in most other films, and to force the viewer to be constantly aware of, and sensitive to, the medium as such. I didn't want to use realism, plot, sound, or many other devices which are normally employed to keep the audience mollified or mesmerized. And I did do that, as well as I could, and made a few films which were black and white not only in look but in their feeling, and were silent as well (although some included written texts). But then the mysterious and less tangible gray areas started to interest me, and I changed—primarily with my last two films, *The Ties That Bind* and *Damned If You Don't*.

In making *The Ties That Bind*, I realized that I had a narrative on my hands: I had my mother's story of her life during World War II, full of personal and political conflict, and although I wanted to explode it, to work simultaneously from many angles, I had to accept the responsibility of presenting it in a way which would be relatively accessible. One simple choice was to have the story unfold chronologically, and as I slowly developed the soundtrack, a moral tale began to emerge. Or, rather, my sense of a moral purpose in making the film emerged. Throughout the editing, I often had to discard formal strategies because they seemed to have no place in a film "like this." At the time, it made me think that I was going to end up with a fairly conventional documentary—and at moments I still fear that that happened. But those of you who've seen the film know that the result is a far cry from a talking heads documentary, and I'm glad of that. Maybe some would even feel that it's a somewhat successful synthesis of radical content and form, but I think that might only be the case when considered in the context of more conventional work. And maybe "context is all," but I'm not satisfied with that excuse. This notion, this formula, seems to exist in some absolute realm above and beyond what most of us are capable of producing, and it's an absolute against which, or with which, I've struggled for many years. And back to the problem of defining what's radical—I could never claim that the film's content is truly radical: it's simply the story of an ordinary woman living through extraordinary times. If that's radical, then what isn't?

But then again with *Damned If You Don't*, I found myself wanting to tell a story, and again one which I thought of as a moral tale. I was ready and, I thought, able to crucify once and for all the Catholic Church, and rescue a poor nun from its clutches. But I found myself unable to be as censorious as I'd imagined; I wanted some of the characters and places and objects to function as a tribute to certain sensual aspects of Catholicism. When I'd forced myself up against the wall, I had to admit that there were some experiences growing up Catholic which I still valued. Perhaps the most subtle manifestation of that is simply in the way the film is shot and edited. It isn't easy for me to articulate how that works, but I'm convinced that my upbringing, with all its repression, idealism, and sense of an unrequited desire for the sublime, has had a direct effect on my way of shooting and editing. So the good and bad were inseparable, and all I could do was use that fact to craft the film as carefully, or perhaps I should say as faithfully, as possible.

The other glitch that appeared, after my initial thrill at the idea of using a radical form to speak of a radical subject, was that I found myself wanting desperately to create a dramatic narrative with, god forbid, a happy ending. And that's what I did, although I fought my impulses all the way, chastising myself for yielding to what I saw as some of the worst devices of that most loathsome film form, the dramatic narrative. Granted, the narrative is interrupted, the story doesn't rely on dialogue, and again, if the context is the world of traditional narrative, the film might be seen as radical. But, if I consider it in the context of my own work, I'm left with mixed feelings. By that measure, I indeed made many concessions to the medium which I wouldn't have borne a few years earlier. And as much as that frightened or worried me, it also gave me a feeling of freedom. Because I really think that the most oppressive situation is one in which we feel we *must* work in a particular way, and that other ways of working are wrong, revisionist, conservative, etc.

When I was first making films, I felt immense freedom in the idea of making films which were drastically different from anything I'd seen before in narrative or documentary films. And it *was* important to look out the back door, so to speak, to turn my back on film tradition. I still do, for the most part. But it always boils down to how one needs to work in order to say what needs to be said in a given film. As I've gone along, it seems more important to allow myself even more freedom: to look out both the front and back doors, as well as all the windows; to still assume that there are infinite possibilities in how a film can be made, and what it can say.

I still ask myself whether I'm being as truthful as possible when I speak in a film, and whether I'm making as many demands as possible on the medium, which is clearly a language that's still evolving. But I just can't abide by a slogan like "radical content requires radical form," because it's too oppressive and too abstract. I don't think anyone sits down to work in order to be radical; one works in order to say something about how it feels to be alive. To put a prescription on that endeavor is one sure way to stifle or discredit most voices, and to ignore the fact that there are so many, many voices in the world. I'm sure we can learn more by respecting each voice as an individual one (of course I'm talking about relatively independent voices, not those of Hollywood), rather than trying to ensure that we all speak the same language. If someone feels deeply moved by the plight of an oppressed group, and thinks that their message should be delivered in a rational, linear, accessible voice, then so be it. If someone else is a gifted storyteller and believes in the efficacy of narrative devices for presenting that story, more power to her or him. And if someone else wants to make a film about walls and floors and sunlight, then I hope he or she does it so that I see those floors as I've never seen them before.

Girls Out of Uniform: Su Friedrich Remembers Being Twelve Years Old and Gay

Lydia Marcus / 1997

From *Release Print: The Magazine of Film Arts Foundation*, April 1997. Reprinted by permission of Lydia Marcus.

Set in the present day and the mid-1960s, Su Friedrich's latest film, *Hide and Seek*, melds documentary footage and fictional narrative. In the documentary sections, adult lesbians share memories of their emerging sexuality in their preteen years. Those stories are intercut with a narrative about twelve-year-old girls, which is based in part on Friedrich's own experience. *Hide and Seek* and other films by Su Friedrich will be shown in April at San Francisco Cinematheque and the Pacific Film Archive, as well as at American Cinematheque in Los Angeles.

A noted experimental filmmaker, Friedrich has been making films since the late 1970s. Her earlier works include *Gently Down the Stream*, *Damned If You Don't*, *Sink or Swim*, and *Rules of the Road*. *Hide and Seek* is her longest film to date, at just over an hour. It recently played in the documentary competition at the Sundance Film Festival where this interview was conducted.

Lydia Marcus: Some of the archival footage that you use in *Hide and Seek* reminds me of the 1931 German film *Maedchen in Uniform*. Was that film an influence on you?

Su Friedrich: I saw that film probably twenty years ago, when the first women's film festivals were going on, and I totally identified with it, and I've seen it a couple of times since then. It's not as if I thought, "Oh yeah, I want to make an updated *Maedchen in Uniform*," but it clearly is an influence in the general scheme of things.

The footage in *Hide and Seek* is from a film called *Our Fascist School*, an Italian film from the late thirties/early forties, which shows all the ways in which a school functions perfectly in a fascist regime. (Laughs) "We are walking together and we bathe together." I never saw the whole film, but it was one of the ones that I got from Rick Prelinger. I love that it evokes *Maedchen in Uniform*. I wouldn't have felt right about using clips from *Maedchen in Uniform* because I consider that an artwork and *Our Fascist School* is more of an industrial film.

LM: Who is Rick Prelinger?

SF: For many years he's run Prelinger Archives and he's done a number of compilation films. He's just sold his collection to Archive Films in New York, but he still holds the rights to some of them, and he gave me everything for free. He's very connected to the experimental film and video community, and I guess when a project comes along that he believes in, he just wants to help out. It was hard to find material with girls in it. Rick had a lot of great stuff, but I also went to the Archives of the History of American Psychology in Ohio—that's where I got a couple of the other pieces that I really love.

LM: The footage of the woman in Africa with the lions—what was that documentary called?

SF: It's called *Simba*, and it's by Martin and Osa Johnson. They were really wild characters, the first people to bring a motion picture camera to Africa. I wanted to use *Born Free* as the reference for the character, but they would not give us the rights to it. We begged and pleaded and they treated it like it was *Gone with the Wind*. Actually, I had a hard time finding a copy of it. It's not like it's a film that people are still running out to see.

LM: The footage from *Simba* represents that whole idea of explorers, and the girls in *Hide and Seek* are explorers. Especially at age twelve, if you are gay, it's more difficult seeking out others like yourself. There are some shots when you cut to the African hunters and then back to the girls, creating a kind of parallel.

SF: I wanted the film to work metaphorically, so that you know it is about another kind of exploration.

LM: I can't think of any other film that shows preteen girls in this kind of sexual stage. I don't think it's ever been done.

SF: It hasn't.

LM: Even for boys it's barely been touched on.

SF: Right.

LM: Has this film been years in the making? Did you think, "God I wish I could have seen something like this when I was twelve"—not that any twelve-year-olds are likely to see this film?

SF: Right. That's why it says on the video sleeve and the promotional card, "This is a film for every woman who's been to a slumber party and every man who wonders what went on at one." Because I don't want people to think this is a movie for kids. It's not.

But it's not as if I wanted to make this for the last fifteen years; I've been really focused on other films. One of the things that got me started thinking about it was the first action that the Lesbian Avengers did in New York in 1991–92. We went to a public grade school in Queens on the first day of school, when all the parents bring their kids, and we had balloons that said, "Teach about lesbian lives." We handed a balloon to each kid as they went into the playground, and the parents were furious. A few parents were cool with it, and the kids were excited—"Wow, I get a balloon!"—but other parents were like, "Let go of that balloon!" Also we had on t-shirts that said, "I was a lesbian child." Seeing that phrase on all these women was so moving to me, I thought, "We have all come from somewhere. There are so many things that went on when I was that age that I haven't thought enough about." So that was a very big part of wanting to do the film.

LM: Were you influenced by Aerlyn Weissman and Lynne Fernie's film *Forbidden Love*?

SF: There are certain things that I'm familiar with and I like doing, but then I also want to do something different. Definitely *Forbidden Love* was something which interested me when I saw it—that they were trying to combine documentary and fiction—but I had also made a film in 1987, called *Damned If You Don't*, which is fiction intercut with the feature film *Black Narcissus*. That was an interesting film to make in terms of how I had to deal with the audience and this whole question of gay film. I think I was still seen as an experimental filmmaker, and then I made *Damned If You Don't* and suddenly I was a lesbian filmmaker.

LM: Because there's lesbian content in that film—the nun has a crush on this woman. Was it then that people started asking you in interviews, "Are you gay?"

SF: They didn't have to ask me; I think I was always up front about it. If somebody would ask me, "Where did you get the idea for *Damned If You Don't*?" I would say, "I was raised Catholic and I had certain feelings about nuns, and I wanted to explore that."

If you do something that's that explicit, and particularly at that time when there wasn't that much lesbian and gay work around, then you really start to be seen as doing work on this one theme—about being a lesbian. I sort of go back and forth. *Sink or Swim*, which was the next film I made, really had nothing to do with being a lesbian; it was about my relationship with my father. So it's kind of interesting to be seen for a while as making lesbian work, and then doing something that isn't, and then the lesbians are like, "Hey, what about us?" and then the experimental people embrace me again because I'm doing something they can deal with. So I'm in a funny place, I think.

LM: Are you able to just make your films and survive financially?

SF: Since 1990, I've pieced my income together from filmmaking. Before then I did paste-up, I did freelance magazine and book production work. I got a

Guggenheim Fellowship for $22,000 in 1990 when I was finishing *Sink or Swim*, a Rockefeller soon after that, so I thought, "Okay, this is safe for the moment, I'll quit this other work. I figured I'd have to go back to it, but so far so good. I do very small teaching things, an editing class at The New School and an optical printing class. But I don't know what's going to happen now. I don't make that much money and I'm not in line to get grants, because I don't have a new project. So we'll see.

LM: You got NEA money for *Hide and Seek*. That's incredible.

SF: Isn't it? I thought, if you don't apply, you'll feel like a jerk, so just apply, even though the odds are about one half of one percent. Somehow the miracle occurred. Then I also got money from ITVS, and I thought, "Whoa, wait a minute, I got money from the NEA and public television for this project about lesbians when they were children. What is going on?" I'm still amazed that it happened.

LM: Do you keep the audience in mind when you are making films—what they are expecting from you or what they want?

SF: I always have cared very much about my audience, in the sense that when I'm making something, I really want to do it so that people will understand it. That's very different than making something that everyone will like it. Even if I choose to work in a complicated structure, I don't assume that I'm just going to have a tiny audience and they're going to be so knowledgeable that it'll make sense to them. I figure, even if it's very experimental, everyone should be able to experience it in some way. I think there's an attitude among some experimental filmmakers that they're above their audience, and that if what they're doing isn't clear, it's just because the person is too stupid. I don't feel that way. I think people are pretty smart if you give them something that works, that makes sense. I've always tried to make things that work in their own context.

Framing Lesbian Angst: Filmmaker Su Friedrich

Erin Blackwell / 1997

From *Bay Area Reporter*, April 3, 1997. Reprinted courtesy of *Bay Area Reporter*.

For someone who never went to film school, Su Friedrich has an enviable reputation as a filmmaker. The forty-two-year-old New Haven native has spent the last twenty years in New York piecing together experimental films she has toured internationally to critical and popular acclaim. Tonight and Sunday she'll present three films that form an incidental triptych on the individual's struggle inside the trap of socially determined identity.

Two early films cut her parents up into conceptual DNA without ever losing the emotional conflict and connection. The elliptical *Ties That Bind* (1984) is a difficult but loving dialogue with her German mother about life under Hitler. *Sink or Swim* (1990) is a harder edged primer on life with and without a father who divorced the family when Friedrich was fourteen. These two films suggest a nature and nurture (if not genetic) genesis of the filmmaker's genius for combining rigorous analysis with deeply sensual forms to express the ultimately unknowable nature of the human heart and mind.

Friedrich's latest film, *Hide and Seek*, is an hour-long homage to her own young lesbian self. Don't worry, this isn't "straight" autobiography. Written with her on-and-off girlfriend of seventeen years, painter Cathy Nan Quinlan, the film encompasses the talking heads of smart urban dykes, vintage educational gender propaganda, and a lyrical narrative featuring some great child performances. It will be shown in this year's Lesbian and Gay Film Festival.

Erin Blackwell: In a 1990 interview with Scott MacDonald you were very articulate about your creative process. To paraphrase, you start with an emotionally charged experience, which you then analyze and put into an accessible and pleasurable form.

Su Friedrich: Going back and forth between emotion and analysis sometimes almost functions like an escape mechanism. I'll start thinking about what it was like to be with my father, or what my mother's life was like during the war, or what it was like to be a lesbian child. Then it may become hard to think about, or just very emotional. So I think, "How am I going to write this sentence better?" Or, "What kind of structure can I use for this series of images?" It removes me from the emotional mess of it. And when I look at the structure, I have to ask if it actually expresses the emotional stuff?

EB: What do you do when you're overwhelmed by the emotion?

SF: I suppose I have a few beers. They weren't easy films to make. But there's a sense of pleasure when I get past a certain hurdle. I may start by feeling I can't think about something. and then I make myself think about it, and once I have, then I *have* it and can start to play with it.

EB: How was writing the film with your girlfriend?

SF: It was really great to work with her, because she's an interesting writer [who] had her own stories about her childhood. We used a bit of hers and bit of mine and a bit of the things we both experienced. She has a good sense of humor and tended to want to find the joyful moments, while I tend to look at the more difficult moments.

EB: In *Hide and Seek* you play a sex-ed teacher who delivers the classic classroom line, "Am I going to have to separate you two?" Are you doing a Hitchcock?

SF: That was never my intention. I just thought, probably the night before, I'II get one of the women on the crew to do it. When the time came, I turned to everyone and said, "Okay, we need someone to put on this ridiculous outfit and say one line." And everyone refused and insisted that I do it. And I was really upset because I hate being on camera.

EB: Are you an artist?

SF: I suppose.

EB: You seem to have a commitment to something other than success.

SF: I don't want to be a hired gun. I've seen that happen to a lot of people. They get picked up after one film that's made from the heart, and they're offered scripts. Maybe they do something that has some significance to them, but they get caught up in making things that will just be bigger or—I don't even want to start using those adjectives.

EB: What's in it for you?

SF: There's an intense pleasure in working. I love most aspects of filmmaking. I love to shoot, I love to edit: I love to write—once I've written it. Writing is not very pleasurable, but the end result is kind of gratifying. There's a simple pleasure just in doing it, just as somebody who loves to swim goes swimming.

So I don't feel like a public servant, because there is a selfish pleasure in the craft of filmmaking.

EB: The term independent seems to have lost its meaning. You've said the same of "experimental." Can you devise another term?

SF: I sort of wish we could just talk about film. When we talk about painting, we don't talk about dependent painting and Hollywood painting or New York painting. There's just this understanding that there are thousands of people painting paintings. Some of them make tons of money selling them, some don't. But they're all working in the same medium. I don't think Ron Howard's new film starring Gena Davis is any more important or impressive than a twenty-minute Super 8 film starring nobody. All the distinctions are really absurd.

EB: How did you finance *Hide and Seek*?

SF: I'd gotten some money from the New York State Council on the Arts and the Jerome Foundation. And then I got money from the NEA. But then I was funded by the Independent Television Service (ITVS) in late 1994, and that made it possible to do the fictional part of the film. The ITVS money pushed the film into a different form than it started out being.

EB: The ITVS gave you $228,000 out of a total budget of $300,000. That's not a lot of money.

SF: It was a lot more than I'd gotten for all the other films combined. I'd made 11 other films for half of that. It's not a lot by Hollywood standards.

EB: The film braids together three separate films, or levels of discourse. Why?

SF: If I had just talked to women and gotten their stories, then I would have had a talking-heads documentary, and that would have been really boring. If I had just used archival clips, they wouldn't have made sense the way they do now when I combine them with the other two elements. If I had just made fiction, then I wouldn't have had all the richness of these real women telling these very amusing stories about their childhood. I love your image of them being braided together, I guess because I had long hair when I was a kid and wore a braid all the time.

EB: Is there a word for this kind of mixing of genres?

SF: Just don't call it docudrama.

EB: I promise.

Film Buffs Are Film Buffs No Matter Whom They Sleep With

Su Friedrich / 2008

From *GLQ: A Journal of Lesbian and Gay Studies* 14.1 (2008): 127–28

I've been out since before I started making films and have almost always had some sort of lesbian content in my work, but I've shown much more often at nongay festivals. I think this has a lot to do with my work being part of the experimental film world and there being (sometimes, although less frequently these days than in the past) more room at nongay festivals for my kind of work.

Queer festivals are best for me when I show a film with substantial lesbian content (like *Hide and Seek*, 1996) and get a rousing response, as I did, for example, at Frameline. They are worst when I show work that doesn't have substantial lesbian content or is somehow "too experimental" and the audience seems disoriented; they're expecting something with two women in bed, and instead I've given them something that's too formal and in which the two women are only part of a more complicated web of ideas and images. I often wonder why my work that is not explicitly lesbian is programmed at gay festivals, and it's usually because the programmer has some affinity with the avant-garde film community and thinks she or he can "bring the audience around."

It's hard for me to talk about the differences between the festivals, and I find that there's more distinction to be made in the scale and intent of the festivals than in the sexual orientation of the work being shown. In other words, the hustle and intensity of Frameline is more like the Berlin Film Festival than like a small-scale gay festival. Film buffs are film buffs, no matter whom they sleep with. I suppose the only very obvious difference is that audiences at gay festivals have tended to be more charged up because of the chance to see work about themselves. In the past, when there was little gay and lesbian media available at the video stores and on TV, it was a big deal to have these festivals. These days, I'm not so sure it's that different from nongay festivals, that is, people go to any kind of festival because they hope to see unusual work, work that won't necessarily get into distribution, or work that will do so later but they want to be the first to see it. With the changed landscape for gay and lesbian media, I think the situation is fairly similar to that of a nongay festival.

Regarding foreign queer festivals, programmers often insist that their audiences understand English well enough not to require subtitles, but the reality is that, without subtitles, the audience misses most of the subtleties of the film's dialogue. But as for attitudes about being lesbian, I haven't found anything that different in foreign film audiences.

I don't think about release strategies because I'm not trying to position my work in ways that will ensure theatrical release—with the exception of *Hide and Seek*, my work hasn't had that potential. Nevertheless, having a body of work that has addressed lesbian identity in various ways, I'm aware of the fact that a new film would likely be of interest to programmers at gay and lesbian festivals, so I always make an effort to have the work shown to them in order to build press.

I don't go to many festivals these days and haven't for the past few years because of the sort of work I've been doing. I suppose if I have to speculate, I would say that festivals are becoming more unwieldy and that makes it harder to negotiate the terrain. It seems they're all getting bigger, everyone's upping the ante, and it's hard to be seen in the crush of that many films and parties. I imagine queer festivals will continue for a while, since more and more people are producing gay and lesbian films and videos and there isn't room in the nongay festivals for all that work to be shown (and as far as I'm concerned, a lot of it shouldn't be shown even in the gay festivals—a little editing would be in order!). I wonder sometimes whether they'll go the way of the women's film festivals, which were so essential, empowering, and wonderful back in the day but which now barely exist except in countries where women still have a much harder row to hoe and the urgency for showing work specifically about women's experiences is still strong.

Su Friedrich's Cinema

Cecilia Muhlstein / 2008

From *NY Arts Magazine*, May/June 2008. Reprinted by permission of Cecilia Muhlstein.

Su Friedrich's work in film is essential in understanding the importance of avant-garde film and history. Since the late '70s she has addressed issues of sexuality, feminism, capitalism, and identity politics. Her latest film, *From the Ground Up* (2007) deals with the production, distribution, and consumption of coffee.

Cecilia Muhlstein: I recently came back from San Francisco where I saw the Joseph Cornell exhibit at MOMA. The ephemeral dreams, found objects, words, important to his work, are refracted in your films. I notice, like Cornell's work, your films engage in dreams which become places, where language appears in the unexpected, and the fantasy—even your scripts read like poems. I keep thinking of the fragile black-and-white images of birds flying in the sky as your mother's voice describes bombs in Germany during the Nazi occupation in *The Ties That Bind* (1984); your looking for something to prune in *The Odds of Recovery* (2002); or the fish, breathing heavily in the market, awaiting death in *But No One* (1982). How does the dream turn logic or dis-logic in your work?

Su Friedrich: I only worked directly with dreams while making *Gently Down the Stream* and *But No One*; I used actual dream texts and also tried to make the film's form respond to the nature of the dream state. I don't mean that I tried to replicate the dream on film, but I attempted to create a dislocating experience for the viewer. By scratching words onto the screen and combining them with images that were only tangentially related to the dream text, I wanted to create that sense of dislocation that one has when one tries to recall a dream—the feeling that one's simple verbal description of "what happened" never quite captures the elusive, convoluted, and illogical narrative that one experienced while dreaming.

Beyond those two films, I suppose there is often a quality or experience in my work that relates to dreaming insofar as I mix so many elements together (both visual and verbal) and, while I try to create credible and comprehensible relationships between the elements, I also refuse to be completely literal or didactic. This results in a lot of slippage, a lot of moments when one is watching one kind of image while hearing some different kind of sound and meanwhile one isn't being told why the two are in conjunction. I want the viewer to be inside the film and perhaps trust that there is a meaning being created by these conjunctions and that the meaning will make itself clear over time even if it isn't clear when it first appears. This might be an unconscious effort on my part to mimic the dream state; I wouldn't say it's often a conscious one. On the other hand, I think that dreams are an incredibly rich source for ideas and images and the way that they function in our lives is quite remarkable, so I see that my films are quite indebted to them even when I don't consciously use dreams or try to work with "dream logic."

CM: The section "Ghosts" from *Sink or Swim* (1990) uses a typewriter to inform meaning on the screen, where for instance, in earlier pieces or *The Ties That Bind* (1984) you scratch letters onto the film directly. What is the relationship to language and sound in how you conceive of a project?

SF: Each film has its own needs or makes its own demands. In the earlier films, the scratched (animated) words were necessary because I wanted to make the viewer read those wobbly words, one at a time, so that the text would slowly reveal itself. The scratched words also had a fragile quality, and sometimes seemed like a child's voice, which was also appropriate to the context. In the other case, using the typewriter was necessary because of its different context: it was a letter, it would have been typed in real life, and so I needed the viewer to understand the "realism" of that scene (which I put in quotes because of course it's shot in negative and the sound fades out halfway through, so it isn't exactly realistic.)

I tend to start my films from language rather than images. I have an idea (of the subject matter) and I think that through primarily with words (talking to myself, making notes, reading, etc.) and eventually the visual elements start to emerge. From then on, it's a battle (or a dance) between the words and images. Sometimes the words dominate or determine the image, and sometimes the images force the words to change. Each time, things work out a bit differently, but in every case I'm concerned about having the two elements work in a sort of sync. In other words, even though I'm not shooting synch-sound of people speaking, I'm creating another sort of sync by having the movement and meaning of the images relate very closely to the movement (the rhythm and changing pitch) and meaning of the words.

CM: Politically your films seem to focus on the fragments of institutions, how individuals are fragmented by different institutions whether it's medicine, racism, sexuality, nationalism, war, or family. Do you feel that your work resonates or feeds into the political agendas of each era?

SF: I always approach a new film with a feeling of wanting to work on two simultaneous concerns: one is my interest in what happens when images and sound are juxtaposed, which is an endless source of fascination and surprise, and the other is my belief that I should speak about something that concerns or affects or engages the body politic. I'm known as a "personal filmmaker," known for making work that's often autobiographical, and that's true; I do tend to speak from my own experience. But as someone who grew up during the '60s—i.e., during the civil rights movement, the women's movement, the gay liberation movement, the Vietnam War, etc.—it's always been obvious to me that there are a lot of things that need fixing, and a lot of ways that my private life was informed by public policy. Consequently, it was a *fait accompli* that I would speak in my films about things that were part of the public discourse.

Perhaps I could explain this more easily by saying that I do believe the feminist motto: "The personal is political." I don't see any break between inside and out; my experiences are shared by millions of other people and what I/we experience is a mirror, or a microscopic version, of the things that unfold on the largest public scale. And because of that, it makes perfect sense to me to have my films confront the most local (personal) issues through the filter of the global, and vice versa.

CM: *The Odds of Recovery*, your auto-medical-biography, *Sink or Swim*, the father as "story," and *The Ties that Bind*, the personal explorations of mother as locus, are highly subjective stories. How does your new work imagine narrative structures?

SF: I can't afford to shoot 16mm film anymore, so over the past few years my work has been tending more towards the documentary rather than a more experimental and interior form, although I don't think that difference is inherent in the two mediums. In other words, one can still make subjective, personal, experimental, you-name-it work when shooting in video, but it has created a different vantage point for me because shooting in digital video allows me to be in a moment for an endless amount of time. By comparison, I always shot film with a wind-up Bolex, which restricted my shots to twenty-seven seconds, and it was a silent camera, so I was forced to deal with sound as a separate element.

I wouldn't say the new work is any sort of conventional documentary, and I don't know how to talk about different narrative structures, but having this often-longer video footage and the live sound of the shots is a change, and one which I'm still trying to figure out. My last three works do diverge from earlier work because of the extent to which I'm looking outward, filming the world more directly, or perhaps just using images of the world in a more direct way than I did previously. For example, *Sink or Swim* tells stories about myself, primarily during childhood, by having written and performed voiceover text with images mostly shot "from life" but disconnected in a sense from the text, whereas in a recent piece, *Seeing Red*, I also tell stories about myself, primarily current ones, but I address the camera directly in a sort of diary format. Both structures have their reasons for being; I don't think either is better or more appropriate as a way of telling a story, but I never would have made *Seeing Red* if I were still working in 16mm, and I don't know if I would have made *Sink or Swim* in the same way if I had been working in video back then.

Su Friedrich

Katy Martin / 2008

From *Yishu Shijie* (*Art World Magazine*), October 2008. Reprinted by permission of Katy Martin.

In the 1980s, Su Friedrich first emerged as a powerful voice in independent filmmaking. Her seminal film, *Gently Down the Stream*, garnered widespread attention for its dreamlike imagery and poetic text which she scratched directly into the film emulsion. Since then, she has created a body of work that makes extensive use of dreams, memory, and personal subject matter that is, at times, emotionally raw. Inward-looking and subjective, yet politically aware, Friedrich's art re-examines personal experience while also commenting on broad social issues.

Since 1978, Friedrich has produced and directed many acclaimed films and videos including *From the Ground Up* (2007), *Seeing Red* (2005), *The Odds of Recovery* (2002), *Hide and Seek* (1996), *Rules of the Road* (1993), *Sink or Swim* (1990), *The Ties That Bind* (1984) and *Gently Down the Stream* (1981). In the following interview, she discusses two important works—*Sink or Swim* and *Seeing Red*—both of which will be presented at MoCA Shanghai in October.

Su Friedrich's film/video art has been exhibited throughout the world in museums and leading film festivals. It has also been broadcast on television across the US and Canada. She has been honored with retrospectives at the Museum of Modern Art, New York; the Whitney Museum of American Art; the Rotterdam International Film Festival; the National Film Theater in London; and the Cinema Shiadu in Guangzhou, China, among others. In addition, her work has been written about in such major publications as the *New York Times*, *Artforum*, *Premiere*, *The Nation*, *Film Quarterly*, and *Flash Art*. Friedrich currently teaches film/video production at Princeton University.

Katy Martin: What first attracted you to film?

Su Friedrich: When I was in fourth grade, I bought my first photo camera, a Brownie, at the local drugstore; I still remember how excited I was when I got it, and I still have it. I then studied black-and-white photography in college (they didn't offer any film classes) and realized how serious my interest was in working with images, but at that time I had no idea about being a filmmaker—that seemed far too big and remote. After college, I moved to New York, which gave me the chance to be exposed to great film culture. I started seeing work by filmmakers like Rainer Werner Fassbinder, Margarethe von Trotta, Chantal Akerman, Luis Buñuel, and Akira Kurosawa, and this gave me a deep interest in the possibilities for telling stories through film.

I started getting frustrated with photography, but I still couldn't imagine that I could make movies; I still only knew about "big movies." Also, back then, there were very few women filmmakers, so that made it seem even more remote. On the other hand, it was the time when women were really fighting to make and show work, so I feel lucky that I started out then instead of ten or more years earlier.

One day a friend asked me to go with her to a Super 8 filmmaking class at the Millennium Film Workshop in the East Village. I went and, as they say, I never looked back. It was clear to me after that first evening that it was what I needed and wanted to do. Within a short time I sold my darkroom equipment and started shooting film. The Millennium also put me in contact with the experimental film community, which I hadn't been aware of, and I started seeing films that were very different from the "big movies." These were films I could imagine making myself. It gave me a lot of energy and courage to see that individuals, with very little money, were making films all by themselves.

KM: Let's talk about *Sink or Swim* (1990), one of your best known works. It's a film about your father, and some of your memories are highly charged. Can you talk about the use of explicit, personal material in your art?

SF: At the time, I had already made a few other films that used personal material, including *The Ties That Bind* (1984) about my mother living in Germany during World War Two. So it was a direction I was already going in, and I think there are several reasons for that.

The first would be that I had a difficult time growing up. I had a mother who had been very traumatized by the war and then by her move to a new country; I had a father who was remote when he was living with us and who then left us, who left my mother to raise three children without any support; and I went to Catholic school and very soon realized that I had strong disagreements with the beliefs and practices of the church. So there were many issues I wanted to address when I finally started thinking about telling stories/telling history.

The other big reason is the influence of the women's movement, which opened up a huge and complicated discussion about how we were formed by society, what the damage was from that influence, and how we could change that to something better.

And last of all, I felt that I would be most honest, or would be most challenged, if I made myself look at the experiences that were closest to me. I love to read fiction, and I admire people who can turn life into a story, but I don't think that's something I know how to do, so I decided that I should try instead to speak more directly about my own life and the lives of people I knew.

It's a tricky thing to work with personal material because one has to try very hard to get some distance from something one is very, very close to. Each time I've made a film like that, I've depended a great deal on the perspective of friends. I ask them many times to read the texts, watch the edit, and tell me when I'm not being honest or correct or when I'm just being stupid and sentimental. The films would be very different, and I think very bad, if I didn't always have the criticism and advice of these viewers.

KM: Can you talk about how the film is organized and the simple device of using the letters of the alphabet as chapter titles?

SF: It was extremely difficult to write the text. I started in the first person ("I was" and "my father") but then understood that I couldn't continue, it was too emotional for me, so I changed it to the third person ("the girl" and "her father"). That gave me some mental distance, because I could imagine some other girl, not myself. But I also needed to create a framework, so that I could generate more stories. The fear of speaking was strong, and I was having a hard time continuing to write. Since my father was a linguist, and language was the cornerstone of his work, I decided to use the alphabet as a structural device. This of course meant that I had to generate twenty-six stories, which was more than I had imagined doing, but at least it gave me an end point, a finite sum of work.

KM: How do you use the process of writing in your approach to making films?

SF: Writing has often played a major role in my films and maybe most markedly in *Sink or Swim*. With the exception of *Hide and Seek* (1996), which included a more or less conventional fiction script that I cowrote with Cathy Quinlan, my films have usually depended on texts I write or find, so I don't think of myself as a screenwriter. Also, since I do all my own cinematography (again with the exception of *Hide and Seek*, which was shot by Jim Denault), I tend to be thinking already about shooting, or be in the process of shooting, while I'm writing or finding texts.

I say that writing was most marked in *Sink or Swim* because it was the first time I had written such a lengthy text for a film, and it was such a hard one to write, and I see that the film depends very heavily on the text. The images are expressive up to a point, but the film really wouldn't make much sense if it didn't have the voiceover.

The only other film that I wrote so much text for is *Rules of the Road* (1993). In most of the others I worked more with a collage approach, mixing things I'd written with interviews, found texts, etc. In recent years, with video, I've also been talking more directly, using the camera to record unwritten/extemporaneous speech.

KM: You reference diary, memoir, and letter writing in *Sink or Swim*. There is even a story of you writing something in your diary that your mother actually erased. Can you talk about art and saying what can't be said?

SF: There are many ways and reasons to make art, and I can only talk about what I do and what I believe in doing. This means, very importantly, that I don't think other approaches or reasons are lesser or wrong; they're only different. I don't think it's better (or worse) to speak explicitly and directly about one's personal life, it just happens to be what I do. So in my case, I would say that it was necessary for me to use art as a way to say what "shouldn't" be said.

When I started making *Sink or Swim*, I looked for literature about children's experiences during divorce. I found almost nothing, so I felt I should tell that story and should speak for, and from the position of, the child. I also found very little about "The Father"—or at least very little that saw fathers from a critical perspective. What I was doing seemed quite taboo (at the time) and I felt strongly that it was something I had to address. In a similar fashion, I started making *The Ties That Bind* because I felt that the story of the ordinary, non-Nazi (and non-Jewish) German hadn't been told and I wanted to tell that story.

I think making art like this can be very useful—not just for the person who makes it and thereby has a chance to put their private thoughts and feelings into the public arena, but also for the viewer who might have had a similar experience and can finally see and hear their story being told.

KM: The stories you tell about your father are horrifying. That could not have been easy. How did you come to make this film, and how did you find your way?

SF: It's very hard to say, because I think there were so many factors at play. I started making *Sink or Swim* in 1988, when I was thirty-four. I had started therapy a couple of years before that. The decision to go into therapy wasn't easy, but at least by the time I started making *Sink or Swim*, I was beginning to understand what you had to do in order to unravel certain issues from your childhood. So I had a few skills, and I had somehow accepted that I had to do this, but I was still very early in the process. A critical moment came when I read the book *The Drama of the Gifted Child* by Alice Miller. The one thing I took from it was the idea that children don't have a voice, that their stories aren't told, or aren't believed or respected when they're told. When she articulated that as clearly as she did, I recognized the truth of it from my own experience. All my life I've been full or rage and unhappiness about how my father behaved in our family, and I never felt that my experience was being heard.

KM: Politically the notion of invisibility and voice is very strong. In the women's movement, it's huge—if we're invisible, we have no voice.

SF: You know, I credit Alice Miller's book, but as I said before, I also very much credit the women's movement, in a broader way, for making me able to think that it was not only necessary but important to articulate those things. Because that's what women had been saying for years. I started making this film long after the modern women's movement got going, so there were years and years of women saying, I will now talk about my abusive husband, I will now talk about my experience being raped—all that—and not feel that I'm the one in the wrong. Otherwise, that's the way they keep people silent. Once you say, no, that's not the way I should be treated, things start to change.

KM: And I'm a witness to that.

SF: Yes, that's crucial to me.

KM: What's important about *Sink or Swim* is the tension it creates, so that we as the audience share the pathos and the whole terrible feeling of invisibility you had vis-à-vis your father.

SF: For me, a critical moment came when I wrote the story about being with my father and his younger daughter from a different family. When I heard him say to her, "Oh, that's not interesting," I recognized myself in her. So when I wrote that story, everything came together in that moment—emotionally, because, in the process of making the film, I was really struggling to understand what my experience had been; and artistically, because I was trying to figure out how to make a film that was both personal and formal. That moment seemed to answer both those demands. The circle closed, and I felt very grateful that happened. It was all about the invisibility/visibility issue, which so many stories had touched on. But then suddenly, it was as if I were speaking for her, but also about myself, on film and off!

KM: You saw yourself. You were finally seen. You took that power.

SF: Yes. And I could finally be the one to tell the story.

KM: This issue of invisibility is a force in so many people's lives, which maybe comes back around to the father, and what a father is supposed to do. What you hope a parent will do is provide certain kinds of nonreciprocal attention.

SF: Yes, exactly. [*Laughs.*]

KM: *Sink or Swim* is about the father as absent.

SF: Yes, it's about the absent father. That was the other thing that was invisible. I don't mean to minimize what feminists had done, but the majority of the discourse at the time focused on mothers, daughters, and wives in relation to men. The man was spoken about, but not so directly. He was still invisible. So that's the other side of invisibility, that you have the oppressed person feeling themselves as invisible, but you also have the oppressor being invisible in their role. They're present—I mean, fathers are present, political leaders all have a public face—but what they *really* are is not what's being seen. Their more benevolent public role is what's being seen, but who they really are is not being seen. Part of making *Sink or Swim* was saying, here, I want to make this girl visible, but I also want to make the *father* visible for who he really is.

KM: Which comes back to the desire to witness. How does that relate to making art?

SF: There is a big difference between, let's say, going to therapy or talking to friends, and making art. There are connections, but it's not the same. If I'm sitting at a therapist's or talking with friends about my father, I may be ranting and raving, I may even be crying. But if I'm sitting in a room, editing or writing, there has to be a lot of control at work. I can rant and rave on a piece of paper, but by the time it's in a film, it has been reworked so many times that it has become a very controlled thing. I think that's a really important distinction to make.

A lot of times people watching films about personal issues see them as a form of therapy (for the filmmaker). It may start out as therapeutic, but it doesn't end up as a therapeutic experience because there's so much craft involved. In making *Sink or Swim,* there was so much rewriting, so much re-editing. Worrying about how to cut together two shots has nothing to do with my father—it's about composition and rhythm! And then there's the problem of how somebody delivers their lines. I recorded many, many takes of Jessica Lynn, the girl who did the voiceover, and I had to decide which ones to use. So when she says, "When he held my head under the bathwater"—well, that may be a traumatic phrase, and when I wrote it, it may have made me throw myself on the bed and start crying, but when I was editing, I was just concerned about whether she read it articulately or whether it hit the right frame. It's an odd thing to start out making something that's so emotionally devastating, and then find yourself, a year and a half later, in the editing room, worrying about things like the frame.

KM: Right. Because then there's the art. Art creates a safe space for the viewers, to think about things that may otherwise be taboo. Maybe one way it does that is precisely what you're talking about, the craft and the aesthetics.

SF: If I think about my experience watching other people's work about traumatic experiences—the Holocaust or rape or you name it—there is always that odd combination of sensations. On the one hand, you're being brought very close to something which is almost unthinkably painful and on the other, you find yourself thinking, wow, that's a great shot, or that's beautifully edited, or they found such a brilliant way to convey their experience. In other words, you can admire the film as a constructed object that's very separate from, or something in addition to, the real, lived experience being described. I don't think there's anything to say about that except that it's a fact of life. That's what art is. Art takes the real world and crafts it into something that's small and coherent. That's just the definition of it.

KM: *Sink or Swim* is beautifully crafted and as a whole, it is very poetic. The text itself sets up layers of meaning, and the relationships of word and image are oblique. Maybe it is those oblique relationships that give me a sense of space. They give me room to reflect.

SF: That was the intention, and I'm really glad that you experience it that way. Other people have said that, and that really was what I wanted to do. I asked a lot of the viewers in the sense that I really left them on their own to make up whatever they thought was going on. There are some places in the film where the relationship between the text and the image is quite literal, and there are some places where it's really disconnected. To me, one of the riskiest moments is when I'm telling the story about my father leaving, and I describe my mother putting us on the windowsill and saying, "What if we all jumped out the window!" and what you're seeing at the same time are images in a hospital. There is no direct connection. The story has nothing to do with medical issues. But since I've had a lot of medical problems, I thought, well, maybe there's a way in which growing up in an environment like that could really contribute to being unhealthy, physically as well as mentally, and maybe I ended up in the hospital with all these weird things because I hadn't grown up right.

KM: You had all these injuries.

SF: Yes. But that's a pretty oblique connection between sound and picture. When I was doing it, I thought people are going to be just completely lost during this. But I decided to go with it anyway. That's the kind of thing you do. You have to play around and hope that people figure something out.

KM: Your recent video, *Seeing Red* (2005) is quite funny. But it's also about anger and explicit, personal material. Your approach here, using humor and the color red, is quite different than in *Sink or Swim*. Can you comment please?

SF: I think part of the difference between *Sink or Swim* and *Seeing Red* is that fifteen years had passed. Thankfully, as you get older (if you do the work), things get a little clearer, a little better. Although in *Seeing Red*, I do complain about doing the same things, being stuck with the same reflexes—but I must say, on a lesser level. I'm not still railing about my father! I'm so glad that I'm no longer subject to those rages, that sort of irrational violence. That's part of why *Seeing Red* has a note of humor in it, because even though I'm still stuck in certain ways, I now can laugh about it some of the time. And I can see that that's how we are as humans. We just are always somehow stuck.

Otherwise, I attribute the main difference to the fact that, the year before, I had begun to work in video, which is cheaper and easier to shoot than film. I started *Seeing Red* because my partner said that I seemed to be suffering from something. When she said that, I simply walked into my studio, set up the camera and started talking to it about how I was feeling at that moment. This was something I would never have done in film.

After that first shoot, I didn't have a plan, but I set up a simple structure by deciding that I would shoot myself talking whenever I had something I wanted to say, and I would go around collecting any image I could find with red in it. At some point along the way I came up with the idea of using J. S. Bach's *Goldberg Variations* as sound. I only shot for a short while, perhaps two months, and had very little footage to work with (maybe six tapes). Then I sat down and started to figure out how to put the piece together.

This was very unlike my working method in film, where I had written texts and devised elaborate plans for the editing structure in advance. In some sense, I needed that structure with film so I could afford to shoot what I needed, and also because editing in film is so much more difficult. Now, with video, I find myself accepting a looser approach in gathering material, but the editing is still a very long and rigorous process. Technically, it's easier to edit on the computer, but figuring out the rhythms and the narrative flow is still as hard as it is in film.

KM: We should explain what the expression, *seeing red*, means in English. Maybe there's an equivalent in Chinese—I don't know—but may I ask, what do *you* mean by *Seeing Red*? Where did the idea for this video come from?

SF: In English, when we say that someone is *seeing red*, we mean that they're very angry. However, red is also the color of passion (in the good sense, not just anger), and I wanted to refer to that feeling as well.

All my titles play with some known expression or adage or part of a song. I try to escape that, but every time that I struggle with the title for a new piece, I find myself falling back on that pattern. So in this case, I decided that *Seeing Red* worked well because of the three part association: 1) seeing red as a reference to anger; 2) seeing the color red and asking the viewer to think about what we mean when we refer to a color, and how we tend to think of it as a simple, single thing when in fact it's a complex thing with many variations or shades; and 3) seeing the world passionately.

KM: The images themselves are pleasurable and funny—you've collected the results of "seeing red" everywhere you look. Can you talk about the camera work in relation to pleasure?

SF: I'm not sure how to answer that question. I don't think there was more (or less) pleasure in shooting material for this piece than in any other piece I've done. It was fun to ride around on my bike looking for red things. And it was interesting to experience how we don't see things until we're looking for them and then, once we're looking for them, that seems to be *all* we see. This was similar to my experience shooting the station wagons for *Rules of the Road*; it wasn't until I started shooting that I realized how many there were.

In general, for me, shooting is a fantastic experience, probably because I'm not usually confined by the demands of narrative, dialogue, actors, etc. When I've shot scripted scenes (like for *Damned If You Don't*), I enjoyed the challenge, but I do prefer to be out and free and using the camera to respond to something unpredictable.

I also have a very intense relationship to the (imaginary) viewer when I shoot. This is hard to describe, but as I'm framing and moving the camera, I have a silent dialogue with a viewer—it's like I'm thinking how the shot will translate, or read, when someone watches it. Or maybe I can say that by imagining someone watching it, I understand what I want the image to convey, so that leads me in the way I shoot it.

KM: How about the Bach music on the soundtrack? In this context, it seems rather funny. Are the *Goldberg Variations* just a touch obsessive, or is neurosis "well tempered" when it is turned into art?

SF: I don't know much about Bach, but I do know that Gould, the pianist, was famously obsessive and I think one can hear it in the precision of this recording. I had loved it for years so I thought it was the obvious one to use, but then thought I should listen to at least five other performances and see whether there was one that would work better. It was striking how different they were, and how fast his performance was compared to the others.

But I don't think writing (or recording, or using) a variation is obsessive. Structure is a foundation of any work of art, and doing what seems to be an exercise in writing numerous versions of a basic structure is not only a great way to learn what works and what doesn't, but it can often yield a valuable work in itself, not just something that comes across as an exercise. The *Goldberg Variations* are a prime example of that—there's so much musical pleasure in listening to them.

But, having said that, I agree that using them as I do (in the context of a film in which I worry over many things) inevitably leads to a feeling that the music expresses a kind of neurotic, obsessive mood that compliments what I'm saying on camera. Perhaps that isn't fair to Bach and Gould, but perhaps they would also be amused by it.

Actually, in *Seeing Red*, the idea of variations is really important. You have the idea of artistic variations, embodied by the *Goldberg Variations*, which presents a musical theme and then reworks it in complex and playful ways; and you have the theme of a person talking on camera with variations occurring in clothing, space, and what's being said; and then you have this color, *red*, and many, many objects somehow using this color. But then you also have the underlying idea of life itself being a very variable and varied thing. So maybe the film is simply asking us to contemplate the fact that life is unpredictable and full of variation. Almost any real life situation can play out in so many ways, either in your imagination or when it actually happens. *Seeing Red* is like the shorter version of that.

KM: Can you talk about the scene at the end? You have on all these clothes, and you take them off, layer by layer. Was that taking away some of the possibilities?

SF: It's kind of going in two directions at the same time, because I'm taking the clothes off but I'm piling up the sound. The sound mix is sampling from the different parts of the spoken segments, and adding more and more layers. But then, at the very end, the one phrase that emerges is, "And part of the problem . . . part of what is so fucked up is that I feel like most of life is about performing for people!"

So it gets denser and denser, and then this one line comes out. Meanwhile, I've got on all the red clothes that I wore in the film and in the end I'm in nothing but my bra. So it's not exactly two opposite trajectories but it comes close to that. I just thought, okay, well, I was wearing all this stuff, so let me just take it all off; and I said a lot but the core of what I said was that we're always performing.

As for my remark about performing: I was surprised when I recorded the scene where I was pacing around saying, "Be a good teacher, be a good girlfriend, be a good this, be a good that." I was a little bit scandalized afterwards because I thought, of all the things that I say in the film, and maybe of all the things I've said in everything I've done—and I've never said this before—but of all the things I've said in all my films, that was the most damning and revealing. And embarrassing! It made me worried, because one shouldn't feel that one is always performing. One should feel that there are places in life where one can be true to oneself.

What was scary was that I looked at that footage and thought, can this be true? Is it true that even with my partner of twenty-five years, I am somehow fundamentally performing, I'm never just pure "Su" (whatever or whoever that is)? It's easy for me to accept and admit that I'm performing when I'm teaching or when I'm at a film festival showing my work . . . but at home or with friends? I found that shocking!

KM: When that happens, do you know you're onto something?

SF: In the moment of shooting, I don't know . . . but later, yes! When I saw that, I thought, "I've probably been thinking this and feeling this for years." I'd probably been saying it to myself for years but had never expressed it as simply as I did at that moment, and that shocked me. So I definitely had to keep that in, even though it might be tempting to hide it!

KM: So then, that moment of revealing, baring your chest at the end?

SF: That was nothing compared to that!

KM: What's the relationship of rage and humor—rage and making art? That's a big one, but can you muse a bit?

SF: In the one film workshop I took (my only training in film was those three nights at the Millennium), which was taught by David Lee, he made us write a list of the ten things that were most important to us. The last item on my list was "fear." I was surprised by, and interested in, the fact that I'd put that on the list. I later found that to be a most useful and necessary realization, and I think a lot of my work stems from doing that list. In other words, a lot of my work has been an effort to speak about my fears. But in conjunction, a lot of it has been about articulating my anger at certain things, so I would say that fear and anger usually live together, and they can be a great spur to making art. Moreover, talking openly about one's fears and anger can be a way to rid oneself of those feelings.

I also have a partner who not only has a brilliant sense of humor but who is also much more of a stoic than I am. She believes that one can often make a point better through humor than through anger, and she has often encouraged and shown me how to foreground the humor rather than the anger, fear, or pain. I am very grateful for that. The nicest thing about using humor in film is that, if you're successful, you can actually know what the audience is experiencing. Hearing the audience laugh during a screening is a very pleasurable thing.

It's Alright, Williamsburg (I'm Only Bleeding)

Cynthia Lugo / 2013

From *Brooklyn Rail*, March 2013. Reprinted by permission of the *Brooklyn Rail* and Cynthia Lugo.

The filmmaker Su Friedrich used to live in a loft on 118 North 11th Street. It's one of the more trafficked sidewalks in Williamsburg. Brooklyn Brewery is across the street, and the clothes reseller Beacon's Closet is half a block away. Just around the corner is the newly opened Wythe Hotel, where one can rent a loft-style room for $495 dollars per night.

Walking around the neighborhood with Friedrich as we discuss her film *Gut Renovation*, she points out the many new luxury condos with the alacrity of a real estate agent. She has been inside several of them, posing as a prospective homeowner to see exactly what is being sold, a lifestyle altogether different from her modest life as an artist. Needless to say, she isn't buying.

Gut Renovation chronicles the rapid transformation of Williamsburg as well as Friedrich's memories of a place she can no longer call home. It is a diary as well as an indictment of the collusion of corporate greed and government that has destroyed the character of the neighborhood. Though grim, the film is punctuated by moments of gallows humor. At one point, Friedrich spray paints the wall of a construction site with the slogan, "Artists Used to Live Here." It's both a jab at new residents and a gravestone for the community that has moved on.

Cynthia Lugo: Your film is very successful at charting the destruction and redevelopment of Williamsburg, as well as your personal struggle to stay in your own house. How did you balance these two angles throughout the film?

Su Friedrich: I have been known to make very personal work. But I've also been known to deal a lot with form, and I've always felt like I owe it to my audience to speak honestly about my emotional situation. Also, I love film, and I love what film can do when it's being unconventional. In the case of this film, I recognized that I was going to be telling something personal, but I also was going to be talking about a very large political and economic story. I was trying to keep the two things in view, and one was trying to balance this personal or more general story, and telling it clearly the way a documentary might, but allowing it to be more playful, or unpredictable in structure than a regular documentary. But I'm also very out there with my emotions, and in this film I got to indulge or take advantage of both sides of myself. On the emotional side I was very angry about what was happening. I was also really sad, and those are two different emotions. When my partner, Cathy Quinlan, started looking at the film she brought a lot of humor into it, which was crucial.

CL: Your outrage is palpable throughout the film. You share that your "crazy anger" started when one of your favorite buildings was demolished. Do you think the film harnessed your anger in a productive way?

SF: Anger was a large motivating factor in making this film, as well as my memory of what happened in the East Village back in the '80s. I lived there and then it started changing; I thought I would remember what had been there, and then I forgot. And I was really shocked that within a year or two I didn't remember whether that place was the old butcher shop or the old bakery. When this started happening, I thought, "My god, it is so easy for us to forget."

Anger can be a great motivator, but you can't continue feeding off of anger—more things have to enter into it. In trying to construct the film there were other emotions in play. It was really amazing to me that three years later, when I was looking at the footage of the building across the street being torn down, I started crying again. That sense of loss takes a long time to go away, if it ever goes away. And so I would say that in the course of editing I recognized my sadness more and more. But I had to keep making this film; I couldn't just dissolve into grief.

CL: This film is the culmination of many years of footage—at what point in the process did you know you were making a film?

SF: I started documenting in late 2005, early 2006. The rezoning took place May 2005. Towards the end of 2006 I knew it was a story I wanted to tell.

CL: In 2005, when industrial Williamsburg was rezoned for residential use, you started recording every demolition and development west of the B.Q.E. I'm curious about what this ritual was like for you on a day-to-day basis.

SF: I had lived in the neighborhood for fifteen years and I knew every street like the back of my hand. I felt a little bit like a journalist doing research, and it was daunting—I had to tell myself that I had to be thorough. As the scale of it increased, I realized I was up against a mammoth project.

CL: For me, your film is very effective at debunking two myths, the first one being that gentrification is a slow, gradual, and inevitable process of change; and the second, that artists catalyze the gentrification process.

SF: I think gentrification is a very complex and very thorny issue. And depending on what neighborhood you're talking about there are differences. People compare Williamsburg to SoHo because SoHo was the classic example, and SoHo didn't get transformed by an edict from the city; it was more organic and more gradual in some ways, but of course it has become what Williamsburg has become: a place for the very rich with very expensive stores and very few art galleries. But what took twenty-five years in Soho took Williamsburg five years.

But I really question this idea that artists ruin a neighborhood. What it implies is that the artists want that transformation to happen. It suggests that artists are "willing" to move into a less desirable neighborhood, but then they want it to be really comfortable and full of amenities, and I don't think that's the case. What I see happen in Williamsburg (and also in Chinatown and Lower East Side) is this: You have a city like New York, that's filled with artists. They need a place to work as well as to live. Usually artists need bigger places—they can't work in a tiny apartment. I've lived in a tiny storefront on North 9th street when I started making films, but I was able to go to the Millennium Film Workshop to edit. We find places to work, often in industrial spaces. In the case of Williamsburg, a lot of those industrial spaces were not being used. The reason for that is because the city was already making it unaffordable for industries to be in those properties. You have an ignorant population—the artists—seeing those empty spaces available, and also knowing that they're not supposed to legally live there, but having all these landlords let them live there. They are, for the most part, living around the existing industries. That was certainly the case for us. We lived near a woodshop that ran industrial table saws all day long, and we put up with it, because we needed a place to live and work.

But then marketing people and developers and people like Bloomberg who are only out to make money turn it into something to sell to other people. And that is not the fault of the artists, or the other families who have been living in the neighborhoods and maintaining the basic amenities. All these people with money and political power turn it into something to sell. It's really weird to me that the artists get blamed.

But there's a way in which marketing people can use artists as a groovy selling point. So artists are being totally used by the people with money, and then they're being thrown out. The thinking is that it's inevitable. And it's not.

And that's why I included all those comments at the end of the film of people saying "Fuck Artists." I can't help thinking that every artist I know moved to New York because this city was the art capital of the world. If you do not have a city that supports artists living here, artists will not live here anymore. Young people are moving to Philly, to Portland, to Chicago, to Atlanta, to Berlin—they are not moving to New York.

To anyone who says gentrification is the fault of artists, I say, "Fuck you." Artists have been living and struggling in this city as long as I've been here, which is thirty-six years.

CL: Throughout the film you seem resigned towards the process of citizen action; there's a "we're screwed" mentality that pervades the film. On the one hand, I thought it was honest, because it's an accurate reflection of how few rights tenants actually have. On the other, the film offers almost no alternatives on how to challenge the system.

SF: For starters, I would say that I am not a social activist as a filmmaker. I very much admire films that try to mobilize people about an issue. Take something like Kelly Anderson's *My Brooklyn*, that really tries to educate people about what happened in Downtown Brooklyn, and how one might think about it in the future. And then you have a film like *Battle for Brooklyn*, which is astonishing in its portrayal of the efforts made by all of these tenants to combat Atlantic Yards. They're both really fantastic films, but that's not the kind of film I was making. I think I recognize my limitations; my concerns as a filmmaker are different than my concerns as a citizen. Though I have been involved in a lot of different activist groups, I never feel like my films are part of that process. They are of course informed by the part of me that's a political being, but I don't think of them as *tools*. In this case, I wanted to paint a portrait of a time and an experience, and let people make of it what they will.

I think you're right in saying that there's a general sentiment of "we're screwed" because by the time I started making it, I knew we *were* screwed. I didn't think there was a damn thing that anybody could do. There could be individual efforts on behalf of one building, but to fight the entire rezoning just wasn't going to happen.

I don't want to depress you, but I feel like the forces of money and power are so profound in this city, that the battle is elsewhere. I don't even know what the battle is. Certainly in the case of Williamsburg, the battle is over.

CL: You never mention the word "hipster" throughout the film—was that a deliberate omission? At one point you joke that an alternate title for the film could have been "I Hate Rich People."

SF: You know, that's an interesting question. I never made a conscious decision to exclude the word "hipster." Now that you ask it, I think, there were ways that I found to point to the new demographic. So in one case, I refer to the fancy dogs. And so when I show the fancy dogs, you do see some people that would probably be called hipsters, like the guy with all the tattoos. But I guess to me the term became so contested, and so tiresome, that even to throw it out as a term of derision would have been passé. And I think it's more to the point to talk about money. Money is not confusing to me, especially when someone has $800,000 to spend on a studio apartment.

Q&A with Filmmaker Su Friedrich

Carlos J. Segura / 2013

From *Cinespect*, March 6, 2013. Reprinted by permission of Carlos J. Segura.

Su Friedrich's documentary *Gut Renovation* looks at Williamsburg, Brooklyn's transformation from working-class neighborhood to "Condoburg." Employing an intensely personal style while looking at the big picture, this film is of interest not just to any New Yorker who has ever had a conversation about gentrification (read: every New Yorker) but to people in big cities everywhere.

Cinespect sat down with Friedrich to talk about the making of *Gut Renovation.*

Carlos Segura: What kind of camera did you use for the documentary?

Su Friedrich: Panasonic standard-def video camera.

CS: Were your choices of digital video and graphics mostly due to cost and ease of use, or were they based more on a preplanned aesthetic choice?

SF: Well, I basically shot film as long as I could afford it. So in 2002, I made a film called *The Odds of Recovery*, which was a mixture of 16mm and video. And the video was so I could film secretly in doctor's offices. But then things were such that I couldn't afford to shoot 16mm anymore. So I shot video. It was mostly practical.

CS: I got the impression from a lot of the footage that you didn't intend to make a documentary to begin with. Was the documentary something that came about more as an afterthought, something you came up with as you shot the footage?

SF: What happened is after the rezoning and after we understood what was going to happen and we started hearing the jackhammers, I thought, "I gotta go out and record this." It started as an act of witnessing. I just thought, "I want to remember what was everywhere." But I became very involved very quickly so then I . . . I didn't have a plan. I guess some more conventional documentary filmmakers say, "Ok, we're going to shoot on X day and we're going to have this crew." I certainly didn't approach it like that. I just went out on my bike with my camera, found a building that was in progress, filmed it, went to another. So it was a bit of catch-as-catch-can. And then, of course, I took my camera along to the sales parties because I wanted to get what they were doing but in an unofficial way. I didn't get permission exactly. I went in and I pretended I was filming so I could show the space to my partner because we were interested in buying. It was a little bit of guerilla filmmaking.

CS: How many hours did you have to work with?

SF: About forty-five hours.

CS: Is there anything you left on the cutting room floor that really hurt to leave behind?

SF: That's a good question, but I don't think so. And there are things I'm really glad I cut out. Since it was partly a story of the neighborhood and partly a personal story, I had gotten very involved in cutting parts about when we had to move and buy our new place and getting a mortgage and all that because I thought the struggle of relocation should be a part of this. And then people who were looking at it said, "That's so boring, people know how to buy a mortgage. Leave it out." But I don't think there was any storyline that I developed and then took out.

CS: Once editing was underway, was there an intent to cause a particular effect, or was it more about expressing frustration and anger?

SF: Well, a lot of my previous work has been based in personal experiences. So I do approach projects from my own experience. But I really felt in this case that this was a huge story, not just my story. I knew so many people in the neighborhood who were being affected in the way we were. And so in thinking about how to put it together I actually paid more attention to the big story than to our own story at first. Also, since it wasn't a conventional documentary, one of the real challenges was representing the space. In a way it's a film about losing a home and the politics of the city and all of that. But it's also just about space and materials and buildings and what buildings do to us and for us. To show this huge thing that was going in a film was very difficult.

CS: When it came to focusing on the big story, what kind of materials did you find yourself turning to in terms of journalism or other film and video, literary sources, etc.? What kind of formal research did you do?

SF: I would say I was reading blogs, news stories about what was going on. Something like *The Gleaners and I* by Agnès Varda was in my mind while I was working on this. I didn't look at it again to see what she did. But I think the way that she approached this activity—gleaning—through lots of different avenues and inserted herself personally I found very interesting. Very intelligent. It wasn't a conventional documentary, although she did have a lot of information in it. But there was this personal component. So films like that were in my mind. But I didn't look at films about housing while I was working on it. While working on a film I might see some things, but I don't work that directly with what's come before. I kind of understand I have to figure out my own language.

CS: Now that it's making its way out there in the world, what has the reception been like?

SF: It's sort of the beginning of it I would say. It premiered at the Brooklyn Film Festival and I took it up to the Flaherty Film Seminar and I've just been in Berlin with it. It was interesting in Berlin because I thought, "I don't know if this story will translate." And immediately people said that exactly the same thing was happening in Berlin. So I think, sadly, that this experience is shared by a lot of people in a lot of places.

I would say that one of things that people pointed to is the anger that I express very directly in the film. Cathy Quinlan, who shares cowriter credit, started working with me about six months before I was finished editing. She put in some of the humor because she felt you can't convince people with anger. You have to have something else. And that was an interesting process for me because I did have a lot of anger while I was filming and also residual anger when I was editing. But then when she started bringing in the humor, I thought, "Yes, you have to look at this from many different sides." So I think that's been good in terms of the audience.

CS: Complete this sentence: Based on what you know now, within five to ten years gentrification turns New York City into . . .

SF: Well, the statistics are that it's becoming more and more white. Which I find horrifying. And more and more housing is for the wealthy. There are way fewer rental apartments. I read a long piece in the *New York Times* this weekend about the fight for available land and how there are these huge bidding wars and how the land becomes so expensive that when the developers finally start building the only thing they can afford to build is luxury housing. They all say they're going to put affordable housing in part of the building but they usually don't. So it does seem that it's getting very skewed towards Bloomberg's friends, let's say.

Su Friedrich

Claudia Steinberg / 2013

This interview, "Su Friedrich" by Claudia Steinberg, was commissioned by and first published in *BOMB Daily*, April 2, 2013.

All through the 1970s and '80s, the sole inhabitants of a grand loft space in an old beautiful, industrial building on North 11th Street in Williamsburg had been pigeons fluttering undisturbed under the splendid cathedral-like ceiling. In 1990, filmmaker Su Friedrich and painters Cathy Quinlan and Martina Siebert transformed a full floor of this rusty palace into a communal place where they lived and worked for many years while the neighborhood changed around them. When the coexistence of artists and light industries came to a sudden end with the 2005 rezoning laws, which allowed the notorious Toll Brothers and other developers to build one brash, shiny apartment tower after another, Su Friedrich began counting—and filming. *Gut Renovation* is a systematic yet highly personal response from this cinematographic auteur to a particularly rapid and ruthless version of urban renewal.

Claudia Steinberg: Your film starts with a bang. You push open the door and there's a gasp of disbelief. What happened? There's this sense of shock: the pigeons have moved back in. Almost twenty years of your life have been obliterated—gone, gone, gone.

Su Friedrich: Well, I found that really traumatic. It made me understand what it means for people whose houses are destroyed by fire or bombed in a war. Here was this architecturally exquisite cast-iron building from the 1890s and we had tried everything we could to maintain its quality. It's one thing to see the walls you put up taken out, but the vaulted ceilings had those bands with finely carved, detailed floral motifs—

CS: —which you had cleaned with almost surgical precision, with dental tools, investing countless hours . . .

SF: It's a nineteenth-century technique that people don't use anymore—unless they're the King of Saudi Arabia. The space had been the design and showroom for Hecla Ironworks, which created the marquees for Carnegie Hall, Saks 5th Avenue, and the Stock Exchange and all the beautiful elaborate cast-iron railings that you see in the old buildings of New York. We felt part of this long history of the city. But the new owners used a spray gun to blast the ceiling with white stucco paint destroying all that work. Then they went into the staircase, which had been preserved in its original form for over a hundred years, and covered its beautiful and extremely detailed sunflower pattern railing with battleship-grey enamel paint.

CS: So you catapult the viewer into this void—the erasure of your own history in this building, as well as the destruction of a precious place. But throughout the film you contrast your emotions with a very analytical approach—these two elements bounce off each other.

SF: I don't necessarily have a completely clear plan about how I'm going to construct something, but I have two primary responses to life: One is to be very emotional and the other is to be very systematic. I wanted to be a math major. I love systems. I love numbers. I love ordering things. I love making spreadsheets. So when I recognized that I should bear witness to what was happening, it was very clear to me that I had to take the act of recording really seriously. When I went out and saw an imperiled building on North 10th Street, I had to know its exact address, who had owned it, what it was being turned into. I ended up with a record of 173 spaces. To approach it that way—record, record, record—I had to dot every "i" and cross every "t" in this neighborhood. And then there was the emotional part. I was extremely angry and extremely sad at the same time as I watched this unfold.

CS: What was the moment that made you decide to document what was happening?

SF: We knew that things were getting really strange. Then, on May 11, 2005, the newspaper carried a banner headline—the kind they reserve for a war or an election— about the rezoning. In that instant I thought, I knew for a while that something was about to happen and now it just happened. Forty-eight hours later I heard the first jackhammer. Within a month, I would find a plywood fence around an empty lot. One could see very quickly that the action was starting up. In the film I talk about one of the first buildings to be worked on, which happened to be around the corner from us, 55 Berry. They were also tearing down the bus depot. We heard jackhammers all summer. I thought, "Ah, this is going to be our reality for years to come."

CS: Strange how it all happened so fast. Once SoHo was the precedent and it provided the "rags to riches" saga, literally, but then this type of urban renewal accelerated. SoHo has even become a model for Las Vegas. Last year I heard about plans for a SoHo there. An architecture firm is inventing an industrial past for Las Vegas which then allegedly "became an artistic center," but is now a shopping and gambling hub.

When was the first time you understood that Williamsburg would not always be your home?

SF: In my film I talk about Isabelle Hill who was a member of the team that surveyed the waterfront for the City Planning Office between 1987 and 1992. They were supposed to determine whether manufacturing was vital and thriving. They determined that it was and the city said, "We don't want to know about this." They already knew that they wanted to transform the waterfront. So I think a lot of what was happening during the '90s—manufacturers getting pushed out, spaces becoming defunct or available to other kinds of people—took place because they had decided on the transformation. I don't think many people were aware of the plan that was being fomented by the City Planning Office and by the Mayor's Office. One community group knew what was happening and proposed a plan that allowed for the coexistence of manufacturing and residents. Williamsburg has a long history of people working in manufacturing and living in walking distance and they wanted to maintain that ecology but the city completely disregarded their suggestions. None of us were aware. But around 1990 *New York Magazine*'s cover story was "The New Bohemia," and we knew, that's it, we're screwed—Williamsburg has become a commodity, it has been branded and somebody is going to come in to make money off of that. And that was fifteen years before the rezoning happened!

CS: So already the first artists who came with a strong sense of creating a new community in Williamsburg, while leaving Manhattan to the rich, were inadvertently laying the groundwork for the City Planning Office. You were among them when you moved across the river in 1990.

SF: I had lived in really tiny places—a storefront in the East Village, a tenement in Chinatown—and I had to work outside my home, at places like the Millennium Film Workshop. In Williamsburg I could live not only with my partner but with roommates too—potentially with other artists and filmmakers—and I could also have a huge studio. People I knew had already moved to Hoboken or other places where they lived in industrial buildings. I always envied them but I never had the money or the wherewithal to do that. Artists who moved into commercial spaces in Williamsburg with unprotected leases lived with the risk of rents being tripled overnight. Like many others, we as tenants did all the work and spent all the money—about $80,000 in materials alone— and the three of us renovated every day for eight months. We also paid all the expenses of the building and were living adjacent to manufacturing. There was a furniture-making place across our courtyard so all day long we heard buzz saws. It was very loud. But for us, it meant: Somebody is working, they have a job, and I get to have this place where I can work! The kind of people who live in Williamsburg now do not want to live with the sound of a saw all day long.

CS: And the cleaning trucks with the noisy brushes—every morning at 6 a.m. there was this elephant herd streaming out into the city. But there was also peace.

SF: Back then you could walk for an hour along Kent Avenue on a weekend and not see a single person. This was such a treasure for me having grown up in Chicago where I could go to the lakefront and not see a soul, and also after living in Manhattan, which is always so loud and crowded. Our loft was a block and a half from the river, so even in terms of my development as an artist, to have that privacy and sense of peace in a modest environment was really great.

CS: What did that do for you as an artist?

SF: It gave me some time away from all of the pressures of living in the city—just to go somewhere and sit for hours and stare at the water and think my own thoughts. Also, we were right up against all of the industries along the river. Our own building contained small industries and we were mostly surrounded by those kinds of buildings, not the little row houses like in the rest of Williamsburg. It meant that every day I was seeing people at work. Not like in the city where people are going into office buildings or into shops, but people making cardboard boxes or labels. Over time I developed such a respect and a real attachment to it. I could go out and see people producing things that we need on a daily basis—it was something that became very much part of my feeling: this is a necessary and important thing and I'm glad to be around it.

CS: Especially as a countercurrent to the increasing abstraction of work that is taking place in Manhattan where everyone seems to reside in a numerical and intangible sphere that becomes less and less comprehensible.

SF: That has been true for the last ten years but during the '90s outsourcing to China really increased and all those basic items for daily life were being made elsewhere. And now everyone is doing virtual work. I'm a very hands-on, DIY kind of person and to see somebody make a cardboard box is actually exciting to me. I made a film called *From the Ground Up*, which I finished in 2007 and which is about coffee. It originated with seeing the coffee carts arriving and leaving from a place just around the corner from us—I thought, "Oh, we have a part of the production chain right in our neighborhood."

CS: In many parts of Manhattan one is mostly surrounded by banks, and the Halal stands are among the few signs of production in otherwise increasingly sterile neighborhoods.

SF: It's also evidence of the labor of the immigrant population in New York. The vast majority of the people who work in the manufacturing spaces still in existence in Williamsburg, who run the coffee carts and who run the Halal stands, are recent immigrants. Our neighborhood had also been a vital center for art production and showing art and having performances and screenings for a long time. And then that all fell apart.

CS: You and your partner Cathy Quinlan were part of that production and you lived with your roommates in your own art community that attracted other artists.

SF: We lived in this beautiful space which soon became a gathering place, and more officially so in 2004 when my partner, Cathy Quinlan, started the Temporary Museum. We'd have a show, an event, or a discussion with an artist and lots of people would come and passersby would stop in from the street—it really was a salon environment and people loved it. Cathy has been a painter all her life so when she started her museum she said, "This is for painting and drawing." Period, end of story. And she proceeded to mount really good shows of only painting and drawing month after month. People would say, "Thank God I have come to a space where I can just look at paintings and drawings and not have some monitor over in the corner yammering at me." There were people who had that kind of seriousness of purpose and focus in Williamsburg.

CS: I think it's interesting that art now is employed as a cure for social ills—the NEA puts a little art center into the slum of Atlanta so the neighborhood will blossom! It has become almost like a social strategy.

SF: Yeah. But there's also blurring of lines between what it means to be an artist and what it means to work in the commercial realm employing certain art practices without being an artist. This is what we started hearing back in the early 2000s when people would say about Williamsburg, "Oh, it's just filled with creatives!" And we'd be like, "What the fuck is a creative?" I had been a creative if you consider that early in my life in New York I worked in advertising and magazine and book production, so I was around people who were trying to sell a product, and I was helping them because they paid me and then I'd go home and make art. But what's happening now is that somebody who works at the Gap designing their website is thinking of themselves in the same realm as me or a friend of mine who's a painter or a poet. And I'm not making a value judgment, but I'm saying there really is a difference between being paid to design a website and sitting in your room not being paid to write a poem or paint a painting. I think if they just called themselves advertising executives like the people who used to do that kind of work did, I'd be fine with that. Because then we would have understood the difference between Allen Ginsberg and somebody who worked on Madison Avenue.

CS: An artist like Warhol promoted something like this himself by mixing the high and low, the trivial and the noble. However, if the artists themselves play with the commodification of art, that's one thing, but if whole industries commodify art for their own purposes, that's still another. You can probably market the poison in the Gowanus Canal in the name of authenticity as a bohemian asset.

SF: In the late '80s when people like David Byrne were in Gap ads in the subway, we were like, "No way!" but that was one of the first incursions of getting artists to basically market themselves. I remember so well how we all talked about that: If the Gap asked you to do that would you do it? It was one of those terrible moral questions that people hated to be asked. Now it's just absolutely ordinary.

CS: I've always admired the work of the photographer Camilo José Vergara who has specialized in showing the opposite process, starting with a slightly endangered neighborhood and documenting what happened to it all the way down to the very ruin of the buildings and then in the end the fortification of a neighborhood with all the fences and concertina wire. And, like in your case, the systematic process in connection with an aesthetic concept gives a more powerful understanding than just reading a book about it. Did you know what a long breath your project would take?

SF: No, at first I thought, "Wow, the building at the corner, I'll go watch them jackhammering it." And then, "Oh, the one on North 10th" and "Oh, the one down on South 3rd." And suddenly it became so huge. I would get on my bike with my camera and ride around and check up on the construction sites that I knew already and then find new ones. Over the first two years I was just periodically continuing this record. Eventually I started logging just to get an idea of how much material I had and what I might need to follow up on. Then the Icon on McCarren Park was having its big fancy party so I went to see what these buildings were like inside. It was a process of recognizing additional layers. And, of course, I talked to various small industry people in the neighborhood who I knew, like the guys across the street with the forklift company. Then I talked with other artists—Amy Jenkins threw a party when she was finally thrown out of her loft along with many of the original Williamsburg artists I've known for years. We were witnessing virtually every building around us being either transformed or torn down.

CS: In spite of the tragedy all around you there is also a lot of humor in your film.

SF: One critical evolution of the film came when I had constructed a two-and-a-half-hour rough cut. At that point it was mostly my voice. Then Cathy Quinlan entered the picture and she was the one who brought in a lot of humor even though she was as upset as I was about losing our space. She said, "This is an important story to tell but you won't win people over, or you won't even get them to listen, if all you are is angry or sad." There needs to be humor because there is a tragicomic side to the way these developers behave toward the people who are moving in. The whole situation is just preposterous. And so she did some extensive rewriting and cowriting with me. That made all the difference.

CS: In the film you quote Cathy suggesting you should just call it *I Hate Rich People*. There is certainly a great deal of absurdity in these pseudo-glamorous buildings and the way they are marketed.

SF: It's always a really bad idea to tell people what they're seeing but if you say that the sales agents love to brag about their subway tiles and twenty minutes later we see a developer talking to a client and he says something about the subway tiles, there's always laughter in the audience. People remember.

CS: And then there is the piece de resistance, the stoic, irremovable boulder, which for a gleeful little while becomes your ally.

SF: One summer they had torn down the building across the street, which I found absolutely heartbreaking and then this huge rock was unearthed. I just put my camera on a tripod by the window in the kitchen so I could record their efforts over many hours—it turned out to be many days—as they tried to get rid of this poor rock. And so that became very emblematic to me of what was going on, the losing battle we were fighting against these people.

CS: If the architecture was not as offensively hideous as it is, if this had been done with more sensibility, would you have felt at all differently about it?

SF: Of course one wants things to be more pleasant and more interesting to look at, but it wouldn't take away from the fact that the buildings drove out other people. The one couldn't happen without the other. And not just people in the industrial buildings but all the people who lived in the small two-story and three-story houses in the neighborhood. Those mostly were not rent controlled or rent stabilized and so the rents skyrocketed. The owners of the corner deli on Driggs and 9th Street tried so hard to stay. Now their rent is $30,000 a month—for a deli! Only those who own the buildings can remain, everyone else has been driven out. So, yeah, the buildings for the most part are crap. I couldn't believe what I was seeing when I went to those showrooms. Karl Fischer is famously horrible. He was the architect of a good number of buildings in the neighborhood and there's a lot of stuff online about just what devastation he's wrought, architecturally, visually, esthetically. We used to joke about how fifteen years from now Williamsburg is going to be like a scene from *Blade Runner*—all these buildings will be falling apart. All the rich people will have moved out. People are going to start squatting them. I kind of hope that happens.

CS: Moving to Bed-Stuy, you have embarked on another chapter in your life, another interesting, complex situation. To me, that would be another film—the irony of having been kicked out of one neighborhood and then being seen as the gentrifier in another, eyed with suspicion. It just seems like a never-ending New York story.

SF: I insisted that we buy something because I'm in my later fifties and I just couldn't imagine going through this again. We had very little money. We looked and looked, and eventually got a place in Bed-Stuy. I was very aware that we would enter into a neighborhood that had been largely a black neighborhood for about forty years. Before that, it was different—it had been German and Jewish. Knowing what had happened in Harlem, I was sensitive to what it might mean to move to Bed-Stuy. I tested the waters a bit before we had found this place and decided to buy it. I was met with varying responses. Some people were saying, "Don't do it," or, "We don't want your kind in this neighborhood." And other people were saying, "Do it. We need stability. If it's a home that isn't occupied, we need people to be living in these homes and maintaining them and keeping up the block because we want a safe, friendly, good neighborhood." And so some recognized us as people who might possibly do that. The day after we closed, we went over to start working on the house and a van drove up with three women in it who jumped out and said, "Hello, we're the block association of this block and we'd like to welcome you to the block and please come to the meeting next week." We went to the meeting and have since been incredibly involved with our block. We've done tons of work with our neighbors. I read Bed-Stuy Patch every day and there's lots of talk about what all this means. It's debated a lot on the internet. I feel like it's a thorny thing. Just like living in Williamsburg, living in Bed-Stuy to me means eating at the local restaurants, shopping at the local grocery store, and joining my neighbors, who have lived here for ten or thirty or even forty years, doing things that they think are necessary to make it a nice neighborhood to live in. I did that when I lived in Chinatown. I renovated my crappy old apartment so it was a nicer apartment and I ate at the local restaurants. So I think we can be a part of a neighborhood without destroying it. The people who live in Williamsburg now would never have wanted to live in the old Williamsburg. They wanted their Williamsburg. I don't move into a neighborhood in order to turn it into my vision of some glittery place full of palaces and flashy restaurants.

CS: One last question: how do you see this film in the context of your other work?

SF: I've been making films since 1978 and I'm known as somebody who makes work that is seen as quite personal or as something that originates with the personal. A film about my father, *Sink or Swim*, or the one about my mother, *The Ties That Bind*, or *Hide and Seek* about lesbian children—I'm a lesbian so, yes, it's sort of about me. I have always wanted my work to originate in the personal but extend out from there in all kinds of ways. And sometimes that happens because of a formal device that I use or sometimes it happens because I introduce other characters, but I don't want it to just be about me. Judging from people's responses, my approach does speak to them. So I would say this film is in keeping with my other work. Back in 2002 I made a film called *The Odds of Recovery*, which was about medical issues and it was seen as more of a documentary with a capital "D" compared to my earlier work. When I made *From the Ground Up* about coffee I wondered, "Am I turning into a documentary filmmaker?" I love documentaries but I didn't ever quite see myself as a documentary filmmaker before. *Sink or Swim* is a document about my relationship to my father but aesthetically it is very far apart from documentary. *Hide and Seek* uses interviews with women about their childhoods but there's also fiction mixed in with it. I think of *Gut Renovation* more as an essay film, more in keeping with what Agnes Varda might do in *The Gleaners and I* or what Chris Marker might do in some of his films. It's trying to step back a bit from the immediate and allow people to think of it as a conversation about something that applies to many other situations. If you watch a documentary about steelworkers in Mongolia you might think, "Oh, this is like what steelworkers in Pittsburgh experience." *Gut Renovation* is very much about Williamsburg but at the same time reaches beyond that.

Su Friedrich Returns

Adam Schartoff / 2016

From *Filmwax Radio*, Episode 377, November 12, 2016. This interview first appeared as part of the podcast *Filmwax Radio*, www.filmwaxradio.com. Printed by permission of Adam Schartoff and *Filmwax Radio*.

Adam Schartoff: The reason we're talking is because your new documentary, *I Cannot Tell You How I Feel*, which is about your mom, is going to have a screening at BAM in a matter of days from when we're sitting here. So that's the underlying focus of why we're talking, but it's also nice to have you back on this podcast. We can now divulge that last time you were on we sort of did a hoax on my listeners. Do you remember?

Su Friedrich: I don't remember. What was it?

AS: You're gonna laugh. Well, you were late. Then you came into DUMBO, but I wanted to get into the car with you and drive around Williamsburg to do an audio documentary of you pointing out spots and mentioning what happened to the neighborhood and your experiences in the neighborhood.

SF: That's right!

AS: And you had this great idea, because the time was tight. You said, "Well, can we go into the car, drive around so you get the atmosphere, but I'll just fake it and pretend that we're in Williamsburg.

SF: [*Laughs*] That's true!

AS: So we just drove around DUMBO for about twenty minutes, but it came out very well.

SF: So nobody will believe anything I say this time! Here we are sitting in Trump Tower . . .

AS: [*Laughs*] Right. Well, just for some more context, this was during a period a few years ago where there was a crop of documentaries about New York, but more so Brooklyn, and what was happening to our neighborhoods with rezoning and development in general. *Gut Renovation*, which was your prior film before this one, was about your experience of losing your home in Williamsburg. So you've been here in Bed-Stuy now for . . . ?

SF: Seven years and some months. Yeah, basically in 2008 I started looking and we moved in 2009.

AS: You have dealt with family in a number of your films already, so this new film is kind of going back to that. Right?

SF: Yes, although one thing that's funny about the screening at BAM, which is on November 17, is that they decided to program it with *The Ties That Bind*. So that's a film I made in 1984 about my mother, and, of course, this one is about my mother.

AS: Thirty years later.

SF: Yes, and so they thought, "Well, let's see what happened in the last thirty years," and I said, "Well, that's fine. You're the programmers." But I never thought that this film was a sequel, or was in any really related to *The Ties That Bind*—except for the fact that they're both about the same person, because the other film tells the drastic tales of her life, growing up in Germany during the second world war. It was the first long film I made and it was sort of looking back at the past of this other person. And when I started making this recent film, I didn't have *The Ties That Bind* in mind at all, except to think, "Well, I did make another film about her." But it's not as if I meant to mirror this earlier film in any way. I just didn't think of it in relationship to my recent film because *I Cannot Tell You How I Feel* is very much about the present. It's about, "Wow, look where we are and look what we're going through." And so, it'll be interesting for me to see them together.

Actually, as I went along in the edit of this film, there were a couple of moments when I wanted to show very briefly something about my mother's character or her activities in her daily life. And so, I did use some clips from *The Ties That Bind* showing her swimming. But then I even wonder, "Well, if somebody sees this without knowing *The Ties That Bind*, will they understand where this footage comes from?" It might just look like home movie footage. So, it's a funny thing.

AS: Let me ask you a question, and I assume you don't mind divulging the answer. Let me know. [*Laughs*] I'm sure you'll tell me otherwise. How old was your mom when you made *The Ties That Bind*?

SF: She was born in 1920. I finished it in 1984. So, sixty-four.

AS: Now, you were roughly how old when you made *I Cannot Tell You How I Feel*?

SF: I am about to turn sixty-two.

AS: Okay. So, now this is something you reflected on at some point in the film itself, but you kind of noted something about being the age your mother was . . .

SF: Yes, that was a very weird moment and that does have to do with *The Ties That Bind*. Because, in the new film, I visit her in Chicago and somebody takes a picture of us—it's the summer and we're walking along the lake. This picture then fades into a picture that was taken of us when I was making *The Ties That Bind*. In that photograph, she's sixty-three. I have lived for all these years with that photograph, knowing that I'm getting older, of course, but still it's always my mother, the woman with the gray hair who's a lot older than me in the photograph. And suddenly, I'm only two years younger than her. And that was, aside from many other things, very confusing. Or it was a wake-up call [*Laughs*].

AS: It is odd, because I certainly have memories of my father at my current age and being an adult then, albeit a young adult. The point being that I know what you mean.

The phrase that gives your current film its title, "I cannot tell you how I feel," is something your mom says in the film because she's so overwhelmed. I should mention, the backdrop of the film is that she's being moved from her home of like fifty-two years in Chicago to just outside of New York City, which for anybody is a big deal, but for somebody who is as old as your mom is . . . she's in her nineties, right?

SF: Yeah, she was ninety-four when we started moving her. She just turned ninety-six. Her birthday's on Halloween.

AS: I guess my question would be, she's not really putting things in the context of aging—because she's been older for a while—but are you [*Laughs*]?

SF: [*Laughs*] Actually, one day she said to me, "You know, I'd really love if I were twenty years younger." I was like, "Mom, that would make you seventy-five. That's not exactly a young person" [*Laughs*]. But I think everything's relative, so . . .

AS: That's right. Well, she was probably pretty darn youthful at seventy-five, because at ninety, she's still very mobile. Because of her forgetfulness, if she were diagnosed, my guess is the doctor would say, "She's ninety-three." At ninety-three . . .

SF: Things start to fade.

AS: Yeah, it's a lot of years to remember, let alone just a lot on your mind. In the epilogue of the film, she's now in New York and you go to visit, and she doesn't remember that you were coming that day. Again, it's just being ninety-three. My mother, if I go visit her, she doesn't know my name. She doesn't know what our relationship is. She knows she loves me—she'll tell me that—but she doesn't know who I am.

SF: That's the next level. I know that hasn't happened yet, but the day that she says, "Oh, hi. Do I know you?" It's gonna be pretty rough. I went through that with my grandparents, but it's different when it's your parent.

AS: Yeah, and my mom is a good sixteen years younger than your mother. So, it's a different thing. But I think a lot of people are going to be able to identify. To see somebody who's in their early sixties and still grappling with those difficulties with their parent, it's quite a universal thing.

SF: One of the feelings I had when I was doing it, and certainly just in living my life while I was making the film, was the fact that we never got any training in dealing with this stuff. Of course, any of us could have taken a workshop about what happens when your parents start going through this. We could have read books. But we don't. When you're our age or younger, you're just thinking about your life. You're just doing what you're doing. And somebody else who's a little older may say, "Oh God. My grandfather has Alzheimer's." You may hear about it and think, "Oh, that sounds terrible," but I don't think any of us think, "Well, I'm going to be prepared." Suddenly it happens and you have no guidelines. It's actually kind of reminiscent to me of what happened when we did have to leave Williamsburg and decided to buy a house instead of rent again. I'd never owned anything and the learning curve for, "What's a mortgage? How do you do this? How do you even begin," was really steep. I sort of got through it. We got a place. It all worked out, but this is sort of similar, but of course much more emotionally charged.

I was really lucky that my sister and brother live here too—they're both in New York. My sister's in Park Slope and my brother lives up in Westchester. They're both very capable and responsible. So, between the three of us, we were able to figure out what to do, like, "Okay Pete's going to find the lawyer and my sister's going deal with the doctors. I'm going to deal with the real estate." We could kind of cross-reference what we were doing and work it all out, as opposed to doing it alone.

In making a film, you're always meeting people and talking about the subject. I premiered this film in Vienna, and I talked to people there and was meeting people who are alone when they do it, either because they're the only child or they have siblings who just won't lift a finger. I feel so sorry for people who have to do this alone, because it's overwhelming the amount of stuff that one has to do.

AS: It is true. I have a sister, so it was very helpful. I was visiting friends upstate and they were telling me that they both had just gone through two years or more of drama with all four of their parents. But I did learn quite a bit and I knew the right questions to ask—I learned what I had to do to get my dad the help he needed, because he's just not that ambitious. I didn't know this. He was always a provider when I was growing up; he always got home after work and provided and was there, present. It wasn't until my mom was gone that I realized who was really the force behind the family—and that was my mother. When she was gone, my dad was really just willing to go status quo every time—given he's in his eighties, so that has something to do with it. It's like having a car and you never do anything preventative, like tuning up the car. You just wait till things break down. As they break down, you get them patched together. You just have this kind of lemon. He wouldn't do anything proactive. And he's losing and spending his money. So, I just had to dig in my heels.

SF: This summer my father passed away and, for two months before, my brother was dealing with him about all his finances. Then there was the funeral and all of that. Looking at it the day after it happened, I thought, "Oh, well, this is also another big step or something that you should know about." I talked to Pete and he said, "Yeah, and you know what, the whole funeral industry in this country is such a rip off, like so many other things" [*Laughs*].

AS: The wedding industry, too [*Laughs*].

SF: Yeah, the wedding industry. So, there you are, totally in grief and suddenly, there's this funeral director saying, "Well, maybe you'd like the most expensive coffin."

AS: Grieve in style.

SF: Yeah. So, my father was cremated and there was an urn. It was like a five-minute walk from the funeral home to the cemetery, and the funeral director asked my brother if he would like to have the hearse drive the urn to the cemetery. My brother's like, "No, I'll carry it." It was like five pounds. How much would they have charged for the hearse to transport it? Again, I think there are so many things about this that we don't really want to think about. We don't want to know about them until it happens. But buyer beware. Sometimes it helps to know things ahead of time.

AS: Oh, absolutely. So, you realize you were moving your mother down to New York and that was of course a huge obstacle. I'm assuming she put up something of a fight.

SF: Yeah, a bit.

AS: We see some of that in the film, although it seems like it's already resolved by the time the film is in the present. Were you feeling the urge to tell this new story or was this particular story just speaking to you? Perhaps a better way of putting it is that I'm wondering how you knew it was time to start making a new film.

SF: Yeah, that is a good question. It's always a good question. When anything is done, how do you start the new one? What's the new one going to be?

AS: Well, *Gut Renovation*, for instance, had much more universal context.

SF: Right, the whole neighborhood was experiencing this thing. So, yes, that came from this sense of a shared experience. One of the things about this current film is that I really tried, also with the help of my partner who's a very good editor and has a good sense of humor, to inject some humor in film, because this could potentially be a really dreary and depressing subject. So, early in the film, my mother asks if I'm going to come along with her as they leave the house, and on the screen (because I use a lot of text in the film), I say "Yes, but I'm going to be hiding behind my camera." Now, that was written after the fact, when I was editing and I heard her ask me that question on camera.

AS: Oh, you recorded it after the fact?

SF: Yeah, I was looking at the footage of the day she leaves and this particular shot where she asks, "Susi, are you going to come with us?" And as I was editing, I thought, "Yes, but I'm going to hide behind my camera," because I kept thinking about the fact that I had my camera on during so much of this and I knew that I wasn't thinking at the beginning, "I'm going to make a film about moving my mother." That absolutely was not my thought. I thought, "Holy shit. We have to do all of this. It's going to ruin the summer. It's going to be a nightmare." And I realized that my little Sony pocket photo camera also shot video, so I just started using it and she wasn't aware of it. It was partly just because I thought, "Well, maybe I'll just look at this footage later so I remember what happened, because I'm so freaked out that I'm not going to remember what it was like." In one case, when we were looking at the place where we were going to move her, I was recording for the same reason you would when you buy a house, just to have a record of what street it was on, what the house looked like, etc. So, there were various ways in which I picked up and used the camera. But, at some point early in the fall after we had done the whole move, I thought, "I've got a lot of footage here. I've got a lot of ideas. So, let me see what happens if I start editing." So it kind of went like that.

AS: And then a story emerged.

SF: Then a story emerged. Plus, as I said before, when you're having this experience, you just start meeting tons of people who are having it: friends, strangers, whatever. And so, the more I was in the experience and talking to people, the more I thought, "Well, this might be something that other people would like to see—either because it will reflect their own experience or if they're younger, it might be instructive in some way." Actually, when I showed it in Vienna, the film's first screening to a big audience, and I had no idea how people would feel, a number of people came up to me afterwards and said, "That was so liberating." And I was like, "It was liberating?" They said, "Yeah, because I also think those things and I'm afraid to think them. I think I'm a really bad person if I think them. So, I'm really glad you said those things."

AS: Do you have a sense that you're more outspoken than the average person when it comes to personal feelings or your personal life?

SF: Well, I might be a little bit more outspoken [*Laughs*].

AS: Well, you might be so accustomed to it because you've made how many films . . .

SF: Well, they're not all about family. But I've made twenty-four films and a bunch of them are pretty frank about stuff that goes on between people in families, or . . .

AS: Yeah, or what you're going through.

SF: Yeah, like *The Odds of Recovery* was about medical problems and I think there were some very frank moments in that. So, I do try to say it like it is.

AS: Yeah, and there are certain parts of the world where that's not what people do or it's not the way you're supposed to be. But I think people do want it or, maybe as this person admitted, I think a lot more probably wish they could be more frank or not be ashamed of their feelings.

SF: It's like reading *Fun Home*, the Alison Bechdel book, or Roz Chast's book, *Can't We Talk about Something More Pleasant?* I read those and think, "Thank you so much for being so upfront about what really goes on in these situations." I don't know if Roz and Alison had somebody sitting at their elbow, but in my case, I had Cathy. I'm editing and, once in a while, I say Cathy, "Hey, could you look at this? Tell me what you think." There's this one moment in the film where I was saying something about my mother and feeling like, "Oh, yes, and I'm so much like her. I'm her daughter," and Cathy said, "That is so euphemistic and kind of wishy-washy, and that's not how you really feel." I responded, "Oh, you're right. So, what do I really feel?" I kind of know, but I'm not going to say it [*Laughs*]. And she said, "Well, let's talk about this," and I ended up sort of writing this little statement with her, which I thought so exposed me. I did a recording of it, but then she said, "Yeah, but you know what you should do? You should whisper it." I was like, "That's a great idea!" So, I sort of performed it in this desperate whisper.

So, I wouldn't say I'm always able to be as frank, but with her prodding me a little bit, I get a little more frank.

AS: Keeps you honest. Did your mom get a chance to see the film?

SF: No, that's not gonna happen.

AS: It would be too painful?

SF: I think it would disturb her. I don't think it would do her any good, so to speak. Also, it's really bizarre, when somebody is in the state that my mother is in now (which is to say that she forgets three minutes later what happened), I don't even understand what it would mean for her to see it if five minutes later she would forget that she had seen it. You want to show something to somebody because then you will talk, they will reflect on it, they will get back to you. With her, it would just sort of disappear. So, I don't know. I just don't want to do it.

AS: Has she seen a lot of your work?

SF: Yeah.

AS: What does she make of it?

SF: She likes it. She's interested in it. She's happy that I'm a filmmaker. So I don't feel like I wouldn't show it to her because she hasn't been supportive of me. And, of course, the real experience of showing her a film of mine was when I did *The Ties That Bind*, so it was a completely different situation before. And I was working in film then, which meant all the expense and trouble of getting a print, so I showed it to her when it was still on the editing table so that I could be sure that what I had said was correct, how I represented her was correct. I felt that was really necessary and we worked it out fine.

AS: Also, I understand why BAM is pairing these two films about your mom together, because it's specific to the career of Su Friedrich. I think your films do talk to each other and I think there's something that is different about your body work than a lot of other documentary filmmakers who are looking for the subject. They kind of work together. I've only seen four or five, but I feel like they work together. You're seeing your life in stages.

SF: It's weird because there are so many thousands of people at this point who know so much about me. I'll have somebody come up to me at a screening who says, "I've seen all your films," and they'll start talking about my father, my partner, and my this and my that. It's so weird because they really know tons of stuff about me and I don't know who they are. I don't even know their name. It's odd, but of course that's going to happen if I do the kind of work I do.

Another thing about showing those two films together that just occurred to me—I had made about four or five short films (also silent films) before I made *The Ties That Bind*, so that was sort of like my big breakthrough: I'm going to start working with sound, it's going to be fifty-four minutes instead of fifteen minutes. It was really a leap for me. It was also going to be a documentary of sorts. But because I had come out of this experimental film tradition and had all kinds of principles and beliefs about film, I chose not to do any talking heads in it and I didn't shoot any sync sound (I shot everything with the Bolex, you hear her in voiceover, and I mixed incredible amounts of images together to tell the story). So, on one hand, it was my first "documentary." I've made a bunch since, but it was the first of what has been a series of films which some people could call a documentary because it's a record of somebody alive in the real world (as opposed to an actor). But, on the other hand, it's quite unconventional in its form from a regular documentary, and so is this current film. I feel like, thirty years later, I still am really interested in picking up my camera and shooting the world in front of me, but that doesn't mean I'm going to do a talking heads documentary. I have no objection to that kind of film. I see lots of them. I think they're great, but it's not who I am. In a way, I think this shows that, in all these years, I haven't really left some of those early principles or ideas that I had.

AS: That's a great way of putting it. There's a through line.

SF: Except there's more humor now than there was in the past. I suppose I was very serious [*Laughs*].

AS: You've lightened up a bit?

SF: Well, I just think humor is a really important part of life.

AS: Yeah, especially when you're confronting all this mortality stuff.

SF: Yeah.

AS: You really have to use it or tap it because otherwise . . . [*Laughs*].

SF: "Getting old isn't for sissies," as Bette Davis said [*Laughs*].

AS: Again, the name of the documentary is *I Cannot Tell You How I Feel.*

SF: Can I say something about the title? So, I have made twenty-three/twenty-four films, all of them have a title that's some form of idiom, aphorism, saying, whatever you want to call it: *Gently Down the Stream, Damned If You Don't, The Ties That Bind, Rules of the Road, Sink or Swim, The Odds of Recovery, From the Ground Up*. Every time I've made a film in the last decade or more, I've thought, "Don't do it this time. Come up with a title that isn't a known thing." But I always end up with a known thing. So this time, again, I thought, "I've no idea what the title is. Let's see what happens. Please let it not be . . ." And I like the titles. I don't mind them. I just think sometimes you shouldn't do what you've always done. So, when I shot what is the first scene of the film of her talking, sort of traumatized the day she's leaving, I thought she finished what she was saying so I turned off the camera, but she continued talking. So, I quickly turned the camera back on, but it meant that the shot kind of fell to the floor and then got back up on her. When I was editing, I thought, "Well, that's a mess. That looks terrible. What am I going to do? How am I going to cover it? I'll find some old photographs of her." So, I just put black over it. Then, I was editing, and I heard her say, "I cannot tell you how I feel," and then continue talking when she came back on camera. But this phrase was where the image was a mess. And I just thought, "Well, that's the title." I really loved it because I could make the title come up on the screen while you heard it being said, but also because it's her saying it (because it's her voice) as well as me saying it (because it's the title of my film). There's a great irony in it, because she does tell us how she's feeling and so do I [*Laughs*]. I was just like, "Yay! I love this!"

AS: [*Laughs*] Finally, you've been liberated.

SF: That's right [*Laughs*].

AS: Again, the screening again is at BAM.

SF: Thursday, November 17.

AS: Which is coming right up.

SF: Right, and it's only that one night. Sometimes people think, "Oh, it's a week run." Hopefully I'll show it at other places around the city, but at the moment, that's it. And it's the New York premiere, so I'm very excited.

AS: It's a great venue for your premiere.

SF: Yes, it is.

AS: Did you just submit it, or what?

SF: Yeah, I sent it to one of the programmers and just said, "Let me know what you think." She wrote back and said, "We'd love to show it."

AS: That's a nice answer that maybe you were hoping for [*Laughs*].

SF: Exactly [*Laughs*].

AS: Thank you.

SF: Well, thank you.

Su Friedrich in the Swamp of Images

Giovanni Marchini Camia / 2016

From *Fandor*, November 13, 2016. Reprinted by permission of Giovanni Marchini Camia.

Avant-garde filmmaker Su Friedrich has been making intimate, self-revealing cinema for close to four decades now. In her twenty-four films to date, she's tackled subjects such as the conflict between her Catholic upbringing and homosexuality (*Damned If You Don't*, 1987), her difficult relationship with her abusive father (*Sink or Swim*, 1990), and getting evicted from her Williamsburg apartment by way of gentrification (*Gut Renovation*, 2012).

By candidly confronting personal struggles, Friedrich's films invite reflections on broader, often universal concerns. This is again the case with her latest, *I Cannot Tell You How I Feel*, which premiered at this year's Viennale. A documentary about the experience of moving her ninety-four-year-old mother—already familiar from Friedrich's sublime 1984 exploration of identity and history, *The Ties That Bind*—into assisted living, *I Cannot Tell You How I Feel* offers a moving, tragic, frequently funny, and profoundly empathetic consideration of mortality and filial responsibility.

Giovanni Marchini Camia: When you started filming your mother's move out of her apartment, did you know you would make the film? Or do you have a habit of filming important events in your life?

Su Friedrich: I didn't know I was going to make this film, but I don't just film events in my life. I'm not a diary filmmaker; I start working when I have an idea. I need to have some sort of goal. At the beginning of this film, when I say, "I'm going to be hiding behind my camera," it suggests that as soon as we decided to move my mother, I decided to make a film about it. But it wasn't like that at all. I thought, "Oh shit, this is going to be such a terrible experience, my summer is ruined!" When I picked up the camera, it was to have something to think about aside from all this terrible stuff we had to think about.

GMC: So there was a therapeutic aspect to making this film?

SF: No, because this isn't art therapy. Art therapy is something very particular: People have troubles and they go to an art therapist. They aren't artists; they're people with problems who use a paint brush. I'm a person with problems who also is an artist. I don't disrespect art therapy, but it's not at all the same thing. If I start thinking about working on a film because the subject has deep emotional resonance for me, I know it's going to be really hard and that I'm going to have to go to places in my mind that I don't want to. But it's also going to be hard because I'll have to get good footage, good sound, I'll have to write good texts, and then I'll have to edit so that it all makes sense and works well. There is a huge, huge, huge amount of craft and thought and planning and consciousness in the process that completely takes over from the emotional stuff.

Also I think the goal of art therapy is that you understand how you're feeling and you get better. That never happens when you're making a film! [*Laughs.*] You have a better understanding of what you're thinking, but afterwards, you have this product, this object that follows you around for the rest of your life and makes you recognize—I will speak individually, other people may have had different experiences—it makes *me* understand that I never really come to the end of my feeling about the thing. The film can only be a limited discussion, and I will continue, forever, to experience whatever it is—my mother, my father, being thrown out of my house . . .

GMC: And why is it important for you to share this process and discussion with an audience?

SF: There's two parts to it, which are equally important. One part is the content: the emotion, the story, the revelation, the confession—whatever you want to call it. The other part is the craft: the shooting, the editing, and writing. The first part I want to share because of something I first learned in 1981, when I made *Gently Down the Stream*. This will sound immodest, but somebody came up to me afterwards and said, "Thank you so much for making that film, because I've had the exact same experience. Nobody has ever expressed that in the way you have and it's really great for me to hear somebody else say they've had this experience."

It's not as if then I thought, "Ah, I'm the savior of the world!" But I have also sometimes gone to see a film, read a book, read a poem, or seen a painting in which I've recognized something about my own life and thought that the person had suffered like me, laughed like me, had sex like me, eaten too much chocolate like me. . . . No matter what it is, we share this life. That's been my experience all along: I make a film about my father, everybody comes up to me: "My father, my father, my father . . ." I make a film about medical issues, people come up to me: "My operation, my this, my that . . ." Every time I make something, there will be a lot of people who have the same experience and want to hear it talked about.

That was the one side of why I show it to people. The other is simply that I'm a filmmaker and I love films and I work incredibly hard, especially in the editing, to create things that—I hope—move in ways that are interesting, exciting, funny, make associations between images, between texts and image, that somebody likes to see on the screen. So, of course, if I work so hard to do that, then I want to show it to people! [*Laughs.*]

GMC: You've been making very personal films since your debut, in 1978. Personal films have a long tradition in avant-garde cinema, but over the last decade or so, the zeitgeist seems to have become all about laying yourself bare—most obviously on Facebook, Instagram, etc. How do you regard this shift in attitude, and do you feel it has any relation to your own practice?

SF: The idea of making very personal films, laying oneself bare, is interesting, because if I read Dickens or Jane Austen, or if I see a film by Agnès Varda or Steven Spielberg—to me all art is laying oneself bare. Even if a writer or filmmaker takes somebody else's story, they're still, almost always, working from a place that means a great deal to them emotionally, that touches their heart very, very deeply. So, on the surface, they make a film about another character, but it's very much about them. We're always laying ourselves bare when we make work. I just do it more obviously, let's say.

This thing now, though, about the zeitgeist, it's very difficult for me. It's very difficult for everybody. Everybody I know who makes work is saying, 'Oh my God, what do we do now in this environment?' Because everything is media! Now everything is conveyed through a moving image. The carefully selected, thought-about, worked-over thing that we have known as film starts to become part of this big swamp of images. It does make me feel like people will have less and less of an ability to differentiate between the two.

I don't know what that's going to mean for us, and what that's going to mean for us as makers. I thought about it when I was making *Gut Renovation*, and I thought about it very much while making this film: Maybe I should just stop making films; or, fuck it, I'm going to continue making them in the same way I always have. I have no control over the world, and if until the day I die I still make my carefully crafted films that you should watch in one sitting with the lights off, and no one is watching them that way anymore, I can't do anything about it. [*Laughs.*] But if I stop doing that, if I only make one-minute videos that I put on Facebook, then I'll just kill myself. It would be so pointless.

MC: I read that you gave your mother final approval of *The Ties That Bind* and that you wouldn't have released it if she'd had objections. Since she's no longer capable of making such calls, why was her approval not a preoccupation this time?

SF: It was a preoccupation, from the first day until today. I could go to her tomorrow and say, "Mom, I made a film about you, is it OK?" And if she said yes, five minutes later she would forget. So I could ask for her approval, but that would be completely dishonest and stupid of me. I had a lot of ideas and feelings about it, the whole time, for the last two years, and I finally thought, "It is what it is." I hope people don't think I'm making something that discredits her terribly, but if they do, I have to live with the consequences. I know I can't show her this film. She would be upset by certain things in it. And so I finished it, and I premiered it the other night, and mostly what people said was, "This is not critical of your mother. This is not a negative portrait. You say things that sound negative but she comes across mostly in a way that we admire her." And I'll live with that, that's OK with me.

GMC: I was at the premiere, and in the Q&A afterwards many people commented on the scene in which your mother tells the ludicrous story about her doorman robbing her and balancing a bowl of hot soup on his head. I'd like to bring that up again because, I must admit, that scene was excruciating for me to watch. I'm having difficulties judging whether it was because of the scene itself, or because of all the laughter in the auditorium.

SF: As you say, there was a lot of laughter in the audience. That surprised me. I felt it was nervous laughter. People who aren't familiar with that experience don't know what to do with it. When I was editing the film, I kept thinking it was a miracle that one day, by chance, I had the camera sitting on the dining table, her sitting on the couch, and she suddenly started telling the story. For me it was great that I could have it in the film, as evidence of how crazy and painful it all was. Then this laughter in the audience was very strange for me.

GMC: Generally, there was a lot of humor in the film, and other scenes were genuinely funny. Why was it important for you to make this dimension so prominent?

SF: If you make a film about something like old people losing their memory and getting stuck in assisted living, ugh, who would want to watch that? I wouldn't! But if you do go see it, then at least you won't just be dragged through the dreary mud. That's one part of it. The other part is that life is pretty funny, really. It's terrible, and then, my God, if you can't laugh at it, what will you do? And this is something I've learned over many years from my partner. She learned to laugh about some tragedies, and I understand how important it is. Then, some things are truly ridiculous, so to me it's a mixture of trying to make a joke about a terrible thing, and then simply making a joke. In this case, just like in *Gut Renovation*, I couldn't just be angry through the whole film. I was angry when all of it was happening, but in the film you have to have some levity. I love comedy, I should just make a comedy.

GMC: In the film you say you don't like your mother very much, which is something you reiterated in the Q&A. And yet the film expresses such strong affection—I didn't believe you when you said it in the film, and I didn't believe you when you said it in the Q&A.

SF: [*Laughs.*] Damn it, believe me!

GMC: Do you think your films give expression to your subconscious despite yourself?

SF: The simple words, "I don't really like my mother and I don't want her to live near me," are true. When I'm sitting in a room talking with her, all I wanna do is be somewhere else. Because I find the conversations either difficult, or boring, or upsetting, or something. And I'm not talking about now, I'm talking about the past. In the sense that we can meet a new person and feel like, "Wow, I wanna be friends with them!" I would say that if I met my mother as a stranger, I would never think that. But of course she's my mother, so I have a lot of sympathy for her, I have empathy, I have pity, I have attachment. One feels in the film that there's that kind of loyalty that you have to somebody because they're your family, and I guess people call that love, and that's there, of course, because that's in me.

GMC: When you were making the film, were you familiar with Chantal Akerman's *No Home Movie*?

SF: I love Akerman's films, of course, but I hadn't seen it. Often, while I'm making something, another film or book will come out on *exactly* the same subject. It happens a lot, because we all share these stories. There were probably ten movies about people and their mothers when I was making this one. So in the case of Akerman, her influence is so great, and what I understood the film to be about was so intense, that I thought, "No, I can't handle it. I will wait until afterwards to see it." I still haven't seen it because I was just finishing the film and too busy, but of course, I will see it.

GMC: I know I'm projecting here, but in several instances it almost felt as if you were in direct dialogue with Akerman. There are obvious thematic and also some aesthetic parallels, but this feeling was especially strong in the last line of your film, when you talk about contemplating suicide and then rejecting it in favor of "putting one foot ahead of the other."

SF: Wow, that's interesting, because I didn't mean it exactly that way. I do talk about "the exit strategy" that all people my age talk about, which one can call suicide. But that's meant when you're eighty-five, or ninety. When I'm talking about putting one foot in front of the other, I'm talking now, so the sequence is important. Just to clarify: For now, I'm going to keep going, but when I get to eighty-five, then I might use the exit strategy. But I think we have dialogue with other filmmakers all the time, intentionally or not. For you, or anybody else, to see a dialogue between my film and Akerman's makes sense to me, even if we haven't seen each other's film. Sadly, she's gone; she can't see my film and I have yet to see hers, but I can imagine that there's dialogue.

Interview for *Dykes, Camera, Action!*

Caroline Berler / 2016

From an interview conducted in service of Caroline Berler's documentary *Dykes, Camera, Action!* (2018). Printed by permission of the author.

Caroline Berler: I enjoyed this piece I read of yours called "Mea Culpa," published in the feminist journal *Heresies* in 1977. What were you exploring in this essay and what point were you trying to make?

Su Friedrich: Well, I did "Mea Culpa" when I was still basically being a photographer. I had focused on photography in my studio artwork in college. Then, I came to New York and joined the collective of Heresies that published a feminist art magazine which was so fantastic. I joined partly because my partner then, Amy, was a member of the collective. We were always looking for other people's work, but we would also often put in work of our own. I wasn't very happy doing photography, but I was still trying because I had no idea that I would become a filmmaker. I would do sort of photojournalism projects, but I was also doing these studio pieces.

You know, there was a lot of talk then, like there still is, about women's appearance—how you're judged by the public. I was very conscious of the fact that the way I might be dressing as a young dyke was not exactly the norm, and that I would never dress in what was considered a normal way. I thought, "Well, why not put on these characters?" I mean, it's not like I'm a performance artist or anything, or much of a fashion person, but I really wanted to look at those stereotypes. I also lived for a while in a collective house with a woman who was a total thief and a pack rat. She would constantly go to flea markets and vintage stores, and she had so many clothes, so I kind of had all the outfits on hand, thanks to her kleptomania.

Anyway, it was just interesting to put myself into these different guises and also to think about the different places in which these women might work, or the ways in which women would be expected to dress depending on where they worked. Then, you know, I've always been interested in writing, and I've read huge amounts my whole life, so I could have let the photographs live on their own, but I wanted to do this written piece with it. Not to make this too long an answer, but I also was earning my living doing paste-up and mechanicals (magazine and book production). One of the many places I worked was *Vogue* magazine (I also worked at *Us* and *People* and a few other magazines). I was always looking at these *Vogue* magazines and thinking, "Oh, please." That's why there's a lot of quotes from *Vogue* in "Mea Culpa."

CB: You've said that the personal is the political. Can you talk about the relationship between political involvement and one's personal life in relation to your work?

SF: I didn't say the personal is political. I was quoting the brilliant woman who thought up that phrase back in the early '70s. All the credit to her, whoever she is. When I heard that, I thought, "Well that's really true." I think it's super complicated, and maybe one can't go into all the nuances of it; but, at bottom, I think one's immediate life, one's personal life—with the people who you're around, the kind of work you do, the kind of house you live in, and all of that—totally informs the way in which you see the world. The world, in the larger sense, is this political entity because it has to be organized by governments. But the two are totally intermingled. Of course, the "personal is political" phrase came out of the women's movement because what happens in the home is being influenced by the larger body politic, etc. That's what I meant by that phrase and why I think it's true.

CB: How tied is your sexuality to your filmmaking?

SF: I don't think that's a question a person can answer. If I was straight, I'd say the same thing. I would say it for this reason: if you're straight, you don't have to think about the fact that you're straight; if you're gay or lesbian, you do, because everybody makes you think about it. It seems like being aware of one's self as a gay or lesbian person would then mean that the way you approached making your work had a lot more to do with that than if you were straight. I think whatever it is that's in us, the desire to have sex or be with a person, you can't pin it down, right? You could look at art by straight people and say, "Well this is clearly structured in the way that a heterosexual has sex or in the way in which a woman looks at a man." But who can really say that? I think there's this tendency to look at gay or lesbian art and somehow see a correlation. I don't want to do that because I think it limits things so much.

I could also say, "Well, how much does my growing up in an academic family inform my art? How much does growing up white inform my art? How much does having lived outside of the country, in kind of extreme circumstances, and then returning to this country, inform my art? How much does reading the kind of literature I read inform my art?" There are so many factors that go into who you are, that then go into what happens when you pick up a camera or sit in front of an editing station. It's not necessarily because I'm thinking about having sex with a woman, but it could be.

CB: Tell me about *Gently Down the Stream*. What is this film about?

SF: *Gently Down the Stream* came about after I had only made a couple of short films, and I didn't know what I was going to do next and was very naive about filmmaking. I started jotting down my dreams every morning, though I'm not even sure that I did that because I thought I would make a film out of them. Maybe I was just having really fucked up dreams all the time, so I started recording them. Then, I wrote out a lot of the dreams on single index cards and I showed them to a couple of people to ask what they thought of them. At some point along the way in this process, I had started to think about working them into a film.

As you know from the film I did end up making, I worked with these dreams in a very reduced way. I made them into succinct, little texts instead of the long, drawn-out dream that I had originally written down. I then experimented with scratching words on the screen to go along with the images. I think I did that because I wanted to get at what was strange or surprising in dreams. For example, in the film, there's a dream about somebody putting spermicidal jelly on my lips—why? In one sense, it's just to sort of toy with these unexpected elements that emerged from a dream, but it's also very much to play around with this formal question about what happens if I put the text on the screen. What happens for the viewer if they have to read text instead of hearing it? What happens with attention to the visual if there's an image framed while you're trying to read, or if the words are scratched on top of an image? I was very much coming out of the experimental film world and was seeing lots of films that were very challenging, intellectually and aesthetically. I was very excited by that. I wanted to be a part of the making of that kind of work. Much of making *Gently Down the Stream* was precisely this excitement about formal play. Really, at bottom, I was just loving the way the images and the text worked together.

I want to say that a very surprising and very informative experience I had with *Gently Down the Stream* happened the first time I showed it, which was at the Millennium. I had only had one or two dinky little shows in a bar before. I was so excited and freaked out, and I thought, "Everyone's going to hate this film." Afterwards, this straight, Scottish man came up to me and said, "I loved that film because I totally identified with it. I have the exact same dreams." I had originally thought I made a film that was completely weird and that only a few lesbians—white, American lesbians who dream like this—will identify with, and suddenly there's a straight man from another country saying that my work spoke to him. What I took away from this interaction is an understanding that you can never know who your audience is; you can never know what kind of response you're going to get and you cannot make work based on some notion of who that is. If you do, you're just going to shut yourself up and make stupid, whatever work. You just have to speak in your own voice and let the chips fall where they may.

That was an incredible thing to happen because that's how I've felt ever since about the work I've made. It has always been borne out that, invariably, I make something about something and somebody who has nothing to do with it comes up to me says, "I really identify with that." I say this all the time to film students because if you try to be too general, if you try to reach too many people, you say nothing. If you are very specific, then the person translates it. We all do that. I do that. I go to a movie about a Bolivian coal miner, and if it's a good film and I'm really paying attention, I translate that to something that I understand and feel, and it works. You can't be translating for the universe. You have to speak from your own place. Thank you to the guy from Scotland, whoever he was.

CB: I love that. Especially because in film marketing there's a huge emphasis on identifying your audience for the purpose of selling the film, but fuck it.

What inspired the film *Damned If You Don't*?

SF: Okay, in 1984 I was living in Berlin. I had a grant, and I had finished *The Ties That Bind* and was showing it. I was very lonely and I drank huge amounts. I called America all the time. This was before email. I used up all my stipend money on phone calls to America. I was talking to my friend Leslie Thornton, a filmmaker I was very close to at the time. So, I was really drunk one night and I said I wanted to make a film about a girl who falls in love with a nun. I started laughing hysterically, and she was like, "Okay." I woke up the next morning and I thought, "I am going to do that, actually." That wasn't just a drunken moment. That was a drunken moment that revealed to me something that I would actually really like to look into.

There I was in Germany, which was filled with Catholic imagery. I was also lucky enough to go to Venice during the time I was living there (1984–85), and there were nuns everywhere. Then I went to Israel from Berlin to visit a friend. Again, Catholicism was everywhere. I started collecting images of the Catholic world. Then, I came home and thought more about creating a film from that initial idea. The inspiration for it was a very drunken moment in Berlin, but also the fact that I had spent my childhood going to Catholic schools (grade school and high school) played a part in it. I just wanted to look into that.

There had been a few books written on the subject of lesbians within the Church. When you start thinking about a film, you start looking all around and you notice, "Oh my God. There have been six books written about this and three films made." This always happens. I started thinking about this lesbian nun movie, and then there's like two books that had just been published by lesbians about this topic. However, it turned out that it was very interesting to read these books, and it didn't make me feel that I shouldn't make this film because the topic had already been covered. It also did seem like a time when more and more LGBT history was being brought to the surface, and that religious life was of course a big subject. So, I decided to go ahead and make the film.

CB: *Damned If You Don't* seems to celebrate sex and even has a happy ending, which wasn't the case for a lot of lesbian representation in film. Were you trying to make a different ending for lesbians? Can you go into the sex scene in particular?

SF: When I was thinking about the film, there were various considerations. One of them was the fact that I was dealing with a nun as opposed to a non-nun woman. In what way would I handle the presentation of her sexuality, her sexual activity? I didn't feel vindictive—I didn't feel like, "Ha ha! Now I'm going to show what the nuns are really doing!" I didn't want to do that. I had fantastic teachers, wonderful women, women who had made huge sacrifices, as one can imagine, because of the time. I thought they may have had their passions, which they either realized or didn't. I wanted to be, not tasteful, but respectful. However, I still wanted it to be sexy and I wanted her to have sex.

The other thing I took into consideration was that this film was finished in 1987 and one of the first places it showed was at the Flaherty Film Seminar, which is a sort of famous, notorious, great, questionable, film event that happens every summer. It is a great thing, but famously, by the middle of the week, everyone's seen too many films, and some film just gets the shit. I showed *Damned If You Don't*, and a woman—not a man, a woman filmmaker—raised her hand and in effect said, "It's not yet the time when we can show women on screen in this way." These were the years of the male gaze and of everyone being very critical (and rightly so) of the ways in which women were portrayed in films made by men. There was great discussion about, "Well, then how are women going to show women?" In the case of this woman, in her opinion, I showed women in a way that was not yet acceptable—like there will be time when somebody can get naked and roll around with somebody, but not yet. I was just like, "Are you kidding me? I'm a lesbian. I'm a filmmaker. I made this film. Really?" Anyway, that was strange and unexpected.

As I said before, I really considered how to portray the nuns in a respectful way. I also really wanted there to be a positive ending, a happy ending. I didn't want her to jump off the bell tower of the church. I didn't want her to see the other woman walk by with a man in her arms. I wanted her to come to end of this question that she was having and have the woman sort of mysteriously enter . . . Like, how did that happen? How did she get in the convent room? For my audience, I was definitely counting on suspension of disbelief.

The funny thing was, I've talked to other people who've had to film sex scenes, and we all agree that it's incredibly awkward and difficult. When it was the day to film this scene, I started talking to Ella and Peggy about it and I said, "Well, I was thinking, you know, it would happen like this." Ella says, "Well, I'm not going to get naked." I responded, "Yeah, but you're not the scared nun. You're the sexy babe." She was like, "Yeah, but I'm not going to get naked." Anyway, plan B, she ends up stripping the nun down and Ella's got her little teddy on. It was very goofy to actually film it, but they looked pretty great.

CB: Was the '90s a turning point for lesbian film, or is that idea of the New Queer Cinema a false idea?

SF: What happened with New Queer Cinema was that lots of people were making films and then B. Ruby Rich wrote a story in the *Village Voice* and it put New Queer Cinema on the map. My impression of the piece was that she talked about gay male filmmakers who were making feature-length films, and lesbian filmmakers who were making experimental shorts. It created this sort of split image of the kind of work that was being made within the context of the New Queer Cinema.

Ruby was always very supportive of women filmmakers prior to writing this. She was a great champion of women filmmakers. I don't think she meant to create the sort of bifurcated image of the scene and create this different impression of the kinds of work that was being done, or the capabilities of men versus women, but that was the impression I got from the piece. I had a problem with that as the sort of launching notion of New Queer Cinema. Otherwise, I would say it was good that it was written, because it sort of put these films on the map and made people aware of the amount of work being done. Again, for me, in terms of my own work, I never see myself as part of a category. I mean, I will say to somebody, "Yes, I'm a woman filmmaker. I'm a white filmmaker. I'm a lesbian filmmaker. I'm a this, that, blah blah, you know." I can say all those things, but I never feel like I'm a card-carrying member of the New Queer Cinema, or any of the new cinemas. I don't feel like it had that much of a direct impact for me. But it certainly was a way for people to start recognizing work that was being produced.

CB: I want to talk about *First Comes Love*. What were you trying to express in this film, and how did you feel about the institution of marriage then? How do you feel about it now that same-sex marriage has being legalized, and are you married?

SF: After I finished *Damned if You Don't*, I was living my life and sort of casting out for something to do. I was with my partner and there was the beginning talk about gay marriage: "Is it a possibility? It's wrong that we can't get married." That kind of stuff.

For whatever reason, one day I thought, "Well, why don't I sort of think about this?" My partner and I had a very difficult relationship, but I really loved her. I would have moments of thinking, "God, what if we could get married? Would we get married?" It was just somehow in the air and I thought I would pursue the idea. I decided not to do a film in which I interviewed gay men and lesbians about getting married. I thought, "No, I'll approach it another way." I'd always resisted working with music, but I had used a bit of a song in one film and got so excited editing to music that I thought, "Well, let me see what happens now. I'm going to go out and I'm going to film these weddings, these very traditional weddings, and think about the kind of music that I really associate with my life and my partner."

That was in 1991. I made *First Comes Love* and showed it, and there were conversations about, "Well, what would happen if there was gay marriage?" The first half of the film is the bride and groom going into the church, and then right after they go to the altar, there's a three-minute scroll that says, "If a gay man or lesbian want to get married, they couldn't in the following countries." It's every country in the world except Denmark. At the end, it mentions that Denmark has legalized it. Then, in 2011, what would be twenty years later, I was at a screening by a lesbian filmmaker at Rooftop Films and she got up for the Q&A and said, "Hey everybody, thank you for coming, but I have really big announcement before we start talking about my film. They just legalized gay marriage in New York." Of course, everybody exploded in cheers. Then we had the Q&A and we left. On the way home, I sort of stopped short and said, "I made that film twenty years ago." That gave me such a sense of how long it had taken, from the beginning of the conversation to the actual passing of the law in New York state.

It was kind of funny to think that you can make this little "let's do this" kind of film, and then twenty years later, it comes to pass. My partner and I are married, but really only because I have health insurance for her through my university and the way the law changed, they could no longer cover her insurance as a domestic partner. They gave us a cut-off date. They were like, "By October 18 (or whenever it was), you have to get married." We went to city hall and got married and then went and had breakfast. We're not the marrying kind. I mean, we've been together forever. Of course, we own a house now so that sort of helps to be married.

CB: I really love the music in *Rules of the Road*, which is the next film I'd like to talk to you about. How did that film come about? What was behind it?

SF: Well, *Rules of the Road* happened because the partner who I had been with when I made *First Comes Love*, and imagined getting married to, broke up with me. Actually, we got back together after I finished *Rules of Road*, and we've been together ever since. In fact, we met in 1979 and we're together, now, forever. There have been breaks. After I finished *First Comes Love*, we broke up and I was devastated. I moved out of where we lived together into an apartment a few blocks away in Brooklyn. One day, I saw a car drive by that seemed to be the car we shared, and I freaked out. I went back to where I lived and I started scribbling these notes about it. Then, I thought, "Well, I should do this because I had such a strong experience associated with the car." Of course, when one breaks up, one has millions of thoughts about things, but something about that car really hit me.

I just went out and filmed station wagons in the style of ours—the older kind with fake wood paneling on the sides—whenever I could find them. I never made a point of trying to find her car, though I always wondered if I would. I also incorporated the card playing as a way to talk about chance. It really was about the randomness of how you can be in the world after something like a breakup and, unbidden, you'll see something that just reminds you of the person and you'll just break down in tears. I sort of filmed in that spirit: that it might be her car.

After I did *First Comes Love* and worked with popular music in the way that I did in that film, I really wanted to continue doing that. One of things I did in *First Comes Love* was that I used these hard cuts from one song to the next. It was really, really fun for me to figure out how to get the rhythm to work so you weren't totally thrown off. But I was cutting on film on a flatbed, and that was a nightmare. When I started doing *Rules of the Road*, I first wrote the vignettes and collected the footage, then I wanted to put music in the intervals between the stories. Again, I just did hard cuts. At the time, there was a young woman working for me a bit and at one point, she was looking at the edit and was really upset by the hard cuts. I was like, "Well, I'm going to do them that way. Sorry." I think I put in a little fade out on one of them, just to sort of mollify her, but I like working with music in that way. Once I did *First Comes Love* and worked with music, the floodgates opened and I've worked with music in various ways ever since.

CB: I thought maybe this approach to music in *Rules of the Road* was like tuning the radio in the car.

SF: Yeah, since the film was so much about us sharing this car, and we associate music so much with being in a car or being on long drives, it very much fit with the theme of the film. Simply put, music is a huge part of my life, like it is for most people, and certainly part of a relationship. It had to be in the film.

CB: Thinking about *Hide and Seek* now, I want to talk about lesbian childhood. What themes are you exploring and what are you trying to express in this film?

SF: I first thought about making *Hide and Seek* when I was at the first Lesbian Avengers action and I saw everybody wearing T-shirts that said, "I was a lesbian child." I thought, "Nobody's talked about that yet." My first thought was simply to interview women about their childhoods. I did that: twenty women, two-hour-long interviews, all the same questions. I had all this documentary interview footage and I thought, "Oh my God. This is going to be so boring. A talking heads documentary."

Then I applied for money and got it, so that I could mix the interviews with narrative scenes. I loved the interviews and I really wanted to use real women's stories. I also wanted to work somewhat from my memories and my partner's memories. So, over the course of the three years it took to make the film, I was able to create the narrative of Lou and her friends, alongside the interviews with all the women as well as the archival material I found. I was really happy to be able to mix the two kinds of footage. Also, I would give so much credit to my partner, Cathy Quinlan, because she wrote the script with me for the childhood fictional narrative part of the film. We kind of mixed our childhoods. We were like, "What did you want to be when you grow up? Well, let's have her be this." There was a lot of playing around.

I also wanted to have a three-part film. I wanted to tell stories about three girls—in the '50s, the '70s, and the '90s—because I wanted to talk about these different eras in which somebody might have come up. However, I didn't get enough money for all of them, so I settled on the '60s, because that's when Cathy and I came of age. There were a lot of different issues that were covered in the interviews, like the gay gene, which everyone was talking about at that time, and of course about being a tomboy, and "What was your first sexual experience with a girl?" It also somewhat informed the way Cathy and I wrote the script, because we wrote the script after I had done all the interviews. She didn't watch all the interview footage, but I had, so I could say, "Well, you know, when I interviewed Marty, she told this story about stroking the arm. The way she told it on camera maybe went on for too long, but what if we put it in the film as a narrative scene?" There was kind of a play between the two elements.

CB: Can you talk about visibility and lesbian activism? And can you explain the idea of how film played a role in increasing visibility?

SF: I had been politically active in various ways ever since I graduated from college and was out in the real world. I had been in the Women's Graphics Collective when I lived in Chicago after college. When I came to New York, I'd been part of the Heresies Collective, then I was part of the Lesbian Avengers and various other smaller groups over the years, such as WAC (the Women's Action Coalition). For me, I think the horrible rise of AIDS and then the incredible activism around it was monumental. There had been so much activism among women in the women's movements and also in the gay rights movement prior to the AIDS crisis, but I think that ACT UP found fantastic new ways to convey the seriousness of the crisis and to get people to do something about it. So, that was very inspiring then to the Avengers and to WAC. The AIDS crisis definitely contributed a lot to the notion of how to protest against an injustice or a crisis.

When I started making films, I was already out—but actually I was in because I got involved with this male filmmaker after my first girlfriend broke up with me. But then I met my current girlfriend and the boyfriend went out the window. So, when I started making films, it was a little bit of being a lesbian filmmaker and little bit not. But as time went on, let's say when I made *Damned if You Don't*, I became more aware of speaking from that position and of other filmmakers doing that as well. These notions of lesbian visibility and telling the stories of lesbians became more a part of my life. I felt very engaged with that.

I also had the experience making *The Ties That Bind*, which was my first long film and was about my mother going through the second world war. I finished that in 1984 and that sort of put me a little bit on the map. I got a big review in the *Village Voice* and it was very exciting. It was a fifty-four-minute film and the longest film I'd made before that was fourteen minutes, so to me it was a big leap. Then I made *Damned If You Don't*, and people were like, "Oh, you make lesbian films? I thought you made other kinds of films . . ." which I suppose meant experimental films, films about non-lesbian topics. That was interesting . . .

Returning to an earlier point about lesbian visibility and activism, I have to say that being in the Avengers was an incredible experience. That was in the early '90s, and so during most of the '80s, I'd been aware of other people doing things and other forms of activism, but then suddenly there was this group that was so out there. The first action was mind blowing. All the actions that the Avengers did were really powerful and really did reveal how invisible lesbians were. Because of ACT UP and because of the devastation in the gay male community due to AIDS, people became more aware of the existence of gay men. Unfortunately, people were more aware because gay men were dying, but there were also so many lesbians who were caretakers and that weren't being acknowledged. I was like, "Okay that's really, really major and serious, but there are also lesbians." I think there was something really great about the Avengers because it wasn't saying we've got as big a problem. It was apples and oranges. It was like, "That's that, and we've done a lot to help the gay community during this crisis, and we'll continue to do a lot for it but we have our own issues and we need you guys to listen, and be scared of us, or amused by us, or whatever it was." So, I am forever in awe of what the founding members of the Avengers did by creating the group.

CB: How was the Lesbian Avengers different from previous feminist movements or groups of the second wave?

SF: I don't think I can speak about all the feminist groups in the '70s as compared to the Avengers. There were always groups that did various kinds of public performances, street theater activist things that were great. The Avengers also picked up on things that had happened in the past, but I think there was a sense of playfulness and outrageousness that just was very special to me—things like eating fire. I think they're part of a continuum: whether it was the women's movement, or civil rights, or whatever, there's this long history of the ways in which people have tried to create an awareness in the public of an issue, and it was just one of those many groups, but it did really a great job.

CB: Why do you think the Lesbian Avengers did such a great job of raising awareness about issues?

SF: It was a combination of things. I think the Avengers were successful because of a number of forces and people involved, like Carrie Moyer and Sue Shaffner, who created a lot of great graphics, and we know from advertising about the power of a good logo. Other people thought of performative things to do. There were a number of people involved in the downtown theater scene, so they had a sense of performance. There were a lot of really brave, outrageous women who were willing to do wild things, so I just think there was a real spirit in the group. There were disagreements like there are any group, but there was just a sense like, "Here we are, we're going to do this, and we're really going to make it happen," so it was great.

CB: Can you tell me about the first dyke march and what it represented?

SF: The first dyke march was so great. There was a lot of debate about the first dyke march because many of us in the group had been at the earliest gay pride marches back in the mid-'70s. So, there was this loyalty and love of what that represented to us as New Yorkers, as well as a lot of affection for gay men. One didn't think, "Oh, I've just been treated like shit at the gay pride march. I've got to make my own march." But, again, there was a feeling that we needed to make ourselves utterly visible, and so there needed to be a dyke march. There was debate, but it was agreed on and then it happened. It was fantastic, because there we were, and it was like, "Okay. For this one afternoon, this is what's happening. We're not being diluted or mixed in with anybody else. This is it. Take it or leave it." I thought it was great and, of course, it's continued since then. Marlene Colburn recently did a Facebook post about plans for it next year. I think it's the twenty-fifth anniversary of the first dyke march. It's going to happen. It goes on. I think it also gives somebody the choice if they want to be in the dyke march or if they want to be in the gay pride march, or if they have the stamina, they can go to both. I think it's cool.

Actually, I don't know if it was the first year, but Janet Baus was a good pal of mine, and she's from New Orleans, so she really has this aesthetic of Carnival and dress-up, etc. So for one of the dyke marches, we decided we'd get ball gowns and put on over-the-top makeup and wigs and go. Everybody thought we were drag queens, which was kind of confusing and funny. We didn't expect that.

CB: Could you speak briefly about the documentary you made about the Lesbian Avengers and how you used video in that project?

SF: When I was in the Avengers (beginning around 1991), I'd just finished *First Comes Love* and there were Avengers who were shooting videos during the actions. I was a filmmaker then and wasn't shooting video, so it wouldn't have come naturally to me to pick up a camera and record stuff. I think I might've done some shooting, but there were other people who were collecting material. Janet Baus, who I mentioned earlier, was in the Avengers, and I became friends with her. It was actually more her idea to take all the footage and make a film out of it.

We decided we would coedit the film. She was more the director. She assumed we should get some interviews with the Avengers and she coordinated all of it. I don't even remember if I was present at all the interviews. I would say she was more the choreographer of the material. But then we did the editing together, which was insane, because we went to New Orleans because a friend of hers had a studio there which we could work in for free. It was summer and they didn't have air conditioning, and it was analog A/B video editing. We would sit there and try to put something together, and the machines would break down because it was overheating. Then we'd have to go back and rebuild it. It was so impossible to edit, but anyway, we did it. We finished it. Actually, I watched it again recently and I was really glad to be reminded of the actions, to see the footage of the actions. It was really fun to see it again.

I thought the really fantastic thing about the graphics for the Avengers was that the T-shirt said "Lesbian Avengers" on the front with the image of a bomb, and "We Recruit" on the back. The group was always playing against the worst stereotypes. Just taking them and saying things like, "Yep, we recruit." I loved that.

A Conversation with Su Friedrich

Erin Trahan / 2018

Erin Trahan: Can you remember a film that made you think, "I can do that!"?

Su Friedrich: Seeing [Maya Deren's] *Meshes of the Afternoon*, which is probably everyone's answer. I rented a print from the Donnell Library and watched it three times in a row. I was also really inspired by going to the Bleecker and seeing Fassbinder for the first time or Margarethe von Trotta. I felt a great affinity with a lot of the work I was seeing by European filmmakers. I was already making films, so it's not as if I thought it wasn't possible before then, but there was something about the spirit of Fassbinder's work, for one example among many, that made me feel that filmmaking was something I could be a part of.

ET: How old were you then? What else was going on in your life?

SF: I got out of college in 1975 and traveled for six months throughout West Africa and then came to New York in the fall of 1976. I was doing photography, a kind of photojournalism for feminist magazines, working several publications including as a member of the collective that published *Heresies: A Feminist Journal on Art and Politics*.[1] In 1978, I did a three-night Super 8 filmmaking workshop at Millennium taught by David Lee, and I was totally hooked! I hate those mythical stories about the moment when one finds one's calling, but something serious changed for me in taking that class: I recognized who I should be. I had been really committed to photography. I loved it and imagined I was going to be a photographer, and at that time film was so remote, so far from what I thought I could do. It was really, truly that Super 8 class that made me think about selling my enlarger and dark room equipment.

ET: Were you making a lot of images in childhood?

SF: In fourth grade I saved up my allowance, went down to the local pharmacy, and bought a Brownie Instamatic. I was so proud and excited to own a camera.

Both of my parents were very passionate and knowledgeable about all aspects of culture. I was mostly raised in Chicago and spent a lot of time visiting the Art Institute, looking at great works of art and also being taken to the ballet and music events by my mother. But absorbing art is different than making it, and when I went to college, I didn't have any aspirations to become an artist; I was planning to be a math major. But I didn't do so well at college level math, so I switched my major to French, but discovered that the French department wasn't very good.

At Oberlin, Ellen Johnson taught the modernists. Her lectures were famous, and I was blown away by attending one at the encouragement of a friend who was taking a class of hers, so I switched over to be a combined major in art history and studio art. They had a strong art history program but the studio art was weak and didn't offer any photography courses, so I did photography as independent study and studied African art history also as an independent study with a professor from Ghana who taught political science. Between art history and photography, I had started learning the rudiments of how to compose an image. (I don't think you can claim you know very much in college, or even a few years after college.) And then, of course, with film there's movement and sound, so after a few years of being committed to photography I discovered film, and how the huge, wonderful worlds of movement and sound could be added to image. That was the end of my photography.

ET: Your early film learning was on film—Super 8, 16mm, eventually, in 1994, with synch sound. Shooting on and editing those formats is very different from early video and certainly all of the digital formats now. It seems you've adapted well along with the times.

SF: I didn't do it happily, but I did adapt. Back in 2002, I finished *The Odds of Recovery*. That was the first time I edited on a computer in Final Cut, instead of on a flatbed. The editing was in many ways easier, after editing the 20,000 feet of film I had when doing *Hide and Seek*. But then I did a matchback to film because I wanted to finish *Odds* on film. The process of doing a matchback was such a nightmare, and incredibly expensive. After six months of showing it on film at festivals, I realized that it would live on in VHS or Beta SP, and at that historical point, making prints for rentals and screenings had become somewhat obsolete.

I also couldn't really afford to shoot 16mm anymore. My partner gave me a simple video camera for my birthday and I made *The Head of a Pin* as a first attempt at working in video. Once I admitted I was shooting video, I got a good camera. In some ways I'm a perfectionist and in some ways really not. I'm a perfectionist when it comes to editing. That doesn't mean I do it perfectly; it means I aim for perfection in how it's constructed. With camera and audio, I've made do with what's at hand, so sometimes I just think, "Goddamit, I just need to record right now." And I use whatever is at hand. So some stuff is underexposed, shaky, or the audio isn't clean. If you're a commercial minded person, you might think, "Wow why didn't she shoot in 4k or use a better lens?" I recognize that, but not if you're worried more about the surface than what's inside, and if you can't afford a high-end surface, then you're really forced to deal with the interior, the meaning, rather than just "the look."

ET: That makes me think it's a good time to ask "the woman question." I say that somewhat jokingly and also dead seriously. How has being female impacted your filmmaking?

SF: There are so many categories in which to apply that answer, it's hard. I could start with a few things. I am not an essentialist, I'm kind of the opposite. But I do think there are ways that we are raised and ways in which we're physically different than men, and that informs whatever we do. The fact that I'm female plays a part of every aspect of my filmmaking, but I can't really name what that is, specifically. Back in the '70s people would talk about how women's work was more personal or wouldn't have as much action or was more inclined towards a happy ending. You know, really stereotypical notions of how being a woman comes through in one's art.

But think of Thelma Schoonmaker, the main editor of all of Martin Scorsese's films. Someone once asked her, "How can such a nice lady edit such violent films?" She rightly responded by saying, "They weren't violent until I edited them." And men can also make a heartfelt emotional scene, so I don't believe in those differences. But certainly for me, the fact that I'm a woman is a central aspect of my subject matter. I grew up thinking, "Fuck this world," so my world is going to point a finger at all of those things. It doesn't *just* do that but that's a part of the work.

ET: I'm not proud of this, but I had no interest in keeping up with the technology after studying filmmaking in college in the mid-'90s. At least not on my own, anyway.

SF: I've been going to B&H for thirty years to get my photo and film equipment and the salesmen, who were all men, would always treat me like a stupid little girl. Now I walk in and say, "Hi. Listen, you need to talk to me like I know what I'm doing," and they get all flustered and try to pull the usual bullshit but then they realize they can't. But everyone I encounter is going to assume I don't know enough, so I'm on my guard, being sure I *do* know what I'm talking about. Because—news flash—it isn't just about salesmen at B&H, it's throughout the film world, and the experimental film scene is no less sexist than any other part of American landscape.

ET: And how has the experimental scene treated you, or anyone who also fits an "other" category?

SF: Well, also being a lesbian, back in the early '80s, it was a really fortunate thing that I made *Gently Down the Stream*, it really hit a nerve with people, and was really being recognized, but not as a "lesbian film." And then when I made *The Ties that Bind*, I got a full-page review in *Village Voice* and that blew the top of my head off! I thought I was made in the shade! Amazing! But then came *Damned If You Don't*, and suddenly I was a "lesbian filmmaker." You make one film and suddenly you're *this* kind of filmmaker? How boring and reductive is that?

Sometimes I give a "clip talk" where I give some background about what went into the making of each film along with a five-minute sample clip from it. In the introduction, I list certain things I always try to keep in mind when I work. One item is that my work should speak about the lives of women and my experiences as a woman. Because that's what men do in their work, isn't it? Men have always made things about men. (And if we're going to be fair, then we should call them "men" filmmakers, and "men's" film festivals when we're seeing programs without a single film by a woman.) Now we can talk about pre-#MeToo and post-#MeToo, but we are definitely not yet at a point where women don't have to be vigilant and proactive in respect to sexual harassment but also in regard to women's (lack of) inclusion in the film world. The neglect and disparagement run way too deep and do not change in six months.

ET: One of your other "categories" has been that of personal or first-person filmmaker. That subgenre generates its own set of preformed judgments. Plus, women are again in the minority, and again, judged more narrowly than men. Have you gone through any major phases of feeling you shouldn't or couldn't make a certain film?

SF: Couldn't does happen very often. I'll think, "Oh my God, I'll never have another idea." But that's most of us. There's no telling when that will break, when some idea will walk through the door. I tend to make one film after another and people have said I'm prolific, but there are periods of a real sense of nothing being there. But *shouldn't* make films, I've never thought.

There is the worry about if something is too touchy. In *Damned If You Don't*, I was talking to a friend back home when I was living in Berlin, and was really drunk and said I want to make a film about girl who falls in love with a nun. The next morning, when I had sobered up, I realized, "Oh Jesus, I really can't do that," and turned it into an adult woman so I wasn't making something about a weird pedophile nun.

In *I Cannot Tell You How I Feel*, I wondered, "Should I be making film about my mother without her knowing about it?" And I decided I'll live with what history decides. I cannot resolve this conflict; I have to put it out in world. If somebody thinks I'm an asshole . . . well, when you get older, you think, "If I'm an asshole then I'm an asshole." There are ways, as a filmmaker or writer or painter, to think seriously of your subject matter and its impact on audience. I never take this lightly. Other people would have stopped short of the line. But some people don't have the same kind of access; it can take being in a fortunate situation. For *The Ties That Bind*, I had always wanted to make a film about my mother growing up in Nazi Germany and she didn't talk about it much when I was little, but she miraculously agreed to talk with me then, but it was because I lied to her and said I just wanted to record her stories for posterity, for the family. And for example, my partner has said, "Don't you ever dare make a film about me." But there's *Rules of the Road* (1993); she couldn't stop me because we were broken up at the time. And my brother has said, "Don't make a film about me." But when he said that, I said, "If I did, it would be a love letter."

ET: What's it like to work with you on a film? Do you consider your subjects your collaborators?

SF: If it weren't for the people who looked at my work while it was in progress, I swear to you it wouldn't exist. I learned that really early on. I've never called it collaboration; the other person is not an equal partner. I don't say, "Hey, let's develop it together." But when I start to think about something, let's say with *Sink or Swim*, I started to write all the stories but then I showed those stories to two, three, four people, and they gave me a lot of notes. I recently dug out all of my paper archives and I found a really fantastic page of notes from my friend Steve, "This is saccharine, this is maudlin." Sure, when I read it, I tore my hair out, I had been working on it for weeks and weeks and weeks, but he was right, and it was time to do some rewriting. I always ask people to read the script or look at an edit and be brutally honest. They're people I know well, who are really smart, and I keep going back, rewriting, reediting, going back over and over and over. We are not good enough by ourselves.

ET: Has your work been understood? Interpreted in ways that satisfy you?

SF: Yes. I've never had that question asked of me. It's such a weird question! The lesson I learned, watching the structural films, the system films, or films where maybe the filmmaker was really concerned with composition and tempo, is that cool things would happen, but they didn't seem to be concerned with engaging the viewer in an emotional way. I really want people to keep watching, to hook them. I want them to laugh, and cry, and be freaked out, and all those emotions that can be evoked when we watch something or read something. That's a big part of my drive—to have the films give you an emotional experience, an emotional ride, so I've gotten a lot of responses because people have been able to enter the work.

Even though, for example, I was in Dortmund for the Women's Film Festival with *Rules of the Road*. Germans think they speak English well but it still gets opaque at times. So I'm sitting out in the lobby, the theater door slams open, and in German a woman stalks away saying, "Cars, cars, cars, Godammit!" She's so upset about the film! It's true—it really is about cars, so I figure, "I didn't get you, did I?" But I have been very gratified by the extent to which people have been affected by my work, or moved by it. It has also been a long life lesson in how much people translate films. We all do this. If I read something about sixteenth-century Algeria, I somehow "translate" it into something recognizable to me. And it happened for the first time with me when I showed *Gently Down the Stream*, and afterwards a straight guy from Scotland told me, "I have the same dreams." I was like, "You do?"

ET: What's one of the most important things you teach your students at Princeton?

SF: My experience teaching, for many years now, is that I feel more and more sorry every year for the students. It's exponential: my feeling sorry is getting bigger faster. I feel really guilty saying, "Wow, when I started making films, there was a place we could all go and hang out." But those places don't really exist now. So if they send somebody a file to watch, they think that's the same thing, and it's not. They're not being in the same space. They'll look at it for one minute and then check their email, get distracted. But how do they make spaces? You'd have to be really proactive as a maker. There's a great loss. On the one hand, ooh social media, it connects the world, but yeah, you haven't talked to somebody across a table from you in weeks.

ET: I know you were in New York most of the time that the Association of Independent Video and Filmmakers (AIVF) existed and published *The Independent Film & Video Monthly* (1976–2006). They were community catalysts, too, right?

SF: I loved *The Independent*—that to me was *the* publication when I started making films. It was like my bible. I would read it cover to cover. The back had so much info about grants and the classifieds. Of course, those resources are now online which we didn't have then. But it was really wonderful and gave me such an understanding about how filmmakers were coping with both the technical and financial issues in trying to get their films made.

ET: And your films, and writing, frequently graced the pages of *The Independent*.[2] Switching gears, what do you still hope to accomplish as a filmmaker?

SF: Please, that's a dumb question. I want you to put that part in there, how I said it's a dumb question. How the fuck does anybody know? I'm sixty-three and a half—it's horrifying to say that—but I suppose I'll just keep trying to make films and be good. It's not like now I want to make the really great film, or now I want to make the film that's seven hours long. I just want to keep interesting myself.

ET: Before we go, I have to ask about that moment when you're crying on the couch in *Seeing Red*, worrying that you'd become a housewife. Were you serious?

SF: As you get older, you start living with people, and you have more responsibilities, like grocery shopping and doing the laundry, so you can live together. When I lived alone, I could ignore those things. One morning I opened the fridge and the only things in it were a bottle of vodka and a pair of gym shoes. I must have been drunk when I undressed the night before. But then I started living in a collective loft situation with Cathy who really loves to cook. It grows on you. If you have kids, you really do have to do that domestic stuff, but even without kids, you have to put food on the table.

When I did *Seeing Red*, I was in the middle of making *From the Ground Up*, and Cathy said, "You seem like you're in pain. Instead of making a movie about coffee, turn on your camera and do something more real." It was very real, that feeling of "I'm turning into a fucking housewife," because *From the Ground Up* was boring. So we distract ourselves. We make new pillows for the couch. I think I was doing a lot of that, so I stormed into my studio after she said that and had a tantrum on film. When I showed it for the first time at MoMA, everyone I knew was in the audience. I was sitting in the back with Cathy, imagining they would feel so sorry for me and my plight. But when I started crying on camera, they all started laughing instead in recognition. We all somehow turn into housewives.

Didn't I just tell you I have to go clean the basement?

Notes

1. A feminist publication on art and politics published by the Heresies Collective.
2. Some of *The Independent* articles that feature Friedrich include Martha Gever's "Girl Crazy: Lesbian Narratives in *She Must Be Seeing Things* and *Damned If You Don't*," in July 1988; "Some Like It Hot" by Judith Halberstam in November 1992; "Fit & Trim: A Foolproof Method for Storing Film Trims" in July 1999; and "A Message to the Future" in January/February 2000.

Personal and Collective Memory in Su Friedrich's Films

Allison Ross / 2020

Printed by permission of the author.

Allison Ross: My first question centers around the chronology of your earlier films, many of which, I believe, deal more with the subject of dreams than memories. How do you view the connection between these elements in your first projects? Did you approach them as related or disparate? Over the body of your work, has there been a shift from one, dreams, to the other, memories?

Su Friedrich: I think we have to break this down a bit. You have never seen my first film because I never converted it to digital, and anyway, it's forgettable. Next, there's *Scar Tissue*; *Cool Hands, Warm Heart*; *Gently Down the Stream*; and *But No One*. After that, there isn't that much reference to dream life in my work. In *The Ties That Bind*, in *Damned If You Don't*, in *Sink or Swim*, dreams really don't play a part.

AR: No, they don't, which is why I was wondering about the shift.

SF: Are you asking if *Cool Hands, Warm Heart* refers to a dream?

AR: Yes.

SF: *Cool Hands, Warm Heart* had more to do with performance, more to do with a woman's appearance and all the bullshit that women have to do—or have had to do. And many women still do those things to be presentable in public. I was disgusted by it all. The film had more to do with that than with dreamscapes or dreaming life. However, *Gently Down the Stream* and *But No One* were both based entirely on dreams. I really love how *Gently Down the Stream* turned out.

As a young filmmaker, I experimented when creating that first project, which, as I mentioned, isn't for public viewing. Then I made *Scar Tissue* and *Cool Hands, Warm Heart*. While playing with varied techniques, being young, I also liked talking about my dreams. In those early days, I wrote down my dreams and wondered what would happen if I tried to work them out in some way through a film.

At the time, I hated how dreams were portrayed in standard movies. They're usually filmed in blue light, shot in slow motion, accompanied by weird music, all of which seems completely unrelated to the actual experience of dreaming. As I started toying around with my notes for *Gently Down the Stream*—my scribbles—rather than trying to reenact or replicate the dreams, I challenged myself as to how I could best convey the ideas. Specifically, how best to express them on a piece of celluloid.

Exploring the relationship of dreams to memory wasn't on my mind when making those two films. What I thought about was how to turn a long, rambling text into a few short lines. How do I scratch that onto a piece of film, and what image goes with that? In choosing, I was looking for shots that in no way describe or replicate the text—that live alongside text, but don't function as an illustration.

AR: More of an evocation than a direct linear representation.

SF: I was happy with *Gently Down the Stream* because I think I succeeded in various ways. Also, dreams are very elusive. You wake up in the morning and try to recount them to someone else, and then either you realize that you remember less than half of it, or you trail off into nonsense while the listener loses interest. I tried to present a dream similar to how we imagine a nondream story. In the way we would re-create a real event, like riding a bus. An event that actually might happen. However, it just doesn't work because dreams are irrational.

It's more important to me that, when someone sees the film, it sparks a reaction. You see a weird phrase in *Gently Down the Stream*, like "She calls up a friend from the audience—Asking her—Come and make love to me" and you're thinking, "No one would do that." Then you pause—wait a minute. Or you see another odd passage, like "I make a second vagina—Beside my first one." These sequences might provoke a response that has nothing to do with what my dreams actually looked like or smelled like or sounded like or the feeling they left you with.

You can never predict how an audience is going to take anything you do. You put stuff up on the screen, and a viewer sees it in a completely different way. I totally love that. For example, people have sworn up and down that *Gently Down the Stream* is in color. I've sworn up and down to them that it isn't. And I'm the person who made the film, so I should know. Despite that, they insist that it's in color because they remember the film being in color.

AR: That is fascinating.

SF: Yet, when they were watching it, the movie brought colors to their mind. That happens. You can't plan or anticipate or even worry about that. You say, okay, that's the way it is.

AR: Shifting from dreams to memories, I would like to focus our conversation on the ways in which your personal memories, and what I am thinking of as a more collective memory, intersect within your films, specifically *Hide and Seek, Damned If You Don't*, and *Rules of the Road.*

Beginning with *Damned If You Don't*, I want to explore your decision to focus the narrative on an historical account and a fictionalized storyline, as opposed to your own experience of growing up Catholic. In contrast, other films of yours are perhaps more directly personal. What influenced this choice?

SF: Are you referring to my quotations from *Immodest Acts*?

AR: Yes, and the way the voiceover from the book intersects with the story's narrative segments.

SF: At the start, I wanted to make a film about a girl who fell in love with a nun. Then I decided the next day, after sobering up, that it had to be about an adult woman. So, the genesis of the film was my interest in portraying the kinds of sexual tensions and possible sexual alliances that could occur for someone who is a nun. And that, of course, came out of my own experience, which is to say that I went to Catholic schools from grade three to my third year of high school. I never had sex with a nun, but, you know, stuff was in the air, let's say.

In the late sixties and early seventies, when nuns were no longer having to wear habits, many also were moving out of the convent and moving in together. In some of those cases, we were wondering if they were moving in together because they were girlfriends. There was just a feeling back then that there might be some stuff going on. We certainly knew that the priests were fucking around. Fifteen years later, I wanted to revisit what might be happening among the nuns. I really liked some of these nuns. They were fantastic women, and I just wanted to think about what it would have been like for them to be sexual beings—because we are all sexual beings—having to contend with these feelings coming to the surface. Right? That really was the genesis of the film.

Then, as I do with any film I make, I started doing research, which included looking at all of what I call the "nun films" that were very popular back then. *Black Narcissus*, by Powell and Pressburger, seemed to be the most appropriate one that aligned with the direction I was exploring. Also, I did a lot of reading. One publication, though I don't remember the name, contained first-person accounts by different nuns who had come out as lesbians. In the appendix of a very interesting book, *Immodest Acts*, I was astonished to discover the transcript of a trial that had taken place, which included the testimony of a nun detailing her sexual experiences. I thought it would be funny to include it because it was so vivid compared to what I was planning to do in my film. At the time, I felt strongly that I wouldn't portray anything directly sexual that transpired between the woman character and the nun. I had no interest in showing that. So, I showed what you see in the film—which is the nun being disrobed and the two of them falling down on the bed and starting to make out. I thought having this other account from *Immodest Acts*, as a voiceover, was useful.

My decision to include the graphic description came later; my original impulse for *Damned If You Don't*, and what went into the narrative, mostly stemmed from my own experience and the experiences of the eight women I interviewed. In the film, you only hear one person's voice, that of Makea MacDonald. She was the only person whose interview I used. We were in the same high school at the same time, and what she said really rang true, so I decided to just use her commentary.

AR: This leads to my next question which deals with the *Black Narcissus* footage and how, in previous interviews, you referenced looking at the nun films and specifically that film. As an audience, we are viewing a character watching *Black Narcissus* within *Damned If You Don't*. The focus of this scene are the looks exchanged between the women in *Black Narcissus*. How were you thinking about these expressions of desire in the narrative fictional segments of the film, as indirectly observed or directly experienced? Did you see this implicit exchange and later explicit expressions of desire as enforcing one another? As evoking something broader about the way that desire is operating in the film?

SF: When you're working on a project, you have many options as to how best to approach your theme. You continually play around with the material to get it to convey the things you want to convey. Those elements are varied. In one segment of the voiceover, Makea hints at her sexual feelings towards a nun. In another, my nun and my woman character interact. Incorporating, altering, and integrating scenes from *Black Narcissus* was a third way. *Black Narcissus*, unlike my modified version, has nothing do to with lesbian desire. It centers around a man, the one nun who is obsessed with him, and a few other characters who have a sort of giggly relationship with him.

In *Black Narcissus*, there are a lot of looks exchanged. And I chose to show many of them, occasionally in the way they were edited and sometimes intentionally exaggerating those moments. I admit, I took some liberties with their narrative. But I believe that I was also faithful, in many ways, to the essence of their film. While each of our projects set out to explore similar themes, we went about our messaging differently.

Mine was another way of talking about desire, flirtation, and obsession in relation to somebody who has taken a vow of chastity, done in a way that expressed it as forthrightly as possible without being explicit and pornographic. Honestly, I had no interest in being pornographic. There are lots of porn films involving nuns and priests and that's the last thing I was interested in making.

AR: Sure. That's a very different genre. Those sequences which feel as if they reference subtext in the original film become textual in your work. Though they may not represent the actualization of desire onscreen, might they be seen differently, similar to how desire could be read into *Black Narcissus* by certain viewers? Or would that be a stretch?

SF: No, I don't think so. Powell and Pressburger did not produce a lesbian porn film or a nun porn. In *Black Narcissus*, they were exploring the overheated, sexually frustrated environment of the convent and what happens when you drop a sex bomb into it. Their movie is about obsession, about that nun being sexually obsessed with that man. And on occasion, the events that drive their narrative assume a melodramatic tone, like when the nun falls to her death.

Make no mistake, though, *Black Narcissus* isn't pornographic. However, Powell and Pressburger did take risks. And, I believe, they produced the best film they could, given the times. These risks are among the reasons I liked the film so much and decided to work with it. Compared to the other so-called nun films, especially ones created in America, it was the most explicit, while being almost funny—or at least that was how I reacted to the intense ways in which the characters interacted.

AR: Humorous because their interactions are so overheated. Referencing Cathy's voiceover from *Immodest Acts*, she peppers the voiceover with pauses, interruptions, and times the speaker stops to change the way she's saying certain passages. Was this to achieve a particular viewer experience? By introducing these effects, was it to distance the viewer from the graphic description of the details of the incident? Also, does it draw attention to the fact that this is a voiceover from a different time?

SF: The truth is I asked her to do the voiceover simply because of a lack of money to hire an actor. Back then, I had limited resources. Often people who were doing voiceover for me were people I knew. And so, I asked Cathy. The fact that we were sexual partners adds a certain dimension to it for me. Not that anyone would need to know that when they were watching the film. But Cathy is a bit of a trickster. When she began, she started joking around, which is what you hear in the film. At the time, I was little annoyed. I was like, "Cathy, just read it . . ." But, during the editing, I realized that even if people didn't know we were sexual partners, her performance added another layer to the interaction between the two women.

It's good to add a little levity when you are making a film that could turn out to be very emotional. I mean the text itself is so insane. This puts a little humor into it. My decision was influenced by the era in which I made *Damned If You Don't*. I was working on it in 1985 and 1986, so I hadn't been making films for that long. At the time, I was considering all of the ways in which it was possible to disrupt the seamless flow of a standard narrative that portrays a world you are supposed to enter, live in, and never think about leaving until the story is over. And I was thinking about how to make the viewer more aware of the fact that they were watching a film that's constructed, that breaks the fourth wall and maybe gives the audience a little moment of, "Oh, what is going on here?" which is a form of disruption I've continued to experiment with ever since.

AR: Speaking of how audiences experience film, I want to shift to *Rules of the Road* and the ways you played with its construction, specifically, the relationship between the recollections that occur within the narrative and the card game—the game of Solitaire. Did you intend these scenes to be contrapuntal or did they come after you had cut together all the parts of the station wagon storyline? Do they serve a similar function of taking the viewer out of the narrative and making them aware this is something that has been edited together? Is the effect to give the viewer an experience that has both a symbolic resonance and a personal resonance?

SF: Actually, there aren't that many card-playing sequences, and I didn't think of them as functioning to take the viewer out of the flow of the film. I suppose they could because suddenly you are seeing a person. I mean, you only see my hands, but you assume that the hands playing the card game are the speaker's. So yes, it does remove you from that moment.

But that wasn't my intention at the time, though I don't mind if it does take you out of the story for a moment. We're talking about a film I made in 1993, and it's now 2020. I can't say precisely when I shot that material. I don't recall exactly when I did what I did. I do remember that the Solitaire scenes weren't included after the fact. It wasn't as if I had the whole film cut together and then thought, "Oh, I need to show myself playing cards."

Part of the idea that underlies the film is chance. *Rules of the Road* began because I happened to be out walking around my neighborhood and saw a car that I thought was being driven by my ex-girlfriend. I freaked out, went home, and started scribbling down notes. That was the genesis of the film. And, as I began to write the story, I had in mind that when you're in that situation—when you've broken up with somebody and you're afraid of seeing them—that the chances are that you might cross paths. I wanted to just live in that world of rampant possibilities that can be really upsetting.

When I was filming, I just went out with my camera, rode around on my bike, hoped that a station wagon would drive by, and then tried to shoot it before it drove away. I never set up any of those shots, and I also didn't stand on a corner for eight hours until a car drove by. It wasn't like I was filming wildlife and was having to wait around long enough for something to happen.

To get back to the card game, my girlfriend and I had broken up, and I was living by myself. I was lonely, and I played a lot of Solitaire. I could have been playing some other game. One day, I thought, because Solitaire is also a game of chance—that is to say, you don't know what cards you're going to deal—why not use it? It seemed to function as a good metaphor within the film. That's pretty much why it's in *Rules of the Road*. Plus, I love the way cards look, and I loved how I was able to use them to create the opening title cards.

AR: And because the appearance of cards provides a great textural contrast with the interior of the station wagon, I think so too. I know a lot of your films intersect narrative and experimental and documentary aspects. Would you characterize *Rules of the Road* in this way, or as being more of a personal narrative that maybe doesn't have the additional fictional narrative overtones?

SF: You know, I don't know. I have a problem when people start asking me to place my work in the context of some genre or another. Each film stands on its own and often borrows from one or two or even five genres, many times responding to or undermining them. Elements within each project always are in conversation with one another and with multiple genres—the entire range, from the most experimental to the most narrative. The structure of my stories is very formal and, I would go as far as to say, conventional, given that I always have a beginning, middle, and end. I always have a story arc. I really love traditional fictional narrative for providing that sense of story, and that's also why I read literature all the time. I love a good ending, you know. I really strive for that, no matter how experimental a film of mine might look.

But I also love all the disruption and the questioning and the challenges and the playfulness that occur in experimental films, and I would like that to play a part in my work or be something that I'm in conversation with. And so, for example with *Rules of the Road*, it would never have occurred to me to do a reenactment: to cast two women as the characters and have them act out being together and then being broken up. But the idea definitely informed the way the stories were written.

Rules of the Road starts at the beginning and ends at the end. When someone creates a piece of fiction, they almost always base it upon their own experience, despite what people pretend. That makes perfect sense because what we know best is what occurs personally to each of us. And so, in the case of *Rules of the Road*, I could have talked to fifty people who had gone through a breakup and used their stories, or I could have interwoven their stories with mine. However, I didn't feel that was necessary, and also it would have been a very different kind of film, and one which I had no interest in making.

It seemed the job was for me to go from that initial "shock and awe"—to quote George Bush—of seeing the car and then to say, "Well if that car did that to you, what does it mean that that car carries all of those memories, and why not see what happens when you start describing them?" It was a matter of sitting down and, over a period of many, many months, writing and rewriting the voiceover segments between sessions of filming. Of course, it did end up being a film that was specifically about my memories, which is different than some other films I've made.

AR: When you say "between sessions of filming," would every station wagon you encountered spark new material, or did you find yourself adding to the narrative as time went on?

SF: Interesting. No one ever has asked me that question before. The answer is no. It's actually funny for me to imagine how that might have happened. The cars just became a character in their own right. When I went for that first walk, I wasn't thinking, "Oh, I'm walking past Driggs Avenue, and maybe she'll drive by." I just went out for a walk without hoping to see her car, or dreading that I would see it. But after I saw one like hers, I started hunting for any and all station wagons, not specifically for hers. And, in fact, in those many months, I never saw her car, or her in it.

AR: I like the idea of the car as a character.

SF: I would imagine going to Delancey Street, or wherever else, with the hope of catching a few station wagons that day, hunting for that crazy character who was going to speak to my experience. But it wasn't as if any particular car generated a new story. I didn't see one and think, "Oh my God, that reminds me of, you know . . . whatever it might have been." That wasn't the case.

When I started working on *Rules of the Road*, a task I set for myself was to scribble down a series of prompts. For example, when we went to the country, or when we did this or that. Those experiences would then go on to be described in the film. I elaborated, making details much more specific. Shooting was separate.

To me one of the funniest shots is the one on Second Avenue. I was standing on a corner when a bus pulled up to the light, and then the nose of a station wagon, with a kind of slanty front, popped out in front of the bus. It looked to me like it was saying, "Hey, here I am! Here's another one for you!" When I first showed the film, people really laughed when they saw that shot.

AR: It knows you are looking for it.

SF: Right.

AR: Moving on to *Hide and Seek*, of the three films we have talked about, I feel this one has the strongest narrative, the strongest fictional through line in terms of the story of the young girls. Why choose these explicitly fictional forms and then interweave them with the interview segments or use the interview segments as voiceovers during some of the narrative scenes?

SF: Before I made *Hide and Seek*, I had read a novel called *Aquamarine* by Carol Anshaw. I knew her; she was a friend of a friend. Reading that book was the only time in my adult life as a filmmaker that I felt that a book had been written in order for me to turn it into a film. I had never felt that before, and I have never felt it since. I got crazy, crazy excited about it.

I never had the resources to do a narrative except in making *Damned If You Don't*, which was minimal. It wasn't that much material. The film was only forty-two minutes, and the narrative was only a part of it, and it was silent, with only two characters. So, I had tried my hand in *Damned If You Don't*, and still thought making a narrative film was a project I would like to do if I had more resources and the perfect material. So, when I read *Aquamarine*, that was the one; that was the film I was dying to make.

I tried to option it, and I found out that another filmmaker, Maria Maggenti, already had an option for a year. I got in touch with Carol, and said that I really hoped that, if Maria didn't pursue it, I would be able to get the option later. She responded with a vague, like, okay, maybe, whatever. Without being specific, there was a further effort on my part to option it, but I was unsuccessful. And when it never materialized, I was really devastated. And, by the way, the film has never been made.

That was a really crushing moment for me. Ever since I started as a filmmaker, beginning with my early experiences when I moved to New York after college, I have been extremely interested in narrative. I loved watching European Art Cinema, seeing films by Fassbinder, Margarethe von Trotta, Akira Kurosawa, Agnès Varda, Jacques Tati, Satyajit Ray . . .

Then I got involved with the Lesbian Avengers, and I went to the first action where I saw them wearing t-shirts saying, "I was a lesbian child." It was triggering, though I hate to use that word now, given the terrible associations it has become aligned with. Anyway, that was the genesis, that's what started me thinking—nobody had made a film yet about lesbians when they were kids. Everyone was making coming out films, and none of them were talking in much detail about what their life was like before that, when they were much younger.

Once I got started, I could only afford to shoot the interviews on basic analog video—essentially on a Handicam. As I was conducting them, I felt that turning these stories into a narrative would be great. But I had about $4 to work with. So, that wasn't possible until I received money from the NEA and then ITVS. At that point, I was able to seriously consider the narrative part of it.

The funding gave me the opportunity to launch what might well be called a completely traditional narrative. I had a production designer. I had a costume designer. I had a DP. I had a production manager. It was the real deal.

I could indulge my desire to work in a traditional fictional format by mixing those interesting interviews with tons of archival material, maybe messing with the conventions. The final form grew out of my underlying dream of creating a narrative, combined with my usual sense that a film would be more to my liking or more like what I usually create if it weren't simply a conventional narrative. That's how *Hide and Seek* happened.

AR: In the film, sometimes a tension exists between what is said in the interview segments and what is conveyed by the narrative. Other times, the two are in consort. Talk about your process when editing these elements.

SF: I did about twenty interviews that were each two hours long, so I had plenty of material. However, it wasn't well shot because the women were videotaped with a very basic analog video camera and no proper lighting. I certainly loved what they had to say, their stories. But, also, the kinds of stories they were telling sometimes could be interwoven with my script.

So, when Marie Honan tells the story about the Monkees, I thought, "Oh, perfect, I'll get some footage from the Monkees TV show." But there were other stories that lived on their own, which didn't need any additional images, or images that illustrated the story. For example, when the women are talking about sliding down the banister, it wasn't necessary to show my characters sliding down a banister. It would have just been an illustration of something that was perfectly described, on-camera, in an interview. But by combining Marie's story with footage from the TV show, the old Italian film, and the archival footage I had of the chimpanzee and the toddler, a kind of funny exchange existed. How would I put it? The one didn't illustrate the other: the various elements informed each other.

One case did come from a story that you don't hear in an interview. Marty Pottinger told me about doing the thing with having her arm stroked. I really liked her description of it, but I didn't need to hear her say it in the film. I felt that seeing was sufficient, or even better, so I had my characters act it out. As footage, it's more than just an illustration which otherwise would accompany Marty's voice telling her story. In the end, sometimes additional footage informed what was in the narrative parts, and sometimes one or the other element could stand on its own.

AR: Was the narrative writing informed by the fact that you already had done these interviews?

SF: I began by transcribing the forty hours of interviews. When I got the money from the Independent Television Service, I set about writing the narrative, and Cathy agreed to write it with me. We sat around for months, talking to each other like we were twelve-year-olds. She and I also wanted to have it be set in three decades. I wanted to portray a girl in the 1950s, a girl in the 1970s, and a girl in the 1990s, to show how events and attitudes were the same and how they were different over time. But I didn't have the money or the wherewithal to do all three narratives, so Cathy and I agreed it would make sense to have it set in the 1960s, which is when we grew up.

Next, we had to negotiate which of our memories to incorporate into the film: which were hers and which were mine, and what ones do we attribute to Lou, the main character? Each of these recollections contributed to the story. We had many in common, and those were easily worked out and incorporated into the story. However, when we had to decide what Lou wanted to be when she grew up, a little bit of an arm-wrestling competition took place, and then I ended up saying, "Well, it's my film, so I get it to be my thing"—because my dream was going to Africa. For Cathy, it was being a Native American and being able to walk through the forest without making a sound and living closer to nature. But both of us contributed a lot to the gist of the story.

AR: My last question deals with your relationship to embracing different film styles and film history. How might these relationships influence future projects?

SF: When you refer to film history, do you mean works that inspired me at the beginning of my career versus now? If so, then I'd say that what provoked the most enthusiasm when I started out was a mixture of experimental filmmakers, people like Hollis Frampton, or Leslie Thornton, or Joyce Wieland, or Peggie Ahwesh or Valie Export, or Maya Deren. They were experimental filmmakers who were slightly older than I was, were more experienced, and whose work really excited me.

I learned a lot from them. I could cite a film from any of them and talk about their use of text, their use of music, their use of techniques. Their works were filled with ideas I really loved. And there were also narrative filmmakers. As I mentioned at the start of our conversation, I was influenced by artists like Fassbinder, Kurosawa, and in later years, Kiarostami, Agnès Varda, Margarethe von Trotta, Marleen Gorris, Satyajit Ray. The world of film was so vast, and I was interested in all of it, whether experimental, narrative, or documentary.

But I keep adding to the repertoire of films and filmmakers who have something to teach me. By now, I've been exposed to many artists. It's not, "Oh my God, I cannot believe I just saw this film!" Now, watching a current release, I just don't have the same reaction or experience I did when I first started making films. But seeing something new by somebody that I deeply admire does give me a good feeling. I might think, "That's an interesting way of doing a sound bridge, or that's an interesting way of working with text." How these elements are reimagined in a film gives me an "Aha!" moment, but almost more importantly they make me think, "Yes, it still is worth trying to do things well." And I suppose the best example of a time when I did feel completely blown away by a new "discovery" later in my career was when I first saw the films of Kiarostami and Makhmalbaf. The first one was Kiarostami's *Through the Olive Trees*, which I saw because we had an Iranian roommate who told us about it, and it was showing at a theater in Manhattan, maybe the Quad or Cinema Village? This would have been back in about 2004. Before then, I'd known nothing about Iranian cinema. Since then, I've devoured it, learned so much from it, and feel as if my whole sense of what's possible in filmmaking has been hugely enriched by their films.

It's also possible, after you've been working for so long, to get tired with the idea of making another thing. Does the world need another thing? That's why it's helpful to see something so wonderful and to think, "This is why art is being made. This is why films are being made. And let me please have the energy and the intelligence to try again—to do that myself. Because that's what I tried to do in the past." I believe I've succeeded a few times. So maybe I'll succeed again. It's that feeling and that inspiration which keeps me going, in a bigger picture sort of way, rather than being inspired by any specific film or filmmaker.

AR: That's a wonderful way of looking at it. A very optimistic way.

SF: Yes, I'm optimistic when I see good things. And I'm really pessimistic when I see bad stuff.

AR: Then maybe we need to keep searching for and learning from those inspirational filmmakers like yourself.

Thank you.

Editors' Interview

Sonia Misra and Rox Samer / 2020

Rox Samer: How is quarantine treating you? What has your experience of the pandemic been like?

Su Friedrich: You know, I think I'm very fortunate when it comes to the pandemic in the sense that I have a house, and we have tenants whose rent covers almost our entire mortgage. I'm not financially stressed when it comes to that. We've talked to them about relieving them of paying the rent because of the pandemic, but they're fine with continuing to pay the rent. So we even tried to take account of that question and it's sort of working out for all of us so far, so that's unbelievably good. I have a partner, so I'm not alone. And by a miracle, I was given sabbatical this last spring. So when all of it hit, I wasn't in the position of nearly everyone I know, stuck in this horrible situation teaching through Zoom. And I cannot tell you how grateful I am for that, because I don't think I have the personality to have been able to deal with that well.

All of that being said, I think I'm having as hard a time as everybody else, because it's just mind-blowing what's going on. The feeling of not knowing what the future holds, it makes me crazy. I keep saying, "Well, five minutes ago I was happy, and now I'm sad again. And I know I'm going to be happy again in five minutes, then I'm going to be sad again." It's ridiculous.

I also feel lucky because I have this huge project—a new website about William Greaves's films—that takes up most of my mental space so that I don't have that much time to worry about how horrible things are. In late January, there was a symposium about Greaves at Princeton organized by another professor, Fia Backström, and the artist Martine Syms, and I was really glad about that because in 2005 I had brought him to Princeton just after he had finished *Symbiopsychotaxiplasm: Take 2½* (2005). It had shown at Sundance and then it was going to Berlin, and we snuck in a secret screening of it along with *Ralph Bunche: An American Odyssey* (2001). I had always really admired him because of *Symbiopsychotaxiplasm: Take One* (1968), so it was thrilling to have him there. And then he died nine years later. I only knew his wife Louise a little bit, but when I met her at the symposium, I was talking about how great it would be if the Princeton Library would buy them in addition to the ones that they had already. Later, I looked one up on the website and it said VHS, so I called up Louise and said, "You've got to be kidding! VHS?" And she told me she had been meaning to update the website for years. And then I offered to make a new website. I'm no web designer, but it's something I feel is an important thing for artists to have, so I make them sometimes, like making one about my partner Cathy Nan Quinlan's paintings. When I offered, it was the end of January, and suddenly the pandemic hit. Louise lives in New York, so we met once in person before everything was shut down. Greaves made tons of films and has had a million things written about him, so it's been an all-engrossing job.

RS: Do you do well when you're working? Does the world sort of fade away for you?

SF: Totally. Yes, absolutely. I can get completely lost in the work.

Sonia Misra: It's great to have those coping mechanisms.

SF: Cathy always insists that I should be making films instead, and at times when I talk about working on the website, her eyes kind of glaze over. When I ask her why, she says, "I really wish you would just go out with your camera and shoot." I have to tell her that now, during the pandemic, I don't have the mental space for that. I feel like that takes a certain kind of presence of mind that I don't have now, whereas I can try to find a really good picture from one of Bill's films. That's a great distraction, but the deeper kind of emotionally based personal stuff, no.

RS: So you're not shooting anything at present?

SF: Well, no, except for this Wexner thing. A year ago, Dave Filipi from the Wexner Center for the Arts got in touch with me because they were commissioning twenty people to make short films that would be part of a compilation films called *Cinetracts '20*. Their idea was to have a new film that somehow in conversation with the original *Cinetracts*, which was made in 1968 by a group of French New Wave filmmakers in response to the Paris '68 riots. It's an omnibus film in which each person—and it was very strict—made something that was about 2 minutes and 47 seconds in length, could only be made with still images, and you couldn't use audio but you could use intertitles. And then they strung them all together. The Wexner wanted to redo it in some fashion. They didn't specify that it had to be about the protests for Black lives; it didn't necessarily have to be about a new topical, analogous protest.

I got the idea to use footage that I had shot when I went to the very last performance of the Ringling Brothers and Barnum & Bailey Circus. Cathy and I are huge circus fans. She grew up in the carnival. We're just big on the circus. And it was the most heartbreaking thing that it was ending. I got a lot of footage, and I was going to make my short film be about that.

And then on a beautiful day in May, my neighbor rang the bell. I had been inside working all day on the Greaves website. When I opened the door, there was this glorious late afternoon light. A few people were out, even though it's COVID time, so I ran and got my camera. I went out and decided to do something about the block I live on in Bed-Stuy. I filmed people at one end of the block and the other end of the block, a couple people who were gardening, and a place that gives out free food. Everyone was wearing masks, so it was very much about COVID time. And then when I was coming back to our house, because Peggy Ahwesh was coming over for an illicit visit in the backyard, some people came out of a car with balloons which said "Happy Mother's Day." I hadn't been thinking about it, but it was Mother's Day. These two people, a woman and her son, went into their apartment building, and when they came back out, they had even more balloons. Another son was standing nearby with his camera, and he said, "Okay I'm ready." They called out, "Happy Mother's Day! Happy Grandmother's Day! We love you!" and released the balloons into the air. I couldn't believe I got that shot. So, without planning it, I made a COVID Mother's Day film for *Cinetracts '20*. That's the one personal, creative thing that I've done during this time.

RS: I was wondering if something like that had happened or would happen, because while many of your films are quite deliberate and planned, a couple of them suggest to me that they were not, that you didn't necessarily set out to make a film but somehow found yourself shooting what became a film. I'm thinking in particular of *The Head of a Pin* (2004).

SF: Right.

RS: You didn't anticipate that spider web and the spider catching the bug, but before long you had an entire film organized around that footage. Is that often your creative process?

SF: When you were starting to ask the question, I thought of *The Head of a Pin*, and now I'm wondering whether there's any other film that I could say really happened in that way. I guess *Seeing Red* (2005) did, because it started with me going into my studio and just talking to the camera. Even then, I didn't know what I was doing. But it made me think maybe I could make something out of the first stuff that I recorded. So that sort of comes close to what happened with *The Head of a Pin*. But the other aspect of *The Head of a Pin* had to do with the fact that I had a camera with me. We had gone up to the country, and I had decided I wasn't going to shoot on 16mm anymore and had borrowed a really crappy video camera from a friend. So I was there with the sense of shooting something. But definitely what *The Head of a Pin* ended up being had to do with the spider showing up like it did. Yeah, the spider and the bug were the creative force behind that film.

RS: Sorry, this is a totally random question, but is the Claudia who's in *The Head of a Pin* also in *Hide and Seek* (1996)?

SF: Yes!

RS: Is she the one in *Hide and Seek* who tells the story about admiring another girl's legs, or more specifically, the back of her knee?

SF: Yes! That's Claudia.

RS: And then in *The Head of a Pin*, there are two women lying outside in the grass with their cat, and she's the one who reaches out and touches the other's leg, right?

SF: Oh my god!

SM: Rox!

SF: Good catch, Rox!

RS: I watched *Head of a Pin* this afternoon. And then I was like, "Claudia . . . There's another Claudia . . . *Hide and Seek*. I think the leg person."

SF: That is so funny! No one has ever noticed that before, including me.

RS: She still likes legs many decades later.

SF: She still likes legs, and Barbara's got great legs.

It's also interesting—in light of me talking about my work or us talking together about my work—because we do all have these recurring themes or things we pick up on, or things we don't notice but do happen like that, that create some kind of link. So it's very funny. You get a little prize for seeing something that nobody's ever seen before, including me.

RS: Ha, all right! You're someone who champions in-person screenings and really relishes the experience of watching films with an audience, and has on a few occasions been critical of social media or relying too heavily on online platforms because of the absence of an audience. But maybe you could tell us more about your feelings about social media and online distribution, and also tell us if COVID-19 has changed that at all. Is there anything that you've witnessed in these last few months that's given you a hope about the future of film?

SF: Okay, there are different parts to this. First of all, I don't want to conflate social media and YouTube or Vimeo. To me, social media is more like Facebook where there's a lot of interaction, as opposed to YouTube or Vimeo where you can look at films for free. I'm totally opposed to sharing my films that way. But I don't feel prescriptive. I wouldn't forbid other filmmakers to do that because I've recognized that it's a necessity for some. Either they just really want an audience or they don't care about making money from distribution. But whatever their reason, I think that's a personal choice. Let them do it. For me, having come up through film, where people actually paid rentals or paid to go to a theater, and having seen a decline in income even with DVDs versus film, let alone streaming versus film, it felt like a threat to me, a threat to my livelihood. Plus, when all this started, my distributor absolutely refused to have things available online for free. Why would she want to hand out things for free? You know, she's trying to make money too.

But also it was part of a feeling about the larger picture. A decade earlier, I had lots of musician friends who said, "Oh my God, we're screwed. Nobody's going to pay for our music anymore." We have always assumed that culture costs money. You pay for the talent of an opera singer or a blues musician or whoever it might be. You pay to read a book, unless you're good enough to go to the library. And that's part of the deal for me. Some person or group of people worked really hard to create something, often without earning a lot of money in the process. And if I'm going to benefit from their work, I'm going to reward them by paying them something. I feel like that about myself as well as about every other artist in every medium. Both of my distributors have my films available on Vimeo VOD because we all recognize that many people would prefer to stream a film, or aren't in a place where I might come and show the film, so of course we accept that watching films online is the way things go these days. But that's always combined with the belief that we all need to keep assuming that we should pay a little for the pleasure of experiencing something that someone else has made.

In terms of social media, I'm on Facebook. I share stuff all the time—except for my films for free. I think of it as a perfectly useful, fine thing. I don't live in it. I don't care that much about it, but I recognize its utility.

When COVID started happening, all kinds of organizations put things online that otherwise we'd go to see at a theater. I think that's really fantastic. I think the efforts that people have been making to give us what we need is really commendable. But it's not clear to me what's going to happen later, because people might think, "Why not keep streaming everything?" And that goes back to my other point, which is that it doesn't work. You kill culture that way. I don't know if I have something else to say about the future of filmmaking. That's the biggest question of all.

RS: Sonia and I actually both noticed that *The Ties That Bind* (1984) is included in the recent series "Tell Me: Women Filmmakers, Women's Stories" on the Criterion Channel. I imagine that might have been a project that was already in the works pre-COVID, but maybe not.

SF: Some months ago, my distributor told me that Criterion was inquiring about getting the rights to play *The Ties That Bind* on their Channel, and we made a deal. They bought the rights because it was part of a program that Nellie Killian had curated and shown in 2018 at the Metrograph theater in NY, which Criterion was now reprising on their streaming channel.

RS: Hoping that we do get back to in-person screenings, and reflecting on that not-so-distant past, I was wondering how, if at all, your relationship to audiences has changed over the years?

SF: You know, I was thinking about this and finding that it was very difficult to answer the question. If I think about my first handful of audiences, they were the experimental film community. They didn't necessarily know my work because I was brand new, but it felt like it was a very small, particular group that was seeing the work. And by now, forty-two years later, that's obviously not the case. But I was thinking about how I might go do a show somewhere now and some portion of the audience will know several of my films or a whole bunch of my films, and other people will be seeing a film of mine for the very first time. You never know who your audience is and you never know whether you're speaking to the converted or you're speaking to somebody who's just utterly shocked because they had no idea that that's what they were getting themselves in for.

In a way, I approach an audience the same way now that I did forty-two years ago, which is to think, "I hope this interests them. I hope I can answer the questions they might have about the film." In some way, you're always starting over again every time you deal with an audience, because you know an audience at a film festival is going to be really different than an audience of students who are studying film or an audience at some random other kind of place. It's so unpredictable. So you just have to go in thinking, "Okay, here we go again. I'm not going to take this for granted. I'm not going to assume that it's a shoo-in because it's been a shoo-in a whole bunch of other times." You just never know.

RS: Do you have moments in each of your films that you're more nervous or self-conscious about, or, if you're watching it with the audience, your little antennae are up?

SF: Yes, not with all the films, but there are particular cases where it never stops being an issue for me. With *The Ties That Bind*, there's a shot which I deplore and I just die if I'm in an audience watching the film. It's where the character, Lisa, is sitting on the toilet and she's reading the newspaper with the big headline about the Nazis. I just can't stand that shot and I can't stand that it's in the film. With *The Odds of Recovery* (2002), the fact that I exposed my bruised breast is a little mortifying. I'm also always a little bit queasy in *Sink or Swim* (1990) when I sit up in the bathtub and you see my breasts. You know, I can't think of others offhand. So yeah.

RS: Even though you put yourself in your films and so many of your films are so personal and autobiographical, you're still self-conscious?

SF: Kind of. I wouldn't say that I sit in the back of the theater, you know, scrunched up with my head in my hands at the thought of exposing my personal information. I spent however long making whatever film it is. I've now shown it god knows how many times. So the initial terror or embarrassment or whatever that I feel in the first couple of times I show it certainly wears away over time. I also don't often sit in the theater and watch my films when they're playing. I usually go out and read a book or answer emails or wander around. But if I'm watching it, then I'm mostly just thinking about the construction of the film, what's in it, and whether it works or not. I'm usually not all caught up in my personal stuff when I'm watching my films.

SM: We talked a little bit about Princeton at the beginning of this conversation, but we were really curious if you could expand on your career as a professor, because that's something that's not really covered in the other interviews that we've collected for this book. How has your career and experience as a filmmaker affected your particular approach to pedagogy or your particular approach in teaching video production? And how has teaching influenced your filmmaking, if at all?

SF: I never wanted to teach. I only got into it because the thing I really liked doing, which was paste up and mechanicals (which was the handmade way to make books and magazines before computers existed), was killed by computers. It was a really well-paid job that all my artist friends and I did. Relative to what people are paying now, it was an unbelievably well-paid job. I did that for a long time. And then I had to find other things to do, and I did adjunct teaching at The New School, which I really liked. The students were great, partly because they were older and had more experience, but it paid really badly, like all adjunct jobs in New York. Then I had a one semester gig at NYU teaching an undergrad film production course. I had a really terrible time teaching that course because it was prescribed; they gave you a syllabus and structure that you had to follow.

And then I just got really lucky. The Princeton job opened up. Everybody I knew applied. I got the job, and then I got tenure three years later, which was also extremely lucky. Plus it was half-time tenure, so that was even luckier. So, I found myself in 2003 or something with a tenured half-time job at a school that paid really well. It was a two-hour commute from New York, and I only had to be there two days a week, and I could sleep over there. When you're in your mid-forties and you otherwise have no way of earning a living, it's something that you can't pass up, and you can't leave. It meant that I had to face the fact that, for as long as I could tell, I was going to be a teacher—or a professor, if you will.

That wasn't an easy thing to accept for a number of reasons. First of all, the environment of Princeton was completely contrary to anything that I consider normal, and it still mostly is. The students weren't familiar to me from my experience being in college. They tended to be from a different class, different economic class, which is not to say they were inherently bad or anything, but it was just that they didn't feel like who I went to school with . . . I don't know. Maybe it's misguided of me to say that, since I went to the University of Chicago and then

Oberlin, and they tend to attract students from the same economic class overall. But I was in school in the 1970s, which was a more activist era than when I started at Princeton, with the aftermath of the Vietnam War and all that. I suppose that an experience I had in the first year at Princeton kind of stamped me with a certain impression about the place. I always urge students to register to vote, so I started in with my spiel about it and then a lightbulb went off and I took a deep breath and said, "I want everyone in class to be sure to register, whether you're a Democrat or a Republican." I took a show of hands to see whether I did in fact have Republicans in the class . . . and the rest is history [*Laughs*].

But beyond the specifics about Princeton, I just don't like being in a position of authority like that. I mean, if Cathy heard me saying this, she would laugh out loud, because I can be such a bitch. I can be so bossy. I can be so directive when it comes to whether or not we should, you know, get the blue or the green curtains. But when it comes to being somebody who's telling other people how things should be done, and it's about something that I care the most about, I'm very uncomfortable with that. So, there I am with my own idea of how to make my own films and I don't want to tell other people how to do that. First of all, it's impossible, because how you make something is a very individual thing. It would be impossible to teach somebody how to make a Su Friedrich film, if I even wanted to do that, which I don't. Secondly, the majority of students would never be interested in making the kind of films that I make. They want to learn how to make a traditional narrative or documentary film.

When I started at Princeton, one of my co-teachers was Keith Sanborn, who's also very rooted in experimental film. We taught courses in a very open way, in both the Intro, Intermediate, and Advanced courses. So it was like, "Hey everybody, you're going to decide what to do and I'm going to help you do it." And somebody would say, "I want to make an animation" and somebody else would say, "I want to make a short narrative," and we'd be fine with whatever kind of film they felt like making. But as the years went along, they less and less often wanted to do something that I would consider experimental. So it was really more and more a case of me saying, "Okay, go ahead and write your totally conventional script," you know, or "Go shoot talking heads interviews for that film about your roommate who's on the football team." How I approach making something became less and less relevant. And, considering what I was being paid, I was willing to adapt to that reality, and I've always busted my ass so that the students would learn as much as possible, but it didn't make it interesting for me. When it comes down to it, I feel like I know enough about narrative construction, having made at least *Hide and Seek*. And I know enough about traditional documentary that if a student is doing something like that, I can advise them. I can help them make it in the best way possible. But after sounding so harsh just now, I should mention that I've had some fabulous students who have gone on to be filmmakers out in the world. I'm really happy about that, and I really enjoyed working with them in school because they already were showing the kind of passion and determination that you need in order to be a filmmaker.

But the big question is your last question—how it's affected my own filmmaking or my sense of being a filmmaker. And this is the thing I hate most about teaching. Teaching colonizes your mind. You're forced to care about all of these people who are trying to do something, many of them not even very seriously. They might have just taken the course because they had to do an art requirement, while you've spent your entire life doing this thing. Everything about it matters the most to you, and they're like, "Whatever." Plus, then I come home and I have to sit here, thinking, "Oh my god, how am I going to get Joe or Jane to reshoot that thing because right now it's so terrible?" You two are nodding your heads because you both teach.

I think it's a terrible situation for so many artists. We're utterly dependent on it as a job, so we simultaneously feel immense gratitude for having it while being driven crazy having it. For the years that I was doing paste up, a lot of my friends were teaching. Leslie Thornton was at Brown, Peggy was at Bard. All of us would get together, and they would do nothing but talk about teaching, and I would sit there like, "What the fuck? Can we talk about something else?" But they were obsessed with it. And when I started teaching, I understood why. Because it's a rat's nest. But also because your brain can't get free of it. I would also see that it really affected their filmmaking. Not to diss any of their work. I think they're great filmmakers. But there were just things that led me to think that teaching was affecting their filmmaking. When I started having to teach more, I was very scared of that, and I was very protective about that.

Because I'm half time, I have more time to have my own brain. But I do think that if you're teaching production full-time, your work invariably suffers. The more I hear people saying, "I'm going to get an MFA so I can teach and support myself as a filmmaker," I just say, "Do anything but that." First of all, there are no jobs, and, secondly, you're going to regret it. I could go on, but I'm going to stop.

RS: Is it also because when you're then sitting down to make your own work, you hear the sort of advice you give them?

SF: Well, yes, in a way. What happens is, it might be that I'm working and I remember an issue that I had with somebody, and I think, "Oh, if I showed them this example it might help them." Or, mostly, when teaching interrupts my editing, I think, "God damn it, I would much rather be making my own films all the time than trying to get students to make their own films." It's more this recognition that I'm finally in my own space that I want to be in, and that I've been robbed of that when I'm having to do my job. So, yeah, that's mostly where they come into play when I'm working myself.

Well, the thing is, one of the things about the way I teach is that I never let them see anything of mine until maybe the eleventh week of class (we have twelve classes). Obviously, they can see stuff on their own, but I've known teachers who show their own work right away and the students might then feel compelled to make something like their teachers (either because they admire them or because they feel like that's how they're going to get an A). And I was aware of that. So, week eleven, they finally see whatever it might be and they're kind of like, "Whoa, well that was a cool film," and maybe they had no idea before that I knew how to make films [*Laughs*].

Maybe two or three years ago was one of the first times I was teaching a strict documentary class. It wasn't one of these "Whatever you want to do" classes. So, there it is, documentary. And they think, "Okay, teach me how to make a Michael Moore film." So they're talking about their projects and I say, "We're going to watch a bunch of different kinds of documentaries, and you can make it on any subject you want. But I'm going to beg you not to assume that it has to be a talking heads documentary." The next week they came in with proposals, and one of the students, an architecture student, wanted to do something about living vertically. She'd been in Brazil and talked about how everything is vertical there, and said she'd shot a lot of footage there about it. And she said, "I don't think I'm going to interview anybody. I'm just going to use all that footage and maybe not even use any voiceover." And I said, "Really? That's so fantastic!" She looked terrified, like I didn't really mean what I said about freeing yourself from a talking heads documentary. I kept pushing her to do it as she saw it, and she did and what she made was great. And it was the only film in the class that wasn't a talking heads documentary.

That's the other thing. You can go in and say whatever you want, but if they're too constrained by tradition (and what little they know of it, actually), then they're not going to hear anything you say. They're going to repeat a known form. And not that many people are very free in their thinking. There aren't that many people who really do go outside the guidelines.

RS: Meanwhile, the building across from my building is being levelled, and I have to try not to make *Gut Renovation* (2012).

SF: [*Laughs*] Right.

RS: I have some very similar footage of the brick wall getting pushed.

SF: Wow.

SM: An homage! Su, what film of yours, or films of yours, do you show your students?

SF: It depends on the group and what we've been doing. I would say it's usually *Sink or Swim*, *Hide and Seek*, or *Gut Renovation*. Those are the three.

SM: You said it depends on the group and also the particular context of your teaching, like a documentary specific course versus an intermediate or advanced video production course?

SF: Well, I only teach intro or intermediate documentary. And now I'm also teaching something called the Film Seminar, which is intended for students who are doing a major or a minor in film. With them, I might show two that aren't strictly documentary, let's say. But with the documentary class, I would most likely show *Gut Renovation*. Oh, sorry! The new film, *I Cannot Tell You How I Feel* (2016). I showed that one to the last class I did.

SM: Speaking of teaching, your short film *Practice Makes Perfect* (2013) focuses on a class about West African drumming. Can you tell us how you came to and developed this project?

SF: The Brooklyn Academy of Music was doing a big festival about music and performance, and they wanted to have a bunch of short films made. They commissioned me and a few other people to each make a short film, and I knew about Kam Kelly, the drummer who is the teacher in the film, through somebody in my neighborhood. I thought it would be interesting to make a short film about him teaching music to kids at that school. It wasn't something I would have necessarily done on my own, but I was glad for the chance to go. I've always wanted to learn African drumming. Impossible! But I've always wanted to do it. So I really loved being able to go and film at the school.

RS: Do you think much about your own relationship to learning and your ongoing learning process? And do you have anyone in your life that you would still consider, or think of in some way or another, as a teacher?

SF: Yeah, I think we never stop learning. Or at least I hope we never stop learning. In my case, I grew up in an academic environment. My father was a professor. My grandfather was a professor. My uncle was a professor. But I don't think that's necessarily why one is a student for life, because Cathy didn't grow up in that kind of environment and she's the most curious, inquisitive, no, endless learner of anybody I know. But for me, there's always something new to learn. And particularly when you're working on a project, whatever the subject is. You know, you're at a cocktail party or you go to a film or a dinner party and then somebody says "What are you working on?" And you say what it is, and then they start saying, "Oh, I read a book about that" or "I saw a film about it" or "I've been there." You're constantly hearing things from people that are interesting, and I consider that learning. I also do tons of research on my own, so the learning never stops.

RS: In early interviews we've collected for this book, from before you switched to video, you talk about everyone else switching to video and your resistance to it. And then in later interviews you talk about your need to switch to video, for financial reasons, and how it changed the sort of films you tended to make from then on. And at times, it sounds like video has opened up these possibilities of doing longer takes and using sound, but that you're still a little down on the look and the feel of video itself. I'm wondering if you've come around to that or if it's just become part of your aesthetic.

SF: Right. If I'm in a theater watching something of mine projected that was shot on video (let's say a recent film, like *I Cannot Tell You How I Feel* or *Gut Renovation*), it looks fine to me. I don't sit there thinking, "Ugh, fuck, I can't believe this is video." I'm aware of how much I was able to film because it's video: long takes, or the hidden camera stuff in *I Cannot Tell You How I Feel*. I'm more aware of the benefits that have come from shooting digital. But then, once in a great while, I go somewhere where somebody is projecting a film of mine on film, an older film— and at this point it's like this memory of what it's like to watch a film on film—and I'm stunned by it. I sit there thinking, "Oh my god, it's really a different thing than video. There's no getting around it." But, when it's over, I think, "So what? There's nothing you can do about that. You can't return to film. It won't be projected on film if you do. So, shut up. It's history." And I do feel very grateful at this point for the unbelievable flexibility of editing in the computer. It's just fantastic. As a deep editor, it's super fantastic. You can't live with a regret like that, because it's dysfunctional. It's like you're convincing yourself that you shouldn't continue working. And if you want to work, you can't do that to yourself. You just have to say, that was that and this is this.

SM: That makes sense. I wanted to ask you about your short film *Queen Takes Pawn* (2013) and how you developed this project. How was your process of editing this film or developing it inflected, in any way, by your transition or move into digital editing?

SF: I don't think the way it's put together had that much to do with digital editing. Certainly the way it was shot, because it had live sound. If I had made that with my Bolex, then when the bell fell to the floor, I wouldn't have had the funny crashing tinkling noise, and I wouldn't have had the sound of the wind chimes doing their thing. It would have been silent. And that might have been fine too. I was also sort of laughing when you said, "When you developed this film," because that is such a grand term for this film *[Laughs]*. I'd like to think I developed it, but it was more just something that happened because I went with Cathy to the house of another filmmaker. It was his mother's house out on Cape Cod. Cathy was drawing and I thought, well, I should do something myself. So at some point I picked up the camera, because I recognized that the house evoked something about my grandmother, who had died some years back. It reminded me of her, and so I shot what I shot. I also had *Alice Through the Looking Glass* with me. I'm not sure why I brought that book along with me on this beach trip.

Sort of weird. It's this book from my childhood. Maybe I was thinking about the book unrelated to the house we went to. When I got back, I just started putting it together with home movie footage I had that my grandfather had shot of my grandmother. I approached it with a slightly casual attitude, like "I'm not sure what this is. Is it worth making?" And, by the end, I was okay with it. I hope it's not the only film I'm remembered by [*Laughs*], but I was fine with it.

The really unfortunate experience I had with that film was that the filmmaker whose mother's house it was got incensed. While I was there, I had sent an email saying, "Oh, it's so great to be here, and I even started filming. I hope that's okay." And he said it was fine. Then I wrote him later asking his mother's name, because I wanted to thank her in the credits, and he gave it to me. I then sent him the film so he could look at it. He couldn't believe that I had included certain shots, like a close-up of a prayer card wedged into the mirror in the bedroom, which somehow showed the name of a friend of his mother who had died. He also had a problem with the shot of the recipe box. By chance, when I opened the box while I was filming, I pulled out the recipe card for War Cake. And I thought that was cool because it connected to the chess game in *Alice Through the Looking Glass*. He insisted that the shot come out of the film. And this is what I don't like in the film—the shot of the recipe card that I wrote out at home as a replacement, which I don't think looks real. Stupid. But at that point, I was determined to finish the film. I wasn't going to let this one stupid fabricated shot keep me from releasing the film [*Laughs*]. But it ruined our friendship, which is really tragic because my film is probably going to show twelve times. Nobody's going to care about this film [*Laughs*]. Nobody's going to see this film. And then, here's the best part of it. And I know I shouldn't go on. He had a partner, and they stayed with us, and the partner had a Bolex and filmed in the house, including filming various paintings of Cathy's that were on the wall. And that footage was included in a film that showed at the New York Film Festival . . . without getting permission from us. I really wanted to write them both and point out the hypocrisy of it all, but I didn't. That was sort of the end of it. Speaking of being a lifelong learner, that taught me never to do that again.

RS: To film at your friend's house?

SF: Well, always assume that somebody could take the worst possible position in relation to what you've done. Before you get too invested in what you've done, check on it [*Laughs*].

RS: Sonia loves that film.

SM: I do. I really like it. I was going to show it, Su, when you were going to come to my school before COVID happened.

SF: Oh, yeah?

SM: Yeah, there's something that speaks to me about that film.

SF: Well, thank you. I do like it, but I think my experience of it has become so colored by what happened that it's not just the film itself anymore. It's all of that mess that came with it. I mean, I adore the Lewis Carroll books so much. To have made something from that book and also to have incorporated my grandmother in a film I'm happy about, for me, is quite special, because my grandfather was famous and got all the attention and took up all the air in the room. I like that I gave her a moment on screen, even though I made her the bad Queen.

RS: Villains are better anyway.

SM: They're more fun.

RS: In a few of your early interviews from the '80s and '90s, you express a desire to work more with humor and perhaps make comedy someday. Looking back over your films, would you describe yourself as growing more comfortable with humor? How would you describe your films' senses of humor? How do you think about humor in your films?

SF: I think, "Thank God I'm with Cathy." She has such a great sense of humor, and she's been the force behind the humor that you see in my films—whether it's in writing a script or the text that's on the screen in various films. I try to inflect them with various kinds of humor, but I usually fall a little short, and she always comes in and says, "It would be so much funnier if you said it this way or that way." So I give her enormous credit for that. We were talking the other day about this, and she said, "You should just try to make a comedy. You love comedy. You have a really good sense of humor, but you hide it under all this serious emotional stuff. Why don't you just make a comedy?" I said, "I could never do that." But when it comes down to it, it would be fantastic to have humor be the genesis of a film, not keep it to snarky asides or a few funny moments. I don't know how I would do that, though. It's so intimidating to me to think about it.

RS: What's intimidating about it?

SF: That it wouldn't be funny. There's a great documentary, *Dying Laughing* (2016), about the process of joke writing. It's done in a really detailed way with a lot of great comedians talking really specifically about how they work. Cathy and I watched it together, and we were fascinated by their descriptions about how hard they work, but we also felt that it's absolutely like being any other kind of artist—dealing with the questions of structure and timing and all of that.

RS: So even when it is a very personal snarky comment, you attribute that to Cathy? I'm thinking of *Gut Renovation* when you're yelling out the window at the businessman and on screen we see something like, "How typical. I make a fool of myself, and they don't even care."

SF: That was me. I thought you were going to cite when I put on screen, "I hate rich people." Cathy said, "You know, Su, you say that all the time. Why don't you just say it right there?" There are definitely moments that I've come up with on my own, and I find the right wording. But I give her a lot of credit for many instances in which she'll tweak it a little bit and then the humor will come out. When I was doing the scene in the cornfield in *I Cannot Tell You How I Feel*, she was the one who suggested I record it in a whisper. And that gave it a little humor.

RS: When I think of humor in *I Cannot Tell You How I Feel*, I think of the scene when you have your mom take the photo of you and you add the text about how you're panicking inside.

SF: That was me.

RS: Another example of humor that appears across your films is in certain ways that you use music for juxtaposition. I'm thinking of some of your montages in *Gut Renovation*, which not only lighten the mood but also are so bizarre. Like your use of that one German song.

SF: "Kommt zusammen" by the band 2raumwohnung.

RS: Yeah, there is a sense of humor to your use of music at times, no?

SF: Yeah, no, I definitely try for that.

SM: We talked a little bit about your use of text on screen. That seems very directly related to your sense of humor but also exists beyond it. There's a relationship between synchronously recording your voice in this diary fashion versus inserting your voice via text during the editing process, where these additional, often humorous, interventions are made. I would like to know a little bit more about your process. How much of your process happens while editing?

SF: Yeah, that's another aspect of the question you asked before, about the transition from film to video. I did say how grateful I am to be able to edit on the computer, but I am so grateful for how I can work with text. In one respect, I started doing that with *The Odds of Recovery* and yet, in *The Ties That Bind*, my questions are scratched on the screen and in *Sink or Swim* there are the alphabet intertitles. Which is to say, it's not as if I didn't do all that before, but with *The Odds of Recovery*, I felt that I needed to convey a certain amount of information and make certain remarks on screen. It was a nightmare because it was on film. It's just unbelievably expensive and difficult to do, but I did it. And then, the next film I made that had a lot of text in it was *Gut Renovation*, and by then I was editing in the computer. Suddenly, I could change whatever I wanted to say a thousand times. I could jot down something and rewrite it the way I would have rewritten the script. And it was unbelievably freeing and exciting because it also meant that I could speak in different registers, I could give you information, I could make an aside, I could comment on what you were seeing, I could do anything I wanted textually. I loved that, and so when I was working on *I Cannot Tell You How I Feel*, I continued with that and played around a bit more with it. At this point, it's one of the really great elements in how a film comes together, how a film works for me, and that's thanks to the computer.

And can I just say, also, that I first used text in *Cool Hands, Warm Heart* (1979) and then in *Gently Down the Stream* (1981), and I did it in a more aesthetically interesting way than just title cards. I've always dreamt that one day, when *Gently Down the Stream* shows in public, the audience would start reading the words out loud, which has never happened. In watching the film, I hoped people would hear their own voices. This has to do with my super intense relationship to an audience. An audience is always anonymous, but they're still there in that movie theater, and I'm always talking to them through the film. Even with *Gut Renovation* or *I Cannot Tell You How I Feel*, when I make those kinds of comments, I kind of feel that the person who's watching the film has maybe already started thinking that. Or if I tell them I'm talking to them, as if I'm saying, "Yeah and by the way." And I really like that. It makes a kind of connection between me and my audience.

SM: Definitely. It feels intimate—almost like an inside joke. You mentioned Cathy's influence on your integration of humor into your work. She's also obviously worked alongside you, cowriting *Hide and Seek* and working as an editing consultant. We were curious as to whether you could tell us a little bit more about your working relationship with Cathy. What is it like to work with your partner? How have you influenced each other's work?

SF: *[Laughs]* I haven't influenced her work that much. There's one way in which it's no different than my working relationships with Cindy Carr, Peggy Ahwesh, Steve Barker, Leonie Gombrich, Janet Baus, or Ernie Larsen. These are friends who have put a lot of energy into my films, spending hours going over the writing or the editing with me. They've invested a lot of their time and been very generous with me, and Cathy's another person who's done that.

But there's also a lot more that she's given to my films, because she's around all the time. I get to always bother her, which sometimes she resents—for good reason. Also, she knows me so well, and it can be a source of incredible conflict, pain, anger, and misery. Because if she comes in and says whatever, and I completely disagree with it—and I've spent months convincing myself that what I'm showing her is right—it's really bad. But I've learned over the years to not scream and yell and burst into tears, but to say, "Thank you, that was very interesting," and then think about it and try it out. And half the time she's right, and half the time I'm right. And the times she was right, when I see a film of mine and I make note of what's going on and remember that it was because of something that she said, I thank God that she was there to tell me to do that.

I'll give you the most dramatic example. It took me a year to edit *Hide and Seek*. I was cutting on film, and right at the end, when I was sure I was done, she came by to look at it. Mind you, she had written the script with me. In the script there's a section called "Party Scene," and it describes the different games that the girls play and also a scene where they all dance together. So she comes in and looks at the film, and she says, "You know, I think the dancing should be at the end of the film." This is a long time ago when I still screamed and cried. I was like, "What? Are you fucking kidding me? There's no way that makes any sense! And anyway, do you know how hard it is to do that in 16 on the Steenbeck?" I railed at her. She left, and I thought about it. I would have been too embarrassed not to try it out, so I did. And I thought, "Oh my god, how right she was. Of course the film has to end with this scene, with this song, so that I can segue into the photographs." It's incredible to me to think that, with my solitary brain, that wouldn't have happened.

The other most significant change to a film that happened as a result of her feedback was when she suggested that I use a girl to read the voice in *Sink or Swim* instead of doing it myself, and then when she insisted that I use Jessica Lynne to do it instead of the girl that I thought I should use. It made a huge difference in how *Sink or Swim* works. And since *Sink or Swim* is the film that everybody goes to, I think they might not have been going to it if I hadn't done that. So she has played a big part in my films.

RS: I literally have goosebumps. I'm wondering, what does Cathy think of *Rules of the Road* (1993)?

SF: Haha! She came to the premiere of it at MoMA with her then girlfriend. She had heard through the grapevine that I was making a film about our breakup and about the car we shared. Later, when we got back together and talked about it, she said she wanted to make an animated film of her running me over in the car. I said, "Oh my god, that would be so great. Let's do it." But who can be bothered making an animated film? She still maintains that things in it are bullshit, but I say, "Okay make your own film. This is my film."

The one film that was a very marked experience for me in relation to Cathy was *The Odds of Recovery*. One day I went to her and said, "You know what? I think I'm going to make a film about all this medical stuff," and she said, "Do not do that." We talked about it, and she was really firm. I proceeded to make it, and a bit of a ways into the editing, she came in and saw that I used her name on screen. This is when I had to make all the title cards in 16mm at great expense. And she was furious, so I changed it to say "My companion," and she never looked at it again. Usually she's interested and good at looking at my films, so for her not to look at another edit of it, for the many months that I was working on it, was hard for me. I felt so bereft, and she was so furious about it. She agreed to come to the premiere, which was at the Pioneer Theater in the East Village. She wasn't going to come, and I kept asking her to. It was an hour before I had to leave when she finally spit out, "Su, I've spent too much time in hospitals seeing you in a hospital gown, and I never want to see it again, so why would I want to see it on the big screen?" I had never thought of that and told her she didn't have to go. And then she agreed to go.

RS: That's actually a very sweet reason to not want to go. I was wondering if it was because of how you talk about your sex life in the film.

SF: No, it was the medical stuff.

RS: Before we ask you about *Edited By*, I was wondering if you could tell us what you consider to be good or great film editing, and whether, in your opinion, there is such a thing as an editing style that could be identified with a particular film editor?

SF: This kind of question makes my brain melt.

RS: We're asking you the questions you ask on your website.

SF: I don't know what you mean.

SM: You pulled segments from a *Film Comment* article in which they posed those questions to film editors.

SF: Oh, right. You know, in a way, I think that posing that question to the likes of Dede Allen or Thelma Schoonmaker or Walter Murch makes sense, because they work within a tradition that has a lot of rules, and then they perfect them or add to them. They do a lot within the realm of what people see as editing when one is constructing a narrative or a documentary, and that's not how I work. We can look at a particular editor's work and talk about their style, but when it comes to my work, I find it hard to answer. It's such a process of a million decisions that happen both intellectually and instinctually. It's having a series of shots that are going into a section, and then considering the sequence of them, and then kind of playing around with the sequence and starting to see movement in one shot and how it relates to the movement of the next shot, and then putting some sound in. And it kind of develops and develops and develops. I can't call it a style. It kind of goes beyond language. I don't mean to be coy about it.

If we were sitting together in front of some section of something I'm working on, I could try to speak my actions. I could say, "I'm looking at the shot, and I'm noticing that the bird is flying over there, and I'm thinking about how the truck drives in on the next shot. And if I use that song, there's that cut in the song, and it might work to do that, so now I'm going to do that. And as I watch it, I'm realizing that the bird takes too long for that beat in the music, and so I'm going to need to cut that back. But that's going to be a problem with the next shot, because the truck is too big in the frame until it moves more." That's what my brain is doing very quickly, constantly as I'm editing. There are more obvious things. If I'm doing *Seeing Red*, I decide that I'm going to use the on-screen talking parts interspersed with different sections of the Goldberg Variations, with different kinds of red images. And so, in terms of editing, I'm thinking about what order things should go in; how the music works with them; and whether I'm going to use the sort of chapter headings I use in *Gut Renovation* with the map or the intervals of music in *Rules of the Road* between the talking parts. But then, there's the superfine part of editing which goes beyond language. It's just what it is, and you just have to pay a lot of attention.

There are also these really funny things that happen for me as an editor that nobody notices. In *I Cannot Tell You How I Feel*, there's a passage where we're at an amusement park, and there's a night shot of some lights on the top of a building. When I was filming, the camera dropped or I stopped shooting, and the image went into a blurry swish. And then I was putting it together with the next scene where it's raining heavily out on a porch, and there's a close-up. I wanted the one scene to follow from the other, and somehow in the way I cut them together, the swish of the lights moved perfectly into the closeup of the rainfall. I went crazy. I love that cut. It's so insignificant. I don't think anybody watching the film thinks, "What a phenomenal edit," but that's the kind of stuff I experience when I'm editing; that's what gets me so excited. It's a very nitpicky life I lead [*Laughs*].

SM: What has been the most important influence on your development as an editor?

SF: The most important influence on my development has been coffee, dancing, and African music.

SM: I love that answer.

SF: Yeah, put those three together and that's why I'm an editor. I've learned a lot more about editing as the years have gone on. I was super particular as an editor from the outset. But I didn't recognize it as much then, because the work of shooting was so big. Now with digital, shooting isn't as burdensome. I have a lot more material to work with, but I also have learned so much over the years about what works, what doesn't, and how you get away with murder when you've got some really problematic footage and you're able to figure out how to edit it.

RS: Can we talk about *Edited By*? It launched about a year ago. How did you get into that project?

SF: I was reading the editing chapter of a certain production handbook in preparation for teaching, and I recognized that the director was the only person ever cited. The chapter was all about good editing, and it tripped something in me that had never happened before. I looked up all of the films and found that half of them were edited by women. My favorite discovery, which became this mantra for me when I was working on the site, was who edited *The Wizard of Oz* (1939). I knew that nobody would know the answer to that until I told them, so that was the start of it. I thought, if Blanche Sewell edited something as canonical as *The Wizard of Oz*, then let's talk. I worked my ass off for a year doing all the research. I had four younger women working with me. Three were my former students, and one had been a student at NYU. They did a bunch of later research when I went from thinking it would be a PowerPoint presentation to turning it into a website, and it became so huge that I needed some other people to work with me on it.

SM: What have been some of the challenges in creating this website?

SF: Finding information! If you're talking about editing, which is not particularly recognized, and when it's done by women, you discover that you put somebody's name into Google and nothing shows up. If anything shows up it's one French or Russian website with two lines about that editor working for a particular director. That was the problem at the beginning. Now no matter who you Google, if she's on my website, *Edited By* comes up on the first page and that person comes up on her own on the first page. That was the challenge. This was a subject that really hadn't been talked about, and not written about very much either. There were two good books: *Women Film Editors: Unseen Artists of American Cinema* by David Meuel, which covers about fifteen women editors, and *Fine Cuts: The Art of European Film Editing* by Richard Crittenden, which had a good number of interviews with European women editors as well as men. Otherwise, there was nothing except links to articles about Thelma Schoonmaker and Dede Allen, who are so famous. The challenge was digging and digging and digging and digging until I could find what I found to put on the website.

RS: Do you have a sense of how the website's been received or if it's being used in classrooms?

SF: Yes, it's been used in many classrooms. I did a big launch party at Union Docs, and I sent it out to everybody and put it on Facebook. People started sharing it, and I got many comments through the website and emails from people about it. One of my most encouraging responses was way before it was done. I was having coffee with Amy Herzog, who is a really wonderful film scholar. She was teaching at Princeton when the project was still a PowerPoint and I had maybe fifteen pages done that I wanted to show her. She started thumbing through it, and she said, "Oh my God, Su, I knew none of these women except for Thelma. This is going to change film scholarship, because film scholars never acknowledge the editor." That carried me through grueling long days of the project. I would think, "It needs to be done, and I'm going to do it." That has been my experience since then. People have said, "Thank you so much for this. I just never knew." One person, Samuael Topiary, who teaches out in California, taught a course about women editors, and she gave me her syllabus. There were a lot of other people who helped, but Samuael was the one who actually had already put her all into creating a course about the subject, and that was great for me.

I also started the project after the Electoral College disallowed the winner of the election to become the president. Like everybody else, I was depressed. And when I started working on this, I sometimes would think, "I should be out in the streets. I should be doing something to overturn this terrible situation we're in."

And then I recognized one day that I was putting something incredibly positive into the world. I was adding something to the world that could not be denied, that would make a lot of people feel really good, starting with the editors, who often wrote me afterwards and said, "Nobody's ever said my name." I thought it was a good thing to do that for the world, even though I think that would be really good if Trump was gone. But that was a motivation for me.

RS: Is the project growing and expanding?

SF: Unfortunately, yes, because aside from all the nice comments, I've also gotten emails from people saying, "Hey, what about that woman who did the Buñuel films?" How could I not have known about her? Of course I'll add her! That's why, when I launched it, the site included profiles of 139 women—64 professional editors, and 75 filmmakers who also edit. And then, this past August, I had gotten a bunch of names from people and I felt that I couldn't really leave it at that. So I decided to add to the site and, hilariously, I told myself that I would be done by October 15. I just decided on that date. I told Cathy and she's like, "Why are you working on that again? Make a film." I said, "No, no, no, it's going to be all done by October 15 at the latest." As it turned out, I officially considered it done and dusted in late January. It took so much work. I added about 25 or 30 main editors to it and a bunch more filmmakers who edit, so now the site has 206 women featured on it. If I hear about somebody else, it's going to take me a while before I add them.

Actually, what I stopped working on when I started working on *Edited By* was a book, and I'm going to go back to it after I finish this next website I'm doing. Two and half years ago, I had finished *I Cannot Tell You How I Feel*. I didn't know what I was going to do next, and I got the idea of looking at the journals and photographs from a trip I took through West Africa by myself when I was twenty-one years old. It was a six-month trip in 1976. I transcribed all my journals. I scanned all the black-and-white photographs I had taken. And I started putting them together as a book. Speaking of my use of text on screen, one of the things that started happening was that I started talking to my twenty-one-year-old self. I also started commenting on changes in politics and culture. The other element in the book is letters, because I also still had letters that I exchanged with people back home and letters from Africans that I got when I finally came home. This was twenty years before the internet. I got pretty far along on a first draft, and then *Edited By* happened and the book was put on hold.

RS: Do you have a sense of what the finished book will look like? Will it be a large photo book?

SF: You know, I don't know what it is yet. It's set up chronologically, day by day, with barely any editing of the journal entries. I didn't take that many photographs, but they're there when appropriate. But the other thing I discovered, which actually fed into how I worked on *Edited By*, was searching for and finding images of the places I refer to in the journals. I was blown away by what Google has available, considering that I was looking for images of places that I visited forty-four years ago. The greatest example was of a ship that I begged my way onto. I was stuck in Lagos because there had been a coup. For two weeks, I was living on the floor of somebody's dorm room at the university. All the borders were closed, so I went down to the docks and went from ship to ship saying, "Oh, please, can I get a ride to wherever you're going?" And finally a Black Star Line ship agreed to take me on board. It went from Lagos in Nigeria to Tema in Ghana, which is the port near Accra. The second captain was really great, and we hung out a lot. We corresponded later and he even came to New York once. So as I was working on this section, I thought, "I wonder if there's an image of that ship . . ." And I go on Google, and I keep digging and digging and digging, and I finally get to this weird website where ship nerds share pictures they've taken of random ships wherever they go. I found a photograph of a really rusted junkie cargo ship at a dock in Liverpool in July 1976. It turned out to be the same ship, and the photo had been taken only two months after I had been on it. It was such a weird moment of "Wow, that actually happened."

SM: I think that's fascinating. What a coincidence!

You often get asked questions about your films' resistance to fitting into easy categories. We don't want to rehash any of those discussions. Instead, how has this desire for classification influenced the way that you think about the future of cinema? What would you like to see in terms of cinema that pushes against these more restricting labels? We could go as far as to say the way that things are cataloged in online streaming, for example—has that influenced the way you think about cinema in any way, in terms of production but also distribution and programming?

SF: I find it really hard to answer that, because I'm just who I am. I make what I make. I see how it fits into certain categories for certain people, and I see that one film fits some place and another film fits another place. I feel that that question is for other people to worry about, that if I were to think about it too much, it would constrain what I do and how I do it.

Beyond that, I can't speak to that for anybody else or for the future of cinema, because there will always be people who want to make a Disney movie. There will always be people who want to make the most extreme experimental film—and everything in between. There's no knowing what the results will be. Obviously, economics can drive people into certain alleys or corners. I don't ignore the pressure of money when it comes to this question. I know how some people yield to that, and I feel sorry for them, because they talk about how it's making them do what they don't want to do. But in the best of all possible worlds, I think there's always going to be this huge range of what's being made, and I think that's all for the best.

SM: Expanding on that, do you have any advice for future filmmakers who might work similarly in a way that people read as ambiguous, whose work can't easily be put in one category or another, or who work across categories? Do you have any advice for them on making work or getting their work shown? Things to help them cope or thrive?

SF: Yes and no. We have a friend who answers some questions by saying, "Yes and no and yes and no," which I love. It's so appropriate at times. Yes, there are things I could suggest, but no I don't feel that it's fair, and the reason I say that is because I was really lucky with the way things happened for me.

I happened to start making films when I was living in New York and I could afford it—but just barely. There was the Millennium Film Workshop, which meant there were people around all the time. There was the experimental film community that was all for doing whatever you believe in. In terms of access and a community and a sense of what's possible, I couldn't have been in a better place, and that continued for a long time. I was also developing my work in a time when people were becoming more aware of the fact that women also made films (surprise!) and maybe those films should be shown. There were suddenly all these women's film festivals and then there were also newly founded gay and lesbian film festivals. So I kept developing in environments that wanted what I was doing, and I'm so grateful for that. I knew back then how lucky that was, and I know it now.

These days, where do you show your work, except for free on YouTube or Vimeo and a few little places here and there? How do you have community when you sit at home alone editing on your laptop instead of being able to go to a place like the Millennium? I think there are so many ways in which the landscape is so different that I don't know how to advise anybody, except to say if you believe that what you should be doing is making films, then do everything you can to make them. And that's the same spirit that I had and that somebody had fifty years before me. That never changes. But I think the thing of sharing your work in the real world is really important, and that's what I stress most. No matter where you live, find a group of people who you interact with—whether it's at screenings or having them come over to look at your work in your living room or basement. People almost never watch links. It's bullshit. You've got to be in the real world with the stuff. That might sound like a weird or harsh thing to say during COVID time because we're all so dependent on seeing things online, and all the film festivals are creating virtual versions of them, and I suppose some people must be watching it all, but I can't bear to think that that would be the way in the non-COVID future.

RS: One more follow-up question, which is speculative. If we were to time travel one hundred years into the future and read a film history textbook, and you were included in the chapter on queer filmmakers or lesbian filmmakers, how would you feel about that?

SF: What a weird question! I feel like that's a leading question. I feel like you have a reason for asking that.

RS: I'm trying to think of a way to get at what you have to say about which of your films get shown.

SF: So, if it gets categorized as lesbian or queer versus general?

RS: Yeah, in addition to being categorized as either experimental or documentary . . .

SF: Well, you know, I would say it depends on how that person wrote the chapter. If they said, "Su Friedrich has done a lot of work that references her experience as a lesbian, but she's done other films that don't, and the way in which she speaks about being a lesbian isn't always that direct and maybe raises questions," then I'd be fine with it. As long as you can acknowledge the variability or the variety in what I do, it's okay to say I happen to also be a lesbian. Same way if you're talking about films by women about women. Where does *Gut Renovation* fit into that? Those labels or categories work as long as you acknowledge the degree to which they may or may not fit in certain cases.

RS: I would say the flip side is, I don't think they don't fit. It's that we have these expectations for what a lesbian film is, what a film made by and for women is.

SF: That's very true! And what that means to me is that perhaps we should no longer be using any of the pointers. Don't refer to "Black Cinema." Don't refer to "Queer Cinema." You just say "Cinema" and then you figure out some other means of organization and you put everybody together. Because otherwise there has to be a chapter called "Straight White Male Cinema." But maybe if there was a straight white male chapter, then one should only cite films whose topics are either being Black or being queer, so you really fuck with people's minds.

RS: Anything we didn't cover that you would like to add? I think we did a pretty good job of finding things for you to say that you hadn't said in an interview before.

SF: Yeah, and that's a challenge. But, yes, you did. It was really nice seeing both of you. I wish we could have seen each other in person. It will happen!

SM: Sometime in the science fiction future when human interaction is allowed again.

SF: I'm really looking forward to that!

Additional Resources

Interviews Not Included

Botzoman, Anka. "Berlinale Interview: Su Friedrich." *Exberliner.* https://www.exberliner.com/whats-on/film/su-friedrich/#sthash.Sbe8vdFv. February 11, 2013.

Ciampaglia, Dante A. "Newsmaker: Su Friedrich." *Architectural Record.* https://www.architecturalrecord.com/articles/2810-newsmaker-su-friedrich. March 6, 2013.

Elfresh, Sam. "An Interview with Filmmaker Su Friedrich." *American Federation of the Arts Newsletter.* (Autumn 1991): 4–5.

Fear, David. "TONY Q&A: *Gut Renovation*'s Su Friedrich." *Time Out New York.* https://www.timeout.com/newyork/film/tony-q-a-gut-renovations-su-friedrich. March 4, 2013.

Fishbein, Rebecca. "Williamsburg Gentrification: The Movie!" *Gothamist.* https://gothamist.com/arts-entertainment/williamsburg-gentrification-the-movie. March 6, 2013.

Iversen, Kristin. "Gentrification In Williamsburg: Is Your Neighborhood Next?" *L Magazine.* https://www.thelmagazine.com/2013/02/gentrification-in-williamsburg-is-your-neighborhood-next/. February 26, 2013.

Klawans, Stuart. "Midlife Fury, Glowing in Glorious Red." *New York Times* (September 24, 2006): 22–23.

MacDonald, Scott. "Damned If You Don't: An Interview with Su Friedrich." *Afterlmage* 15. 10 (May 1988): 6–10.

Nonko, Emily. "The Hot Seat: Su Friedrich." *Brownstowner.* https://www.brownstoner.com/brooklyn-life/the-hot-seat-su-friedrich/. March 8, 2013.

Richards, Andrea. "Su Friedrich Is Seeing Red." *MAKE/SHIFT* (Fall/Winter 2007–08): 40–41.

Schartoff, Adam. "Episode 118: Su Friedrich." *Filmwax Radio.* http://www.filmwaxradio.com/podcasts/episode-118/. March 3, 2013.

Writings by Su Friedrich Not Included

Friedrich, Su. "Bette Gordon's *Empty Suitcases.*" *Downtown Review* 2.3 (Fall 1980): 16–17.

Friedrich, Su. "The Dilemma of the One Who Wants Both and Neither but Would Prefer to Get On with Her Work Instead of Being Preoccupied with Whether Anyone Will Ever Make Love to Her Right." *Heresies* 3, no. 4 (1981): 2.

Friedrich, Su. "Experimental Documentary Questionnaire/Responses." *Millennium Film Journal* 51 (Spring/Summer 2009): 20–23.

Friedrich, Su. "Fit & Trim: A Foolproof Method for Storing Film Trims." *Independent: Film & Video Monthly* (July 1999): 25–27.

Friedrich, Su. "How to Do a Matchback While Retaining Sync and Sanity." *Release Print* (March 2003): 18–22.

Friedrich, Su. "It Takes Two, Baby." *Millennium Film Journal* 41 (February 2003): 44.

Friedrich, Su. "*Jennifer, Where Are You?*" *Downtown Review* 3.1–2 (Fall/Winter/Spring 1981–82): 8–10.

Friedrich, Su. "Letters: On Margarethe von Trotta's *The Second Awakening of Christa Klages*." *Downtown Review* 2. (Fall-Winter 1979/80): 42–43.

Friedrich, Su. "Mea Culpa." *Heresies* 1.2 (May 1977): 26–29.

Friedrich, Su. "Seeing (through) Red." In *Truth in Nonfiction*, edited by David Lazar, 152–62. Iowa City: University of Iowa Press, 2008.

Friedrich, Su. "Sitney on Cornell." *Downtown Review* 2.2 (Fall/Winter 1979–80): 30–31.

Friedrich, Su. "*The Ties That Bind*." In *Alles und Noch Viel Mehr*, edited by G. J. Lischka, 890–91. Bern: Benteli, 1985.

Book Chapters

Cutler, Jane. "Su Friedrich: Breaking the Rules." In *Women's Experimental Cinema: Critical Frameworks*, edited by Robin Blaetz, 312–38. Durham: Duke University Press, 2007.

Fischer, Lucy. "The Nonfiction Film: 'The Reproduction of Mothering': Documenting the Mother Daughter Bond." In *Cinematernity: Film, Motherhood, Genre*, 179–213. Princeton: Princeton University Press, 1996.

Freeman, Elizabeth. "Love among Ruins." In *The Wedding Complex: Forms of Belonging in Modern American Culture*, 1–44. Durham: Duke University Press, 2002.

Holmlund, Chris. "Feminist Makeovers: The Celluloid Surgery of Valie Export and Su Friedrich." In *Play It Again, Sam: Retakes on Remakes*, edited by Andrew Horton and Stuart Y. McDougal, 217–37. Berkeley: University of California Press, 1998.

Holmlund, Chris. "When Autobiography Meets Ethnography and Girl Meets Girl: The 'Dyke Docs' of Su Friedrich and Sadie Benning." In *Between the Sheets, In the Streets: Queer, Lesbian, and Gay Documentary*, edited by Chris Holmlund and Cynthia Fuchs, 127–43. Minneapolis: University of Minnesota Press, 1997.

Kotz, Liz. "An Unrequited Desire for the Sublime: Looking at Lesbian Representation Across the Works of Abigail Child, Cecilia Dougherty, and Su Friedrich." In *Queer Looks: Perspectives on Gay and Lesbian Film and Video*, edited by Martha Gever, Pratibha Parmar, and John Greyson, 86–102. New York and London: Routledge, 1993.

Mayne, Judith. "Su Friedrich's Swimming Lessons." In *Framed: Lesbians, Feminists, and Media Culture*, 193–211. Minneapolis: University of Minnesota Press, 2000.

Renov, Michael. "Domestic Ethnography and the Construction of the 'Other' Self." In *Collecting Visible Evidence*, edited by Michael Renov and Jane Gaines, 140–55. Minneapolis: University of Minnesota Press, 1999.

Rich, B. Ruby. "Collision, Catastrophe, Celebration: The Relationship between Gay and Lesbian Film Festivals and Their Publics." In *New Queer Cinema: The Director's Cut*, 33–39. Durham: Duke University Press, 2013.

Rich, B. Ruby. "New Queer Cinema: Director's Cut." In *New Queer Cinema: The Director's Cut*, 16–32. Durham: Duke University Press, 2013.

Russell, Catherine. "Culture As Fiction: The Ethnographic Impulse in the Films of Peggy Ahwesh, Su Friedrich, and Leslie Thornton." In *The New American Cinema*, edited by Jon Lewis, 353–78. Durham: Duke University Press, 1998.

Russell, Catherine. "Zoology, Pornography, Ethnography." In *Experimental Ethnography: The Work of Film in the Age of Video*, 119–56. Durham: Duke University Press, 1999.

Sitney, P. Adams. "The End of the 20th Century." In *Visionary Film: The American Avant-Garde, 1943–2000*, 419–20. 3rd ed., Oxford and New York: Oxford University Press, 2002.

Straayer, Chris. "Discourse Intercourse: A Compendium of Sexual Scripts." In *Deviant Eyes, Deviant Bodies*, 184–232. New York: Columbia University Press, 1996.

Street, Sarah. "Revival and Appropriation." In *Black Narcissus*, 75–84. London and New York: I. B. Tauris, 2005.

Wees, William C. "Leslie Thornton, Su Friedrich, and Abigail Child: No More Giants." In *Women and Experimental Filmmaking*, edited by Jean Petrolle and Virginia Wright Wexman, 22–44. Urbana and Chicago: University of Illinois Press, 2005.

Weiss, Andrea. "Transgressive Cinema: Lesbian Independent Film." In *Vampires and Violets: Lesbians in the Cinema*, 137–61. London: Jonathan Cape Publishers, 1992.

Articles

Hanlon, Lindley. "Female Rage: The Films of Su Friedrich." *Millennium Film Journal* 12 (Fall/Winter 1982–83): 78–86.

Holmlund, Chris. "Fractured Fairytales and Experimental Identities: Looking for Lesbians in and around the Films of Su Friedrich." *Discourse* 17.1 (Fall 1994): 16–46.

MacDonald, Scott. "Avant-Doc: Eight Intersections." *Film Quarterly* 64.2 (Winter 2010): 50–57.

MacDonald, Scott. "Avant-Garde Film: Cinema as Discourse." *Journal of Film and Video* 40.2 (Spring 1988): 33–42.

MacDonald, Scott. "From Zygote to Global Cinema via Su Friedrich's Films." *Journal of Film and Video* 44.1–2 (Spring/Summer 1992): 30–41.

MacDonald, Scott, "Su Friedrich: Reappropriations." *Film Quarterly* 41.2 (Winter 1987–88): 34–43.

MacDonald, Scott. "Up Close and Political: Three Short Ruminations on Ideology in the Nature Film." *Film Quarterly* 59.3 (Spring 2006): 4–21.

Spence, Louise, and Esin Paça Cengiz. "Pushing the Boundaries of the Historical Documentary: Su Friedrich's 1984 *The Ties That Bind*." *Rethinking History* 16.3 (2012): 377–92.

Wees, William C. "'Making it through': Sickness and Health in Su Friedrich's *The Odds of Recovery*." *Jump Cut* 54 (Fall 2012). https://www.ejumpcut.org/archive/jc54.2012/weesFriedrich/text.html.

White, Patricia. "Lesbian Minor Cinema." *Screen* 49.4 (Winter 2008): 410–25.

Index

About the Editors

Photo credit: Jennifer Green

Sonia Misra is visiting instructor of film and media at Franklin and Marshall College and a PhD candidate in cinema and media studies at the University of Southern California. Her dissertation, "Queer (Post-)Cinematic Futures: Temporality, the Digital, and the Limits of Representation," focuses on contemporary queer cinematic production to explore how queerness becomes reoriented around the shifting relationships that define our digital age. She has published in *Film Quarterly*, *Spectator*, and *Media Practice and Education* and coedited the "Technologies of Knowing" special issue of *Spectator*.

Photo credit: Stephen DiRado

Rox Samer is assistant professor of screen studies in Clark University's Department of Visual and Performing Arts. Rox has published in *Feminist Media Histories*; *Jump Cut: A Review of Contemporary Media*; *Ada: A Journal of Gender, New Media, and Technology*; and *Transgender Studies Quarterly*. They are the editor of *Spectator* 37.2 (Fall 2017), the first journal issue devoted to the study of transgender media, and the coeditor of *Spectatorship: Shifting Theories of Gender, Sexuality, and Media* (University of Texas Press, 2017). Their monograph, *Lesbian Potentiality and Feminist Media in the 1970s*, is forthcoming with Duke University Press (Spring 2022).

CPSIA information can be obtained
at www.ICGtesting.com
Printed in the USA
BVHW081953090222
627929BV00001B/1

9 781496 838179